MY YEAR WITH MERYL STREEP

52 FILMS IN 52 WEEKS

BRIAN ROWE

All rights are reserved. No part of this book may be used or reproduced in any manner whatsoever without written permission from the author.

Copyright © 2015 by Brian Rowe

First Paperback Edition: February 2015

My Year With Meryl Streep is a work of film criticism. At times Brian has pulled information from the Internet Movie Database, Wikipedia, Youtube videos, and DVD behind-the-scenes documentaries and audio commentaries. No books by other authors have been quoted in this work.

Articles on the following films were previously published in different versions on brianrowereviews.com. These articles have since been revised and expanded on. Brian has retained all ownership of this content.

My Year With Meryl Streep
ISBN-13: 978-1507781647
ISBN-10: 1507781644

For Meryl

INTRODUCTION

Who doesn't love Meryl Streep? She's the most acclaimed, awarded, nominated, beloved actress of our time, and as the years tick on, her status becomes more and more legendary, to the point where Meryl herself has become less a person in the public's mind and more an almost mythical icon who can do no wrong. Year after year she surprises us with wholly original characters, unexpected genre turns, an unwillingness to do the obvious. Whether she's the lead of a movie or a smaller part of a large ensemble, she always steals the movie she's in, is always fantastic each time out.

When did my love affair with Meryl Streep begin? With five glorious words: "I can see my ass!" It might not be the best line Meryl has ever uttered on film, but it was memorable to me at age seven, when my mom took me to see *Death Becomes Her* in the summer of 1992. When the film came out on VHS, I watched it over and over, more than *Aladdin*, more than *Beauty and the Beast*. I was taken by this dark and hilarious black comedy even at a time when I didn't know what half the lines meant, and I recognized even then how amazing Meryl was. Over the next two decades, I found myself drawn to anything she appeared in, from her action heroine in *The River Wild* to her poignant turn in *The Bridges of Madison County*, from her singing and dancing in *Mamma Mia* to her charming portrayal of Julia Child in *Julie & Julia*. She has truly done it all, and even more remarkably, she never repeats herself. How in a film career that has lasted nearly four decades has she stayed so fresh and relevant? So courageous and daring? So endlessly fascinating to watch in one movie after another?

At the end of 2013, I had an idea. I had been thinking of doing a year-long series in which I examined an actor or actress' films in order, one week at a time, from early January to late December. I needed someone who had been in about fifty-two films and whose career excited me to the point of wanting to spend an entire year watching his or her movies. At the time I thought I should pick an actor who was no longer alive so that my journey could have a definitive ending, but on the eve of seeing *August: Osage County*, a film that netted her a record eighteenth Academy Award nomination, Meryl became my easy choice. Instead of playing the same role in movie after movie, Meryl transforms herself in every film she appears in, and instead of making the same kind of movie, Meryl has appeared in multiple genres, not just dramas and comedies, but also action, thrillers, musicals, westerns, and science fiction. Of her many films, there had been about a dozen I'd never seen, including *The Seduction of Joe Tynan*, *A Cry in the Dark*, and *Dancing at Lughnasa*, and I was excited at the prospect of completing the canon. And in 2014, she was to release her fiftieth, fifty-first, and fifty-second movies, making for a perfect filmography for a yearlong project. A major task this was, but to say it was rewarding is an understatement; a film fanatic my whole life, I have never had such an extraordinary movie watching experience than I have had in viewing Meryl's work one week at a time for an entire year. Even in her more mediocre films—yes, she has made some stinkers—she delivers moments of brilliance, and more often than not, I was stunned by a performance one week that in no way matched anything she had done in the film I watched the previous week. No living actor has done what Meryl has, a career of unrivaled excellence that will hopefully continue for many more years to come.

My Year With Meryl Streep features reviews of Meryl's films, as well as a TV movie and two mini-series. I look at her hits, like *Kramer vs. Kramer*, *The River Wild*, and *Mamma Mia*. I discuss her underrated and lesser-seen work, like *Falling in Love*, *Marvin's Room*, and *Music of the Heart*. I talk about her occasional disappointments, like *Still of the Night*, *Before & After*, and *Rendition*. And I examine my all-time favorite Meryl movie, a choice that will likely surprise many a reader (it's not what you think). Almost every film and TV project Meryl has appeared in is included here. Each review includes my analysis of the film and her performance, as well as where the film fits in her career. You will also find essential film facts, award wins and nominations, and trivia and fun facts.

Not all projects Meryl has been affiliated with are covered. Her 1977 television movie *The Deadliest Season* was unavailable to screen, as were her 2003 TV series documentary *Freedom: A History of Us* and her 2006 short film *The Music of Regret*. Her voice-work in *The Ant Bully*, as well as in *The Simpsons* and *King of the Hill*, are not given their own separate entries, although they are mentioned in my essay about *Fantastic Mr. Fox*. I almost included a week looking at her funny cameo in The Farrelly Brothers' *Stuck on You*, but in the end there wasn't enough in that movie to warrant a fifty-third entry. And her quick appearance in *The Earth Day Special*, which aired on ABC in 1990, is so bizarre that it feels wrong to ignore it, but ultimately it serves more as a question mark rather than a project worthy of discussion. Lastly, this is not a book that focuses on Meryl's personal life. While I occasionally mention an aspect of her life—that she has two daughters who are working actresses, for example, as well as her tie to the actor John Cazale—this is a book about her movies, and the movies themselves.

The films are discussed in order, from *Julia*, her 1977 film debut, all the way to her 2014 musical, *Into the Woods*. Are you ready to take the journey?

WEEK 1
JULIA
(1977)

FILM FACTS

DISTRIBUTOR: 20th Century Fox
RELEASE DATE: October 2, 1977

DIRECTOR: Fred Zinnemann
WRITER: Alvin Sargent (based on the novel by Lillian Hellman)
PRODUCER: Richard Roth
ALSO STARRING: Jane Fonda, Vanessa Redgrave, Jason Robards, Hal Holbrook

REVIEW

Where does greatness begin? Even the best actors working today endured trying beginnings in their careers. Know what Tom Hanks' first film was? A schlocky 1980 horror movie called *He Knows You're Alone*. Leonardo DiCaprio received some of the best reviews of his career for *The Wolf of Wall Street*, but do you know where he started? *Critters 3*. Sandra Bullock, who gets better and better each year and was acclaimed the world over for her work in *Gravity*, started in a terrible, barely released B-movie called *Hangmen*. Of course there are your exceptions: Kate Winslet's film debut is the haunting *Heavenly Creatures*, and Edward Norton somehow bypassed a turkey on the resume by dazzling audiences in *Primal Fear*.

So where did Meryl Streep, the greatest living film actress, get her start? You may be disappointed (or relieved) to learn that of Meryl's fifty-two motion pictures I'll be looking at, there are very few stinkers in the bunch, and that even her earliest work showcases not just her talent but her tremendous taste in material. Meryl could have taken whatever work she could get (and has even said in interviews she did just that), but her first few films she made in the late 1970s include three Oscar winning films still wildly viewed and discussed today, along with a hugely popular TV mini-series that became her first major introduction to audiences around the world. She shot a little-seen (and currently unavailable) TV movie called *The Deadliest Season* in 1976 (and voiced a role in a film called *Everybody Rides the Carousel* a year earlier), but her first major part in a motion picture came in 1977, with her brief but memorable role in *Julia*.

Born June 22, 1949, as Mary Louise Streep, she first called Summit, New Jersey her home. Her mother was Mary Wolf, a commercial artist and art editor, who Meryl went on to say in her Golden Globes acceptance speech for *Julie & Julia* shared Julia Child's verve and had a joy in living. Her father was Henry William Street, Jr., a pharmaceutical executive who Meryl described in an interview with Charlie Rose as a romantic, and she has two brothers, Dana and Harry. She received her Bachelor of

Arts degree in Drama from Vassar College in 1971, and a Master of Fine Arts degree from the Yale School of Drama.

Her stage career started in the mid-1970s, with featured roles in such plays as *The Taming of the Shrew*, *Henry V*, and *Measure for Measure*, the latter of which she starred opposite John Cazale, the powerhouse actor from *The Godfather* who she entered a relationship and stayed with until his death in 1978. She started auditioning for film roles, and didn't succeed right away. (One film she didn't get was *King Kong*, because producer Dino De Laurentiis didn't find her sexy enough.) She continued to appear on stage, receiving a Tony Award nomination for Best Featured Actress for her role in Tennessee Williams' *27 Wagons Full of Cotton*, and she also played in Anton Chekhov's *The Cherry Orchard*, which Meryl later claimed caught Robert De Niro's attention. She was doing such good work in play after play that it was inevitable that she would make the seamless transition to the screen, and the first director to give her a shot was director Fred Zinnemann.

While her second major film role in *The Deer Hunter* went on to garner Meryl her first Oscar nomination, her role in *Julia* is fleeting and only lasts a few minutes in the two-hour film. Zinnemann was so impressed by Meryl in her audition that he considered her for the title role of Julia, which eventually went to Vanessa Redgrave (who won the 1977 Oscar for Best Supporting Actress). Unfortunately, she was a total unknown as a film actress at the time, so he decided to cast her in the smaller, less pivotal role as Anne Marie. It's probably the only major film she appeared in that doesn't give her a single title card in the credits—she's listed in the beginning but among seven other actors—and it may be her shortest time on screen in a movie ever. But even though she's given little to say and work with, boy, does she make an impression.

Julia tells the story of Lillian Hellman (Jane Fonda), a struggling writer who reminisces about a magical childhood she spent with a best friend named Julia (Redgrave). After she finally writes a hit play, she becomes the toast of New York, and she's invited to a writers' conference in Russia. Julia, who has been battling against Nazism in Germany, asks Lillian to smuggle money on her trip to Russia to assist in Julia's anti-Nazi cause.

Meryl plays Anne Marie, an old friend of Lillian's who, in her first of two scenes, tries to make conversation with the newly celebrated playwright. Wearing a fancy pink dress and a long black wig, Meryl makes her first appearance on-screen in a major motion picture commanding the frame in what is otherwise Fonda's movie. Meryl's facial reaction upon seeing Fonda walk into the restaurant is priceless—she instantly infuses her character with a recognizable personality—and the disappointed look she gives her when she's ignored allows backstory for the character, with almost no dialogue uttered at all.

Her second of two scenes offers the real meat of her performance in *Julia*, the only time she gets substantial dialogue and the opportunity to really play off Fonda. This time, she dips her head a lot, and glances all around the bar, looking less excited to see her than she did the other night. Wearing an over-the-top red dress and a fur around her shoulders, she barely gives Fonda a chance to speak. And then, just when the viewer has become intrigued by this supporting character, she walks off, never to be seen again for the remainder of the picture. She's so striking in these two moments that it's a shame her character couldn't have received more screen-time.

Meryl's film debut doesn't have the pizzazz of Winslet in *Heavenly Creatures* or Norton in *Primal Fear*, mostly because her screen-time is too limited. But there are far worse ways for an actor to get his or her start than in a major motion picture starring Jane Fonda, one that went on to be nominated for a whopping eleven Academy Award nominations, and winning three. While the movie today is a bit dated at times and only works in certain sections, never as a cohesive whole, there is a lot to love about *Julia*, starting with Meryl's oh-too-brief debut. At the 2014 AFI Lifetime Achievement Award to Fonda, Meryl began the ceremony by thanking Fonda publicly for recommending her to other producers and directors, which likely got Meryl her second job, and her third, and her fourth. Who would have thought after appearing in less than five minutes in *Julia* all the decades of brilliant work that were to come.

AWARDS WATCH

Meryl received no awards or nominations for her first film role, but the movie itself received multiple. It earned eleven Academy Award nominations, and won three—Best Adapted Screenplay for Alvin Sargent, Best Supporting Actor for Robards, and Best Supporting Actress for Redgrave. In addition, the film received seven Golden

Globe nominations (and won two) and ten BAFTA nominations (and won four). Zinnemann was nominated for a DGA Award, and Sargent won the WGA Award for Best Adapted Screenplay.

FUN FACTS

Meryl's film debut.

Fonda was originally cast as Julia.

Faye Dunaway, Julie Christie, and Barbra Streisand all turned down the role of Julia.

Jack Nicholson was offered the role of Dashiell Hammett. He would go on to star with Meryl in *Heartburn* and *Ironweed*.

Meryl would appear in another movie with the word Julia in the title—2009's *Julie & Julia*.

WEEK 2
HOLOCAUST
(1978)

FILM FACTS

DISTRIBUTOR: NBC
PREMIERE DATE: April 16, 1978

DIRECTOR: Marvin J. Chomsky
WRITER: Gerald Green
PRODUCER: Robert Berger
ALSO STARRING: James Woods, Rosemary Harris, Michael Moriarty, David Warner

REVIEW

Even though many consider Meryl the best feature film actress of her generation, many forget to mention how fantastic she has been on the small screen, too. A lot of actors start in television, work their way into movies, then never look back, but Meryl has never fully turned her back on TV projects. By the time she won her Oscars for *Kramer vs. Kramer* and *Sophie's Choice*, she was a full-fledged film star, highly respected, with no need to ever return to television. However, she appeared in a TV movie in 1997 called *...First Do No Harm*, then gave not one but several tour-de-force performances in the HBO mini-series *Angels in America*, in 2003. She even appeared on Lisa Kudrow's *Web Therapy*, as a sex therapist named Camilla Bowner. Meryl goes where the stories are, where the rich characters dwell, and such was the case for her first true breakthrough: an eight-hour miniseries called *Holocaust*, which aired on TV screens all around the world in 1978.

While she had appeared briefly in *Julia* the year before, and had a pivotal role in *The Deer Hunter*, which would be released to enormous acclaim that following December, *Holocaust* was the first production that truly introduced Meryl Streep to mass audiences. Aired over four nights, the mini-series received great critical acclaim, and Meryl won an Emmy award for Outstanding Lead Actress in a Limited Series, her first major nomination and win in a career that would bring her accolades almost every year since.

Meryl plays Inga Helms Weiss, who in the first scene of the mini-series marries Karl (a young James Woods) and becomes a member of a German Jewish family. The opening in many ways has shades of the opening of *The Godfather*, in that both start with a happy celebratory wedding before the darkness shows its ugly face. The series makes the many members of this Weiss family the eyes and ears of the Holocaust, starting in 1935 Berlin and taking us well into the 1940s. The production includes a who's who of character actors of the time, like Michael Moriarty as Erik Dorf, David Warner as Heydrich, Ian Holm as Heinrich Himmler, and Rosemary Harris as Berta Palitz Weiss.

Unlike *Julia*, in which Meryl wears a black wig, she has her signature long blonde hair in this, looking how she did in real life at the time. She gives a relaxed performance, one that shows already how assured she is in her craft. Also, unlike *Julia*, she plays a major role here, giving plenty of memorable moments throughout this long and involving story. An early scene between her and Woods expressively shows her love for him, and her fear in losing him. Another moving scene involves Meryl begging to see, or at least write, to her husband. Again, she doesn't go overboard in her emotion, and an outburst she gives at the end is controlled and warranted. (Another outburst she gives, in which she throws milk into a solder's face, is even more necessary.)

Her emotions go up and down throughout the mini-series. In some scenes she's trying to be the one in control. In others, like when she's informed of a death in the family, she breaks down crying. Her most touching moment of all comes when she finally reunites with her husband and tells him, "Because no matter what happens, I will be with you." This scene had the possibility of playing maudlin, but she brings it a humanity that feels just right, and in no way sentimental. And, finally, her most raw moment in the entire mini-series comes when her husband leaves her again, and she breaks down sobbing in his arms. She knows this is the last time she will see him, and that nothing will ever be the same.

Of course these scenes ring even more true to viewers if they understand what was happening in Meryl's real life at the time. Before his death in 1978, Meryl lived with John

Cazale, a tremendous actor who has the unique distinction in having all five of the films he starred in nominated for Best Picture (*The Godfather*, *The Godfather Part II*, *The Conversation*, *Dog Day Afternoon*, and *The Deer Hunter*). As her co-star James Woods noted at her AFI Life Achievement ceremony in 2004, Cazale was dying while Meryl was shooting *Holocaust*, and he passed away soon after production wrapped. These scenes in the mini-series of Meryl having to say good-bye to the love of her life, not once but twice, must have been difficult for her, considering the tragedy that was slowly occurring in her personal life. While Meryl rarely in public discusses the relationship she had with Cazale, he obviously made a major impact on her when they were together, and the more emotional scenes she had to undertake in this series must have taken a toll on her at the time.

Holocaust is a major time commitment, at a whopping eight hours in length, but it is definitely worth watching if you are a hardcore Meryl fan. This is the best work she had done on screen to date, and while her scenes throughout the series are few and far between, she is in a lot more than you might think, and she shows the spark of her talent that would only grow in the years to come.

AWARDS WATCH

Meryl received the Emmy for Outstanding Lead Actress in a Limited Series.

Holocaust earned fifteen Emmy nominations, and won eight, including Outstanding Directing in a Drama Series for Marvin J. Chomsky, Outstanding Writing in a Drama Series for Gerald Green, and Outstanding Lead Actor in a Limited Series for Michael Moriarty. It also received three Golden Globe nominations (and won two), and won Chomsky the DGA Award for Outstanding Directorial Achievement in Specials/Movies for TV.

FUN FACTS

Meryl's first TV mini-series.

So many people watched *Holocaust* in New York City when first broadcast that when commercials were on, the local water pressure dropped due to so many people using their toilets at once.

The term "Holocaust" didn't exist in the German language until the 1980s. Due to the success of the mini-series, it became common knowledge.

WEEK 3
THE DEER HUNTER (1978)

FILM FACTS

DISTRIBUTOR: Universal Pictures
RELEASE DATE: December 8, 1978

DIRECTOR: Michael Cimino
WRITER: Deric Washburn
PRODUCERS: Michael Cimino, Michael Deeley, John Peverall, Barry Spikings
ALSO STARRING: Robert De Niro, John Cazale, John Savage, Christopher Walken

REVIEW

Meryl Streep wasn't a household name by the end of 1978, despite her widely-seen performance in NBC's *Holocaust* mini-series, but one film certainly brought her closer to such a status: Michael Cimino's Oscar-winning masterpiece, *The Deer Hunter*. Starring Robert De Niro, Christopher Walken, and John Cazale, the film was critically and financially successful, and took home the Best Picture Academy Award for 1978. It is a disturbing, hypnotic film, one that examines the before, during, and aftermath of war—in this case, Vietnam—and how it affects close friends and loved ones. While many films of the 1970s have become dated, this one is as timeless as films get, with a unique narrative structure that is rarely utilized in films today. And while Meryl's role of Linda is not the most important in the film—even she has said in interviews that she essentially just plays the *girl* in this—she is pivotal to the success of the movie, giving her character a heart and soul when it doesn't appear as if there was much of one on the page.

How did Meryl come to be in an epic film of this magnitude? She had mostly worked on stage before *The Deer Hunter*, and she only had TV movies and a bit part in *Julia* for her film and TV credits. Well, it appears we can thank De Niro for giving Meryl her first major break. Meryl said, in an interview with the British Academy of Film and Television Arts, that De Niro had seen her perform in the stage play, *The Cherry Orchard*. Meryl doesn't remember her performance as the maid in that play being particularly memorable, but De Niro must have seen a spark of something, because he himself cast Meryl in *The Deer Hunter*, the one significant female role in the film.

The Deer Hunter is separated into three parts. The first hour of the film allows the viewer to spend time with a group of friends—Michael (De Niro), Stan (Cazale), Steven (John Savage), and Nick (Walken)—before they embark on their journey into Vietnam. The men live in Clairton, Pennsylvania, and they spend most of their time getting drunk at the bar, and attending Steven's Orthodox wedding. It's particularly fascinating to note how long the wedding sequence goes on in this film, with endless scenes of people dancing, saluting the happy couple, then dancing again. In any movie made today, this scene would probably be chopped in half, but Cimino and De Niro had the clout at the time to let the sequence play as long as they wanted.

Meryl plays Linda, Nick's girlfriend. She is a strong, sensitive character who loves Nick with all heart and agrees to marry him. However, after the men return from Vietnam, nothing stays the same. Michael has always had feelings for Linda, and when they both think they have lost Nick, the two of them grow closer together. The role of Linda could have been forgettable in the hands of another actress, but Meryl gives the character immense weight, with moments of joy as well as heartache. Her emotional scenes toward the end of the movie, when she recognizes the love she has lost, make a lasting impression.

Of course her impending loss of her then lover Cazale, who plays a major role in the film and stands right beside her in a few scenes, makes some of the sadder moments in the last third of the movie all the more heart wrenching. Here she is, like in *Holocaust*, playing a woman dealing with the loss of the man she loves, while at the same time in real life dealing with the terminal illness of the man she loved. Cazale was so sick that many balked at his even being in the movie, but De Niro insisted he be involved, and Meryl threatened to quit if they recast the role. They ended up filming Cazale's scenes first, and he passed away in March 1978, nine months before the picture's premiere.

The Deer Hunter is an astounding, impeccably directed, and immensely watchable movie. The scene that everyone remembers takes place during the middle hour, a section that Meryl is not a part of; the Vietnam portion includes the famous Russian Roulette scene, a freakishly intense moment of the film that comes back to haunt and firmly put an end to one of the movie's central characters. There is also an effective storyline in the film that relates to the title itself, when Michael approaches a deer a second time, after having been through the hell of war. As great as the film is, however, this is not Meryl's movie. She is a significant character but only in the beginning and end, which was also the case in her breakthrough movie a year later, *Kramer vs. Kramer*.

But whether Meryl is in one or two scenes of the movie (*Julia* and *The Homesman*), is in a large chunk but not all (*The Hours* and *Julie & Julia*), is there every step of the way (*The River Wild* and *Music of the Heart*), or appears at the beginning and end (*The Deer Hunter* and *Kramer Vs. Kramer*), she always makes an impression. In *The Deer Hunter* she becomes the object of two mens' affections, and we buy their love for her right away. Who wouldn't fall in love with Meryl, then or now? At the end of the film, in arguably its saddest scene, the friends sit around the dinner table and sing "God Bless America." Who at the table starts singing first? Meryl, with that melodic voice that would go on to grace both musicals and non-musicals in the decades to come. She might not be the star of *The Deer Hunter*, but she stands out as a true talent, in an ensemble of some of the most gifted actors working in the 1970s.

AWARDS WATCH

Meryl received her first Academy Award nomination, for Best Supporting Actress. She also earned her first Golden Globe nomination and BAFTA Award nomination. In addition, she won the Marquee Best Supporting Actress Award at the American Movie Awards, and Best Supporting Actress at the National Society of Film Critics Awards.

The Deer Hunter received nine Academy Award nominations, and won five—Best Sound, Film Editing, Supporting Actor for Walken, Director, and Picture. It also won Cimino a Best Director Golden Globe and the DGA Award. Also, the New York Film Critics Circle awarded *The Deer Hunter* Best Film and Best Supporting Actor for Walken.

FUN FACTS

This film earned Meryl her first Oscar nomination.

De Niro has said that this was his most physically exhausting film.

Cazale died shortly after filming was completed.

Walken achieved the hollow look of his character by eating only rice and bananas.

All the scenes were shot on location.

Meryl improvised some of her lines.

To date, the first of three Meryl films to win the Best Picture Academy Award.

WEEK 4
MANHATTAN
(1979)

FILM FACTS

DISTRIBUTOR: United Artists
RELEASE DATE: April 25, 1979

DIRECTOR: Woody Allen
WRITERS: Woody Allen, Marshall Brickman
PRODUCERS: Charles H. Joffe, Jack Rollins
ALSO STARRING: Woody Allen, Diane Keaton, Michael Murphy, Mariel Hemingway

REVIEW

The legendary Woody Allen writes fascinating female characters in his movies, from Diane Keaton's Annie Hall, to Hannah and both her sisters, to Alice and the wives in Husbands and Wives, and of course, to the bluest Jasmine. Think of your favorite actresses and it's likely they have appeared in an Allen film. Julia Roberts? Jodie Foster? Helena Bonham Carter? Winona Ryder? The list goes on and on.

But unless you're a diehard Meryl fan, you might not know that she appeared in an Allen film, one of his best and most famous. You might not know because the role came early in her career—she shot her role in early 1978, months before *The Deer Hunter* even opened—and the part is small, only three scenes long. Released in April 1979, *Manhattan* is Allen's glorious love letter to his favorite city, shot in gorgeous black-and-white, with a stellar cast that includes Allen, Mariel Hemingway (in an Oscar-nominated role), Diane Keaton, and Michael Murphy. While not a huge hit at the time, it has gone on to be considered one of Allen's all-time classic films, and it gave Meryl another leg up in her blossoming career.

Meryl does the best she can with her scenes in *Manhattan*, playing an ex-wife of Allen's who is writing a tell-all book about their marriage. Her role as Jill marks her first contentious turn in a movie; the sweet girl from *Holocaust* and *The Deer Hunter* this is not. She is angry, conniving. You almost see the makings of Miranda Priestly in *The Devil Wears Prada*. In her first scene with Allen, she's walking down a sidewalk, her long blonde hair blowing in the wind, a downbeat frown on her face. She is so confident in herself that she won't even entertain the idea of not writing her book, and all Allen can really do is keep up with her as she tries to get away.

Meryl has played a lesbian on film twice, in *The Hours*, and in *Manhattan*. Despite her previous relationship with Allen's character Isaac, and the fact that they have a kid together, she is seen in the second scene sharing her home with a woman. She is a bit perkier this time, as she welcomes Isaac into her home and offers him coffee. But as soon as he mentions the book she goes ballistic on him again. This scene, like her first, is played in one long shot; it obviously didn't take Meryl long to film this movie. In a 1997 interview for a Premiere magazine article, she said that she worked on the movie for two or three days and didn't really get to know Allen; she ultimately felt he hated her character.

What she's saying is probably right, since Jill is fairly underwritten and doesn't do much of anything but yell at him. In her third and final scene, she says the book is, yet again, "an honest account of our marriage," and her closing line, "I've had some interest in this book for a movie sale," is a little anticlimactic for her character, reducing her in a way to some kind of villain. She's got that great icy exterior we would see from Meryl in many of her later movies—*Doubt* comes to mind—but it would have been nice for Allen to give her character more to do.

The quality of Allen's films has always been up and down, especially in the last fifteen years, but his output in the 1970s and 1980s is almost universally excellent. He made *Annie Hall*, *Interiors*, and *Manhattan* back to back—a true testimony to his genius—and in the next decade he made such winners as *The Purple Rose of Cairo*, *Hannah and Her Sisters*, and *Crimes and Misdemeanors*. *Manhattan* is memorable for its hilarious dialogue—this is one of Allen's sharpest scripts—and its sumptuous black-and-white photography that makes New York look like a dream. It's also noteworthy for being one of the last on-screen collaborations between Allen and Keaton after a successful run of five films (they would appear together in one more movie—1993's *Manhattan Murder Mystery*).

The one creepy aspect of *Manhattan* that harms it a little, especially watching it these days, is Allen's on-screen relationship with a seventeen-year-old girl played by Hemingway. Not only is it weird to watch a forty-two-year old dating a girl still in high school; the details behind the scandal that broke up Allen's marriage to Mia Farrow in the early 1990s is difficult to erase from your mind. If Hemingway's character had been written to be an older college student, the romance in the film probably wouldn't come off so weird.

Not to say that Hemingway is bad in the movie; she is excellent in her role, natural in her acting and mature for her age. She made such an impression that she received an Academy Award nomination for Best Supporting Actress. She ultimately, though, lost out to Meryl, who won for *Kramer vs. Kramer*. Yes, Meryl had a tremendous 1979, appearing not just in *Manhattan* but also in *The Seduction of Joe Tynan* with Alan Alda, and *Kramer vs. Kramer*. Meryl's work that year stood out so much that she received Best Supporting Actress recognition from the Los Angeles Film Critics and the National Society of Film Critics for all *three* of the films she appeared in. While Meryl gave her best and most well-rounded performance that year in *Kramer vs. Kramer*, she did terrific work in *Manhattan*, her first and to date only collaboration with the great Woody Allen.

AWARDS WATCH

Meryl received a BAFTA Award nomination for Best Supporting Actress, and for her performances in this film, as well as for *The Seduction of Joe Tynan* and *Kramer vs. Kramer*, she won Best Supporting Actress from the Los Angeles Film Critics, the National Board of Review, and the National Society of Film Critics.

Manhattan earned two Academy Award nominations, for Best Original Screenplay and Best Supporting Actress for Hemingway. *Manhattan* also received a Golden Globe nomination for Best Motion Picture – Drama, and won Best Film at the BAFTA Awards. In addition, Allen got DGA Award and WGA Award nominations.

FUN FACTS

Meryl shot her scenes during breaks in filming on *Kramer vs. Kramer*.

Allen hated this film so much that he offered to make another movie for United Artists for free if they elected not to release *Manhattan*.

The cinematographer Gordon Willis has said this was his favorite movie he shot.

The title of the book Meryl's character wrote in the film is "Marriage, Divorce, and Selfhood."

WEEK 5
THE SEDUCTION OF JOE TYNAN (1979)

FILM FACTS

DISTRIBUTOR: Universal Pictures
RELEASE DATE: August 17, 1979

DIRECTOR: Jerry Schatzberg
WRITER: Alan Alda
PRODUCER: Martin Bregman
ALSO STARRING: Alan Alda, Barbara Harris, Rip Torn, Melvyn Douglas

REVIEW

Few of Meryl's movies can be considered obscure, but *The Seduction of Joe Tynan* would arguably be one of her least known titles on her resume. Released in 1979, the same year she appeared in *Manhattan* and *Kramer vs. Kramer*, *The Seduction of Joe Tynan* is a competent but unremarkable film, starring and written by Alan Alda. The pacing is slow, the cinematography is flat, and the whole endeavor feels from top to bottom like a glorified TV movie. The actors ultimately elevate the film, though, particularly Meryl; while this is not one of her better performances, she does a fine job, and gives far more life to her character than there likely was on the page.

Alda is considered to this day one of our finest actors. Nominated for an Academy Award for his performance in *The Aviator*, he has been a working actor for nearly five decades, appearing in such memorable films as *Crimes and Misdemeanors*, *California Suite*, and *Same Time, Next Year*. He was at the height of his popularity in the late 1970s, when his critically acclaimed smash hit of a TV show *MASH* was entering its later seasons, and he surely had the clout at this time to do anything he wanted; therefore, he was able to get a screenplay he wrote called *The Seduction of Joe Tynan* off the ground, with him also starring in the title role. Directed by Jerry Schatzberg (*Scarecrow*, *The Panic in Needle Park*), the film features a stellar supporting cast, including Barbara Harris, Melvyn Douglas, and the great Rip Torn, who Meryl would share the screen with a decade later in *Defending Your Life*.

Meryl rounds out the cast, and in *The Seduction of Joe Tynan*, she gets to do a lot more than one might expect. While Alda is the lead in the film, Meryl is in more of this movie than she was in *Manhattan*, as well as her Oscar-winning role in *Kramer vs. Kramer*. She plays Karen Traynor, a southern researcher who helps Joe prepare a case leading the opposition to a Supreme Court appointment. Married to his sweet but clueless wife Ellie (Harris), Joe takes an immediate fancy to Karen, and barely thirty minutes into the movie, he's already making his first move on her. One joy of the film is seeing her show a sense of fun on-screen. There is a moment early on when she and Alda go to bed together, and instead of a maudlin romantic montage, we get Meryl dumping beer on Alda's naked crotch and laughing hysterically. Her character is a bit stiff when we first meet her, but she slowly gets to unwind as the film goes on.

The Seduction of Joe Tynan was the first film Meryl made after the passing of her beloved John Cazale, and even she has said she was on automatic pilot during the filming because she was still grieving. She has said that it was the supportive Alda who helped get her though the process. But again, this is not to say that she gives a bad performance.

She appeared in three films in 1979, in each as a blonde, in each as a supporting player to the male lead, but unlike in *Manhattan*, where she is angry and spends most of her time yelling, and in *Kramer vs. Kramer*, where she is often confused and trying to find herself before she can accept a child into her world again, in *The Seduction of Joe Tynan* she plays a confident, independent woman who knows what she is getting into when she enters the affair. Meryl is more gorgeous in this film than she possibly ever has been on screen, her hair up in a bun, her clothes professional and conservative. And she gets her fair share of emotional highs and lows, especially in a sad scene at the end when she has to say good-bye to a torn-up Joe.

The Seduction of Joe Tynan came out at a time when Meryl's career was about to explode. *Kramer vs. Kramer* was a few months away, which was soon followed by her first

Academy Award, for Best Supporting Actress. After that came the releases of *The French Lieutenant's Woman*, *Sophie's Choice*, and *Silkwood* in the early 1980s, all cementing her status as one of America's finest actresses. *The Seduction of Joe Tynan* is an interesting political film, with solid performances all around, and it offered what was probably the last glimpse of Meryl before she became a respected worldwide figure. It's not among her best work, but it is definitely worth seeking out if you're a hardcore fan.

AWARDS WATCH

Meryl did not receive any nominations or awards for this performance alone, but she did win Best Supporting Actress from the Los Angeles Film Critics, National Board of Review, and National Society of Film Critics for her supporting work in her three 1979 films.

The Seduction of Joe Tynan won Alda a Marquee Best Actor Award at the American Movie Awards, and Douglas won Best Supporting Actor for this film and for Hal Ashby's *Being There* from the Los Angeles Film Critics, the National Society of Film Critics, and the New York Film Critics Circle.

FUN FACTS

Meryl has admitted in interviews she only made this movie to cope with the loss of her lover Cazale's death.

Alda spent three years writing the script. It was his first produced screenplay.

Final lead role in a major feature film for Harris.

The film was originally titled *The Senator*.

WEEK 6
KRAMER VS. KRAMER (1979)

FILM FACTS

DISTRIBUTOR: Columbia Pictures
PREMIERE DATE: December 19, 1979

DIRECTOR: Robert Benton
WRITER: Robert Benton (based on the novel by Avery Corman)
PRODUCER: Stanley R. Jaffe
ALSO STARRING: Dustin Hoffman, Justin Henry, Jane Alexander, Howard Duff, JoBeth Williams

REVIEW

When did Meryl become a star? Some might argue that it happened when she shared the screen with Jane Fonda in *Julia*. Others might argue that it happened when she was nominated for an Oscar for her performance in *The Deer Hunter*. These observations are valid, but few would disagree that Meryl had her first major breakthrough with *Kramer vs. Kramer*, the film that won Meryl her first Oscar, and the film that worked its way into the hearts of millions in late 1979 and early 1980. Winner of the Academy Award for Best Picture, *Kramer vs. Kramer* remains not just one of

Meryl's best films, but one of the best movies ever made. And while she is not the lead, her affecting performance lingers in the viewer's memory long after the film has ended. Her scenes in this film crackle with honesty, intensity, raw emotion. And it's a moment in a courtroom, as she delivers a devastating monologue she wrote herself, that I would argue made Meryl a bonafide movie star.

Meryl wasn't even supposed to play Joanna Kramer. Kate Jackson was initially slated for the part but had to drop out due to her commitment to *Charlie's Angels*. After that, despite interest in Meryl for the role, producer Stanley R. Jaffe didn't even want to consider her, due to her commitment to a play and acting in Woody Allen's *Manhattan*. Jaffe wanted Meryl on *Kramer vs. Kramer* only if she were to drop her other engagements, so it took the enthusiasm of both Dustin Hoffman—who at this point had appeared in classics like *The Graduate*, *Lenny*, and *All the President's Men*—and director Robert Benton to officially bring her on board. Despite her Oscar nomination for *The Deer Hunter*, Meryl was not the likeliest choice for Joanna at the time, and there must have been pressure put on Benton to find a bigger name for the role. Thankfully, he stuck to his guns, cast the best actress there was for the part, and in the end catapulted Meryl into the most incredibly diverse and exciting career any actress has ever enjoyed.

Again, Hoffman was a star at the time, while Meryl wasn't. Similarly, Hoffman is the lead of *Kramer vs. Kramer*, while Meryl has far less screen time. Therefore it was another risky move to open the movie on Meryl's face, as she sits on her son's bed, stroking his back. She appears so calm, so in love with that little boy, that nobody watching can expect her to do what she's about to do in the next two minutes. When Joanna's husband Ted (Hoffman, in one of his finest roles) comes home, excited to talk to his wife of eight years about a major account acquired at work, she gives him back his keys, and tells him she's leaving him. For good. And she's not taking Billy (Justin Henry, who gives one of the best child performances ever put to film). Ted barely has time to process what she's telling him before she enters the elevator and walks out of his life. Ted has never been much of a parental figure to Billy, but once he's all his son has, he transforms from a workaholic advertising executive to a father who truly cares about his kid. And then, just when father and son start developing a real bond together, Joanna returns to New York, feeling like a new person, and ready to take back what she believes is hers: her little boy.

Kramer vs. Kramer is such an engaging film because viewers see themselves up there on the screen, whether they have kids, have been married or divorced, or none of the above. This is the story of a family that becomes broken, then becomes unbroken, then threatens to become broken yet again. Since we spend so much time with Ted and Billy, by the time Joanna enters the picture again, we don't want her there. Her reappearance in the third act of the movie is startling because she's gone from the movie for so long we almost forget she's going to come back. And when she does, the unthinkable becomes a pained reality: when the two Kramers go up against each other in court, it's likely from the get-go that the judge will side with the mother and not the father, as is often the case. But we've seen Ted and Billy create a life together, and we don't want that to go away.

Meryl has the hardest acting job in the film because she is, in a sense, the antagonist. Walking away from your seven-year-old child many would probably consider one of the most selfish acts a mother could do. The audience doesn't agree with her decision, and by the time Ted has finished his character arc and becomes a stand-up dad who will do anything for his kid, her insistence on getting Billy back grates on us. We are on his side, not hers. And yet it's remarkable how Meryl, with the small amount of screen-time she has here, still ultimately makes Joanna sympathetic. We never come to actually hate her, and in the hands of almost any other actress, this character might have become a one-note villain. Meryl, however, always gives Joanna a point of view that makes sense, especially in her long courtroom monologue that brings her, and us, to tears.

She is insanely good and focused and so very real in every scene in *Kramer vs. Kramer*. Her first scene at the beginning is devastating, with a pain in her eyes in each step she takes away from her boy. When she comes back, meeting with Ted at a restaurant after more than a year away, she has a lightness about her, feeling more positive both mentally and physically. For a minute it appears like they might even have a pleasant conversation, but all things turn sour when she brings up Billy. Ted cuts Joanna off almost immediately and says she can't have him. An improvised moment at the end, when Ted shatters his wine glass against the wall, shakes us, almost as much as it shook

Meryl; she didn't know Hoffman was going to push the glass off the table, and Meryl's shocked expression is real.

Meryl's shining moment in *Kramer vs. Kramer* takes place in the courtroom. Not until now do we truly get a sense of what her character was going through fifteen months ago, and what she's going through currently. Benton wrote the scene in full, but days before they shot, he told Meryl he wanted her to write the speech herself, to make it more real. Her acting in this scene is exquisite; that Meryl took the time to write these beautiful words herself is just extraordinary. Just her delivery of "I'm his mother... I'm his mother," her teary eyes focusing on her ex-husband, is enough to take your breath away. It is in this scene that the truth of the character finally comes out, and while it's still difficult to imagine a mother walking away from her child, the personal demons and struggles she was going through make sense to us, and it's not unfathomable to think it was right for her to go away.

Of course, it is still heartbreaking to learn that the judge chooses Joanna over Ted, and so we're left wondering, as the film draws to a close, just how we're going to feel when he finally has to hand over his child. When Billy sits solemnly on the sofa, all packed and ready to go, with Ted doing his best to put on a happy face, it appears that no happy ending is in store. But the final scene changes everything. After the bitter courtroom battle they have both suffered through, Joanna comes to the realization that very morning that she can't take her son away from his father. "I realize he already is home," she says. I defy you not to cry in watching this final scene. Again, with another actress, this moment could read false. She has been fighting to get her son back for the past thirty minutes of the movie. Is she really going to just let him go? But again, her reasoning for having him stay with his father makes sense, and her stream of tears tells us that no matter how much it hurts, she knows she is making the right decision. The film closes on a memorable image, of Joanna standing inside the elevator, staring back at the man she never knew could truly be a father. "How do I look?" she says to him. "You look terrific," he replies. There's no sense that things are going to be any easier from here on out, but at least an agreement has been made to allow Ted to not lose the one thing that he loves more than life itself.

Kramer vs. Kramer was the last of Meryl's three 1979 films to be released, and she couldn't have ended the decade on a bigger high. Not only did *Kramer vs. Kramer* do well at the box office, making more than 100 million; it swept the Academy Awards, winning Best Picture, Director, Screenplay, Actor, and Supporting Actress, for Meryl. In her acceptance speech, she opened with "Holy mackerel," and thanked Hoffman, Benton, and Jaffe for the career-changing opportunity. Would Meryl have gone on to become a big star without *Kramer vs. Kramer*? Sure she would've. But this incredibly moving and affecting film, one that has stood the test of time and still resonates with viewers thirty-five years later, certainly helped paved the way for all that Meryl was to accomplish. She is mesmerizing in this movie, so beautiful and thoughtful and complicated, bringing to life in just a few minutes of screen-time a fully realized character who is one of the most memorable creations in her remarkable career. Meryl can do no wrong. And with *Kramer vs. Kramer*, she did one of her best.

AWARDS WATCH

Meryl won the Academy Award for Best Supporting Actress, her first of three Oscars to date. She also won the Golden Globe for Best Supporting Actress and earned a BAFTA Award nomination for Best Actress (not Supporting Actress). In addition, she won Best Supporting Actress from numerous critics group, for *Kramer vs. Kramer* and for *The Seduction of Joe Tynan* and *Manhattan*.

Kramer vs. Kramer won forty-three awards and was nominated for an additional seventeen. It swept the Academy Awards, winning Best Adapted Screenplay, Actor for Hoffman, Supporting Actress for Meryl, Director, and Picture. It was also nominated for Best Film Editing, Cinematography, Supporting Actress for Jane Alexander, and Supporting Actor for Henry, who at age eight became the youngest nominee for a competitive award in Academy history. The film won Best Picture – Drama at the Golden Globes and received six BAFTA Award nominations. Benton also won the DGA Award and WGA Award.

FUN FACTS

This film won Meryl her first Academy Award. She famous left her just-claimed Oscar on the back of a toilet during the 1980 festivities.

Hoffman planned the moment when he throws his wine glass against the wall during the contentious restaurant scene with Meryl. The only person he told was the cinematographer. In the DVD documentary, Meryl recalls yelling at Hoffman when the shot was over for scaring her.

Hoffman was going through his own marital separation during the making of the movie and thus contributed many personal moments and dialogue. Benton offered Hoffman shared screenplay credit, but Hoffman turned it down. Meryl was originally cast in the role of Ted's one-night-stand, eventually played by JoBeth Williams.

Meryl's *Angels in America* co-star Al Pacino, as well as Jon Voight and James Caan, turned down the role of Ted.

Meryl's *Julia* co-star Jane Fonda, as well as her *Death Becomes Her* co-star Goldie Hawn, turned down the role of Joanna.

The highest grossing movie of 1979.

WEEK 7
THE FRENCH LIEUTENANT'S WOMAN (1981)

FILM FACTS

DISTRIBUTOR: United Artists
RELEASE DATE: September 18, 1981

DIRECTOR: Karel Reisz
WRITER: Harold Pinter (based on the novel by John Fowles)
PRODUCER: Leon Clore
ALSO STARRING: Jeremy Irons, Lynsey Baxter, Richard Griffiths, David Warner

REVIEW

After Meryl's very busy 1979, she took a rare year off from movies, in 1980. While most consider Meryl the greatest actress of her generation, she doesn't get enough credit for how incredibly prolific she is. Since her film debut in 1977, she has appeared in at least one film almost every year, sometimes even two or three films. The only years to date she hasn't appeared in a movie are 1980, 2000, and 2010 (she was also mostly absent in 2001, too, aside from a voice credit in Steven Spielberg's *AI*).

Meryl's film career was finally up and running with her Oscar-winning role *in Kramer vs. Kramer*, and some might think she should have committed to a bunch of movies while interest in her was at a high. Instead, she went right back to the stage (appearing in *Kiss Me, Petruchio*, among other productions) and took her time in choosing not the first film project that came her way, but the best. *The French Lieutenant's Woman* was ultimately a terrific choice because it gave Meryl her first leading role in a movie, an effective showcase of dual characters, and further evidence of her versatility.

The odd, and oddly effective, dual narrative of *The French Lieutenant's Woman* must have appealed to Meryl, because not only does she get to sink her teeth into the complex role of Sarah, a 19th century Englishwoman who enters a doomed love affair with Charles (Jeremy Irons); she also gets to play the actress Anna, who is portraying the role of Sarah in the movie. Confused yet? Some actresses might have been afraid that this unusual structure would alienate audiences and not work in the least. The director Karl Reisz's only major credit at the time was *The Gambler*, starring James Caan. Harold Pinter, who wrote the screenplay, had written mostly TV movies. The novel by John Fowles was well-regarded, but many directors, like John Frankenheimer, considered the book unfilmable. It was not a guaranteed success that this script was going to work, but Meryl committed anyway, making for one of her best career choices, one almost as good as her next major project—*Sophie's Choice*.

The French Lieutenant's Woman is an interesting film more than it is an entertaining one, but it is particularly notable for being the first film in Meryl's career that gives her a ton of screen time. As Sarah, she gets to show off her impeccable British accent; this film marked the beginning of a long streak of projects where her various accents would impress audiences and critics the world over. Here, with her long strawberry blonde hair, and her British accent, she looks and sounds nothing like any character she had played before. Some actors can never disappear into their roles no matter how hard they try. We all love Julia Roberts, but is there a film she's appeared in that made you forget it was Julia up there on the screen? Meryl, on the other hand, has a unique ability to completely disappear into a role. It truly is hard to believe that the actress playing Sarah is the same one who played Joanna in *Kramer vs. Kramer*.

Meryl has a fair share of tender, emotionally complex moments in the period scenes. Just the first shot is a doozy—Meryl standing at the edge of a watery cliff. She's at once beautiful and vulnerable. One of her best scenes in the movie takes place in the forest, where the crisp cinematography makes Meryl look like she's stepped into the world of Errol Flynn. She has fallen in love with Charles but hates that he is committed to another woman Ernestina (Lynsey Baxter). "I am the French lieutenant's whore!" she says, her voice quivering. It appears this forbidden romance has no chance of ending well. And when she eventually disappears from Charles' life, he believes he has lost her forever.

Should we care if these characters end up together or not? *The French Lieutenant's Woman* makes it clear from the beginning that this period narrative is merely a movie within the movie, and that the actual story involves a pair of film actors named Anna and Mike (also played by Meryl and Irons), who are portraying Sarah and Charles. In this second, modern-day narrative, Anna and Mike are both married but are having a love affair on the set of their movie. Meryl would have received accolades for her portrayal of Sarah alone, but her spot-on take on a conceited American film actress is just as impressive. It's not often that Meryl disappears into two characters in the same movie, but she does so here. She seems five or more years older as Anna, more mature and confident. While Sarah often feels lost, Anna knows exactly what she's doing.

The novel was famous for including three alternate endings, and what Reisz and Pinter do effectively for the adaptation is give the audience two endings, one for each narrative. The period story gets a Hollywood happy ending, and the modern day story gets stuck with an unhappier, if more realistic, one. Mike even tries to get Anna's attention in the final scene by shouting, "Sarah!" suggesting that since real life can be messy and filled with disappointment, we often yearn for the hopeful conclusions that fiction so often gives us.

Many remember that Meryl won the Oscars for *Kramer vs. Kramer* and *Sophie's Choice*, but few remember just how close she got to winning for *The French Lieutenant's Woman*.

She ultimately lost out to Katharine Hepburn, who won her fourth and final Best Actress Oscar, for *On Golden Pond*, but Meryl won the Golden Globe award for Best Actress in a Drama, as well as the BAFTA Award for Best Actress. At the Academy Awards, the film was also nominated for Best Screenplay, Art Direction, Costume Design, and Film Editing. Obviously there was considerable support for the movie, so one could argue Meryl got close to her second Oscar not in 1982, but in 1981. Of course she went on to win the following year for *Sophie's Choice*, still her most impressive achievement in a career filled with too many achievements to count.

While it is not one of her best movies, *The French Lieutenant's Woman* is an original, sometimes baffling creation that brings to mind the unique creative structure of two of her later films—*The Hours* and *Adaptation*. Meryl had options after *Kramer vs. Kramer*. That she picked *The French Lieutenant's Woman* shows that she not only values great stories and characters, but that she's not afraid to take risks.

AWARDS WATCH

Meryl received her third Academy Award nomination, her first for Best Actress. She won the Golden Globe for Best Actress in a Drama and won the BAFTA Award for Best Actress. She also won Best Actress from the Los Angeles Film Critics. In addition, Fotogramas de Plata awarded her Best Foreign Movie Performer.

The French Lieutenant's Woman earned five Oscar nominations—Best Film Editing, Costume Design, Art Direction, Adapted Screenplay, and Actress for Meryl. The film also earned a Motion Picture-Drama nomination at the Golden Globes and a Best Film nomination at the BAFTA Awards. The composer Carl Davis also won a special BAFTA Award called the Anthony Asquith Award for Film Music.

FUN FACTS

The film earned Meryl her first Oscar nomination for Best Actress.

The novel doesn't feature the subplot of the actors playing the parts in a modern day film.

Harriet Walter filmed a major role, which was completely deleted from the final cut.

An attempt to adapt the novel was made in the 1970s to star Meryl's *Julia* and *Evening* co-star, Vanessa Redgrave, but the film was stalled due to script issues.

WEEK 8
STILL OF THE NIGHT (1982)

FILM FACTS

DISTRIBUTOR: United Artists
RELEASE DATE: November 19, 1982

DIRECTOR: Robert Benton
WRITER: Robert Benton
PRODUCER: Arlene Donovan
ALSO STARRING: Roy Scheider, Jessica Tandy, Joe Grifasi, Josef Summer

REVIEW

In 2012, on *Watch What Happens Live*, Andy Cohen asked Meryl, "Name one bad film that you have made." She took about two seconds to think before she said, "*Still of the Night*." We all know that one of Meryl's most acclaimed performances was in 1982's *Sophie's Choice*, but some might not be aware that Meryl had a second film released that year: *Still of the Night*, which re-teamed her with her *Kramer vs. Kramer* director Robert Benton. It's not a bad film, so much that it's a disappointing one. It's certainly one of her weaker efforts, a lame Hitchcockian rip-off that is mostly worth a look for it being Meryl's only suspense thriller.

Jamie Lee Curtis got her start in *Halloween* and *The Fog*, and Tom Hanks' first movie was the low-rent slasher flick, *He Knows You're Alone*. Brad Pitt made an early horror bomb called *Cutting Class*, and future Academy Award winners Renee Zellweger and Matthew McConaughey starred together in *The Texas Chainsaw Massacre 4*. So many actors who went on to be mega-stars got their starts in low-budget horror movies, and few began right away in A-list projects.

One could say Meryl also avoided the trap of starting in mediocrity, appearing in *Julia*, *The Deer Hunter*, *Manhattan*. Meryl started out super strong, and following her Oscar win for *Kramer vs. Kramer* and Oscar nomination for *The French Lieutenant's Woman*, it appeared as if she would do no wrong. In 1982, she would appear in *Sophie's Choice*, her best career choice yet.

So how, why, did *Still of the Night* happen? Not only is the film fairly unremarkable, but Meryl is completely miscast in the kind of part Grace Kelly or Kim Novak would have played for Alfred Hitchcock in the 1950s. She does what she can with the role of Brooke Reynolds, an art auction house worker who was having an affair with a man who has been murdered. Brooke visits the man's therapist Dr. Sam Rice, played by *Jaws*' Roy Scheider, and asks him not to reveal the affair. Rice immediately takes a liking to Brooke—her sophisticated bob of a haircut probably reminds him of a Hitchcock blonde, after all—and the two begin an affair of their own, while Rice continues to piece together the mystery of who the killer is. Could it be Brooke herself? Or is it another woman entirely?

The plot of *Still of the Night* is sort of silly, and it's a shame it's taken so deadly seriously. You can see Meryl wanting to crack a smile in almost every scene of the film, but instead, she has to keep her face totally straight. Meryl probably gets more dialogue and screen-time in this film than any other up to that point, maybe even *The French Lieutenant's Woman*, and it's a shame much of the writing lets her down. Watching Meryl here is like watching her sing "Dancing Queen" while sliding down the bannister in *Mamma Mia*—it feels a little beneath her.

Meryl could certainly succeed in a well-written suspense thriller directed by someone more knowledgeable of the genre, but *Still of the Night* is a major letdown in the suspense department, and most noticeably the scare department. Much of the film consists of dull plotting and long scenes of stilted dialogue, without much momentum, with little chemistry between her and Scheider. Worst of all, everything leads to a finale more laughable than exciting.

It's not to say that there aren't moments of interest to be found in *Still of the Night*. While director Benton should have spent an additional few months studying up on his thrillers and horror films, one dream sequence, involving a little girl chasing after a man in a house and pulling an eye out of a stuffed teddy bear, only for the bear to start bleeding, is eerie.

This is the only movie Meryl has made that involves a serious discussion while she's sprawled out naked on a massage table, and Benton does give her a strong monologue (like he did with *Kramer vs. Kramer*) toward the end. The last few minutes of the movie are a little silly, but there is some pleasure to be had in watching what will likely remain Meryl's only time on screen running from a knife-wielding villain. Meryl even belts out a scream at the end that would give Curtis a run for her money as Scream Queen.

Why did Meryl do this movie? She has not gone on record at a later date discussing her thoughts on the film (aside from her comment made to Andy Cohen), but it's likely she played this role as a favor to Benton, who made what her career was up to that time by casting her in *Kramer vs. Kramer*. Actors have done this over the years, taking a substandard role to say thank you to their directors for previous work that boosted their careers. Sandra Bullock starred in *Speed 2* as a favor to her *Speed* director Jan de Bont (the 12.5 million-dollar payday probably didn't hurt either), and Nicole Kidman re-united with Baz Luhrmann for the atrocious *Australia*, after they had done great work together years prior in *Moulin Rouge*.

Meryl has worked with many of her directors more than once (David Frankel, Phyllida Lloyd, Robert Redford, Mike Nichols) but only with Benton did it seem like once was probably enough. *Still of the Night* is worth a look for Meryl die-hards but the only film she made in 1982 that is worth discussing in great detail all these years later remains the Oscar-winning *Sophie's Choice*.

AWARDS WATCH

The film received one lone nomination: Best Motion Picture at the 1983 Edgar Allan Poe Awards.

FUN FACTS

Meryl's character is a take on the type that frequented many Hitchcock thrillers played by such actresses as Ingrid Bergman and Grace Kelly.

The original title of *Still of the Night* was *Stab*, the title of the film-within-a-film in Wes Craven's *Scream 2*.

Jessica Tandy previously starred in one very Hitchcockian film—Hitchcock's *The Birds*.

This film was Benton's homage to film noir and suspense thrillers of the 1940s and 1950s. He and his cinematographer Nestor Almendros considered filming it in black-and-white.

Benton wrote the role of Brooke specifically for Meryl.

WEEK 9
SOPHIE'S CHOICE (1982)

FILM FACTS

DISTRIBUTOR: Universal Pictures
RELEASE DATE: December 8, 1982

DIRECTOR: Alan J. Pakula
WRITER: Alan J. Pakula (based on the novel by William Styron)
PRODUCERS: Alan J. Pakula, Keith Barish
ALSO STARRING: Kevin Kline, Peter MacNicol, Josh Mostel, Robin Barlett

REVIEW

It can be argued that Meryl Streep didn't become *Meryl Streep* until *Sophie's Choice*. Sure, she had impressed in *The Deer Hunter*, *Kramer vs. Kramer*, and *The French Lieutenant's Woman*, but Meryl's Oscar-winning performance in the acclaimed 1982 drama solidified her status as one of the best actresses of her generation. When Sylvester Stallone proclaimed her the winner of the Academy Award, he called her the "marvelous" Meryl Streep. In 1982, only five years into her film career, she was already a national treasure.

Sophie's Choice, based on the acclaimed 1979 novel by William Styron, features what still remains Meryl's most complex and haunting film performance. She apparently got on her knees and begged director Alan J. Pakula (*Klute*, *All the President's Man*) for the role, and it's easy to see why. As Sophie, a survivor of the Nazi concentration camps who is trying to make a new life for herself in New York City, she is almost unrecognizable at times (this was her first of many movies in which she worked with her longtime make-up artist and hairstylist J. Roy Helland), and her Polish accent is impeccable. One of Meryl's great gifts over the decades has been disappearing into her roles, allowing viewers to eventually forget they're watching her up there on the screen. Some of the best examples of this phenomenon include *Silkwood*, *The Bridges of Madison County*, *Doubt*, and *The Iron Lady*, and she's probably never done it better than she did it in *Sophie's Choice*.

Meryl is wholly convincing in her moments of sadness, joy, horror. If the movie was only Sophie in 1947 New York romancing her love Nathan (Kevin Kline) and befriending the writer Stingo (Peter MacNicol), her performance would still have been lauded. There's a freedom and a yearning for fun the character exudes in these scenes that make for some of the most affecting moments of the movie. One that particularly stands out is a scene when Sophie criticizes the English language for having so many words that mean *fast*, when in other languages there is typically just one word. It's a cleverly written scene that Meryl plays beautifully, and the whole time you forget you're watching an American actress whose first spoken language is English, playing a Polish character who speaks multiple languages and is learning English as an adult.

These scenes also crackle with energy because the chemistry she has with Kline has a charged intensity, while the scenes with MacNicol offer a quieter, more intimate look at a close friendship. This was Kline's film debut, and he more than holds his own against Meryl. An acclaimed stage actor at the time, Kline came into movies late, at age thirty-five, and his talent shines through as an unstable man, almost bipolar at times, who yearns to love but sometimes fails to see the good in those around him. It seems unfair that Meryl received all of the awards attention for *Sophie's Choice*, when Kline's memorable performance should have been singled out, too. MacNicol, who later appeared in *24* and *Ally McBeal*, is also effective as the young man who moves to New York to work on his writing. He too was brand new to movies—*Dragonslayer* was his film debut the year before—and he brings just the right amount of tenderness and warmth to the role, one that is just as important as Meryl's; some might forget that, while Meryl is the star of *Sophie's Choice*, the actual storyline is told from Stingo's perspective, not Sophie's.

Flashback scenes offer some of the most raw, emotional acting of Meryl's film career, with a sad early moment when she begs a man to guide her toward finding poetry by a man named Dickens. A later moment, when Sophie begs an officer to free her son from the concentration camps, shows the depths of the character's vulnerability. (Additionally, take note that Meryl's sickly physical appearance in this scene is almost identical to Violet's look sans black wig in *August: Osage County*.)

And then of course there is *the* scene, the one everyone thinks of when they think of this movie, when Sophie must make her defining choice. In the documentary about the making of the film, Meryl said that she only read the scene once in the script, and then during filming, she insisted on only one take, because she couldn't think to put herself through the unthinkable horror of this moment more than once (she was, after all, a mother by this time). Coming at the end of the movie, the scene is so heartbreaking that it overshadows almost everything that has come before it. When her daughter is snatched away from her, Sophie opens her mouth and starts trembling, but doesn't make a sound. Meryl said in the documentary that she the actress thought she was screaming out loud during that moment, and didn't find out until later that she wasn't.

The film as a whole, however, is unfortunately more of a mixed bag. While Meryl's performance is superb, the pacing of the narrative leaves a lot to be desired. At times the film grinds almost to a halt, and it seems likely a half-hour could have been shaved from the running time, without losing any important story elements. The structure always keeps the viewer a little off balance, but not always in a good way. The flashbacks to Sophie's past in the concentration camp and soon after almost seem randomly selected at times, and some of the dramatic power of these moments is lost when they merely serve as a story Sophie is telling in 1947 New York to Stingo. More focus on Sophie and less on Stingo would have improved the picture as a whole.

Meryl is the main reason to see *Sophie's Choice*, with her hypnotic performance keeping the film in the public lexicon for the last three decades. The film itself is not one of her best—sadly, some of her better performances are bogged down in movies that are not worthy of her (*The Iron Lady* is a more recent example)—but her performance in *Sophie's Choice* is one of the greatest any actress has ever given in a film. When she's on screen, she radiates, and showcases every aspect of her glorious talent. When she's not on screen, the film suffers. While Meryl's performance was acclaimed in most award shows and critic associations that year, the film itself was shut out of most other categories (although Roger Ebert did hail it as the best picture of the year).

Sophie's Choice won Meryl the Academy Award for Best Actress, her only Oscar she earned in the leading category for nearly thirty years. She fought hard for this role, and in the end, she made it count. Meryl is always great in movie after movie, but rarely has she been as astonishingly brilliant in her long and varied film career as she was in *Sophie's Choice*.

AWARDS WATCH

Meryl received her second Academy Award, her first in the Leading Actress category. She also won Best Actress in a Motion Picture – Drama at the Golden Globes, as well as Best Actress from the Boston Society of Film Critics,

Kansas City Film Critics, Los Angeles Film Critics, National Board of Review, National Society of Film Critics, and New York Film Critics. In addition, she earned a Best Actress nomination at the BAFTA Awards.

Sophie's Choice earned five Academy Award nominations— Best Costume Design, Cinematography, Original Score, Adapted Screenplay, and Actress for Meryl. Kline was nominated as New Star of the Year at the Golden Globes, and Most Outstanding Newcomer to Film at the BAFTA Awards. In addition, the film was nominated for Best Film – Drama at the Golden Globes, and earned a WGA Award nomination.

FUN FACTS

Meryl won her first Academy Award in the Leading Actress category.

Not until she appeared on *Oprah* years later did Meryl actually watch the famous choice scene.

Meryl literally begged director Pakula for the role on her hands and knees.

Meryl not only learned a Polish accent for the film but also learned how to speak German and Polish so she could have the proper accent of a Polish refugee.

Pakula originally envisioned Liv Ullman in Meryl's role, and at one point Natalie Wood was considered.

Meryl's performance is ranked third on Premiere Magazine's 100 Greatest Performances of All Time.

WEEK 10
SILKWOOD (1983)

FILM FACTS

DISTRIBUTOR: 20th Century Fox
RELEASE DATE: December 14, 1983

DIRECTOR: Mike Nichols
WRITERS: Alice Arlen, Nora Ephron
PRODUCERS: Michael Hausman, Mike Nichols
ALSO STARRING: Kurt Russell, Cher, Craig T. Nelson, Diana Scarwid, Fred Ward

REVIEW

After winning the Academy Award for Best Actress for *Sophie's Choice*, Meryl could have done anything she wanted. She could have taken a break. She could have sold out and made a summer blockbuster. So what did she do? Just two and a half weeks after she wrapped *Sophie's Choice*, long before she reached that Oscar stage in 1983, she started filming *Silkwood*, the acclaimed drama co-starring Cher and Kurt Russell, and directed by the late, great Mike Nichols. That brief hiatus between movies was probably stressful on

Meryl, but she couldn't have picked a better follow-up to *Sophie's Choice*. With *Silkwood*, she began her close working relationship with the Oscar-winning Nichols, who would go on to direct her in *Heartburn*, *Postcards from the Edge*, and the HBO mini-series *Angels in America*. She also stunned in another lead performance, and earned an Academy Award nomination for Best Actress her third year in a row.

While much of *Sophie's Choice* and *The French Lieutenant's Woman* featured Meryl in period roles, *Silkwood* allowed Meryl to stretch her muscles in a wholly modern story, one based on true events. She plays Karen Silkwood, a metallurgy worker who makes plutonium fuel rods for nuclear reactors, where she deals with possible exposure to radiation. She doesn't love her job but does what she has to to stay afloat. She has a steady relationship with her boyfriend Drew (Kurt Russell), and adores spending time with her best friend Dolly (an almost unrecognizable Cher). When Karen and others become contaminated by radiation, plant officials blame her for the incident, and she begins an investigation into the various wrongdoings at the company. But before she is able to bring her findings to a New York Times reporter, Karen dies in a mysterious car crash.

The Oscar-nominated screenplay by Alice Arlen and Nora Ephron (the latter of whom would go on to direct Meryl twenty-five years later in *Julie & Julia*) is delicate in its handling of Karen's controversial death. While the film doesn't offer any answers, it also doesn't glorify the death in any way or use it in a tacky manner to create unnecessary tension. Other directors might have used the car crash as a wrap-around to the central story, possibly opening the movie with the accident and then coming back to it in the end. Director Nichols and screenwriters Arlen and Ephron are interested in Karen's human story, and so the film plays out more like a drama than a thriller.

Like *Sophie's Choice*, *Silkwood* is a two-hour-plus picture, one that has as many moments developing the characters and their relationships as it does scenes that propel the narrative forward. Nichols wants the viewer to really get to know these people, and this town, all of which are on the brink of collapse. The movie is a little slow at times, and, like *Sophie's Choice*, could have been cut down by twenty to thirty minutes. But the film pulls you in from the beginning and keeps you engaged because of all the superb performances. Nichols was always a genius when it came to directing actors, and he cast *Silkwood* with a fantastic ensemble that include the aforementioned Russell and Cher, as well as Craig T. Nelson, Fred Ward, Diana Scarwid, Ron Silver, Josef Summer (who was in both *Still of the Night* and *Sophie's Choice*), and a young David Straithairn (who would go on to play Meryl's husband in the action adventure *The River Wild*).

The most significant actors in the film are the main trio—Meryl, Cher, and Russell. Up to this point, Russell was more known for his action roles in the John Carpenter classics *Escape From New York* and *The Thing*, and not so much for his dramatic chops. He gets few explosive moments in *Silkwood*, but Russell proves here that he can hold his own with someone like Meryl. Russell's real life partner Goldie Hawn would go on to battle Meryl mano a mano in the visual effects black comedy *Death Becomes Her* ten years later, but Russell had an opportunity in *Silkwood* to play a much quieter character than he was used to, one who sticks by his girlfriend's side, even when she's panicking about the levels of radiation that might be eating its way through her body.

Cher, in her second significant role on film following Robert Altman's *Come Back to the 5 & Dime, Jimmy Dean, Jimmy Dean*, effectively loses herself in a plain, make-up free lesbian character Dolly and proves, just like she did in 1987's *Moonstruck*, she can be a commanding film actress when given the right material. She won a Golden Globe and earned an Oscar nomination for her performance, and it wasn't just because she shed her singer image; she is a revelation in this movie, her character so effectively underplayed that she feels like a real person right from the beginning. Few directors at the time would give Cher a chance, but Nichols, who gave the unknown Dustin Hoffman a chance in *The Graduate*, obviously saw something in her that he knew would work beautifully for this character.

From the beginning of her career, Meryl kept topping herself, year after year. *The Deer Hunter*, *Kramer vs. Kramer*, *The French Lieutenant's Wo*man, and *Sophie's Choice*—the performances just got richer and richer. While nothing she's done can outdo the brilliance of her performance in *Sophie's Choice*, *Silkwood* is easily one of her ultimate show-stoppers because Meryl really does become Karen Silkwood, and somehow, almost unfathomably, makes us forget about those memorable characters she had already played before. After *Sophie's Cho*ice, Meryl might have been pigeonholed into period roles, ones like she would go on to play in *Out of Africa* and *Ironweed*, but *Silkwood* showed that she could play a complex lead character who lives in the modern era.

As Karen, Meryl speaks her mind, shows her emotion without abandon, and manages to make a sometimes unsympathetic character one we are always rooting for. The film offers Meryl lighter moments—her playfulness in early scenes at work, and her priceless reaction to a joke told by Ward—as well as terrifying ones—each subsequent body scrub down looks to be rougher, harder. The hope she exudes when the doctors tell her the amount of radiation in her body does not exceed the maximum safety amount shows her willingness to live, and the speck of fear in her eyes when she sees the headlights behind her car as she's driving to the reporter shows her growing panic that all might not end well. The film also gives Meryl a chance to sing, which is always welcome; she quietly performs "Amazing Grace" while driving back home after seeing her children, and the song repeats at the end, in a haunting manner, as Karen's fate is finally met in the tragic car accident. Some great actors don't have great singing voices, but Meryl's is enchanting, and rarely has it been used in a more effective and subdued way than in *Silkwood*.

Meryl would next go on to make two questionable film projects—the entertaining but forgettable *Falling in Love* and the well-acted but lackluster *Plenty*—but with *Silkwood* she capped an extraordinary five-year run of terrific films that started with *The Deer Hunter*. She had this early in her career already impressed audiences the world over with her diverse performances, her impeccable accents, and her almost inhuman-like ability to lose herself in her characters. In 1984, Meryl lost the Best Actress Oscar to Shirley MacLaine for *Terms of Endearment*, but at this point, she had already won.

AWARDS WATCH

Meryl received her fifth Academy Award nomination, for Best Actress. She was also nominated for a Golden Globe for Best Actress – Drama and a BAFTA Award for Best Actress. In addition, she won Best Actress from the Kansas City Film Critics.

Silkwood earned five Academy Award nominations—Best Film Editing, Screenplay, Director, Supporting Actress for Cher, and Actress for Meryl. Cher won the Golden Globe for Best Supporting Actress, earned a BAFTA Award nomination, and got second place honors from the Los Angeles Film Critics, National Society of Film Critics, and New York Film Critics. The film also earned a WGA Award nomination, and a Golden Globe nomination for Best Film – Drama.

FUN FACTS

The scene where Karen sets off the radiation alarms really happened. Her contamination level was forty times the safe limit.

The movie was released nine years after the events depicted took place.

Meryl would go on to collaborate with Nichols on *Heartburn*, *Postcards From the Edge*, and *Angels in America*, and with Ephron on *Heartburn* and *Julie & Julia*.

The first produced screenplay from Ephron.

Lily Tomlin, Meryl's *A Prairie Home Companion* co-star, auditioned for Cher's role.

Jane Fonda, the lead of Meryl's first movie *Julia*, at one point owned the rights to this film.

WEEK 11
FALLING IN LOVE (1984)

FILM FACTS

DISTRIBUTOR: Paramount Pictures
RELEASE DATE: November 21, 1984

DIRECTOR: Ulu Grosbard
WRITER: Michael Cristofer
PRODUCER: Marvin Worth
ALSO STARRING: Robert De Niro, Dianne Weist, Harvey Keitel, Jane Kaczmarek

REVIEW

The 1980s for Meryl marked one triumph after another. *The French Lieutenant's Woman*, *Sophie's Choice*, *Silkwood*, *Out of Africa*. All of these films netted her Oscar nominations and created indelible impressions on audiences all over the world. But, no one, not even Meryl, is perfect. *Still of the Night* was a lame Hitchcock ripoff, and Meryl ended the decade by appearing alongside Roseanne in *She-Devil*, easily one of the most inexplicable choices of her career.

But her 1984 film *Falling in Love*, co-starring Robert De Niro, might be one of her more unusual choices of all, mostly because this movie, while entertaining and highly watchable, is just so damn safe. Here was the one time that Meryl and De Niro, who shared screen-time together in *The Deer Hunter* (and later in *Marvin's Room*), and who are arguably the two finest actors of their generation, were the two leads of a movie. They had wanted to do another film together after *The Deer Hunter*, and could have found something special to do together—and yet they settled on *this*?

Up until 1984, De Niro had impressed with haunting characters in films like *Taxi Driver*, *Raging Bull*, and *The King of Comedy* (all directed by Martin Scorsese), as well as *The Godfather Part II* and *Once Upon a Time in America*. He had at this point won two Academy Awards and was sought after for A-list projects. He hadn't ever played the lead in a modern romantic movie before, so maybe that aspect intrigued De Niro, playing a faithful husband with two children who ends up, most surprising of all to him, falling for another woman.

Meryl had stretched her dramatic chops in movie after movie, and here she plays a reasonably happy wife who feels like something's missing. Unlike most of her films up to this time, she looks and talks just like Meryl the person, with her trademark long blonde hair and normal American accident. Obviously in a movie like this it would have been odd for her to be sporting, say, red hair, and talking with a Southern twang or a Russian dialect, but because she's so known for her ability to lose herself in a role, it's always a bit unusual to see her in a movie looking and talking like herself.

Falling in Love is an odd beast, because, again, it's such a simple movie. The screenplay by Michael Cristofer offers few surprises, and Ulu Grosbard, who directed De Niro in 1981's *True Confessions* and didn't make another movie for eleven years following *Falling in Love*, offers little flash or point of view to the proceedings. The plot goes like this: Frank and Molly (De Niro and Meryl) bump into each other in a bookstore during the busy Christmas season, then see each other again on a train three months later. They get to talking, then talking again on the next train ride, and soon they're spending more time together, first as friends, but quickly as lovers.

The movie has all the required scenes: the moment Frank realizes he's in love with her, the moment Molly realizes she can't be with Frank any longer, the moments both spouses (David Clennon and Jane Kaczmarek) realize what's going on and make their fiery confrontations. Even the ending, which takes place on a train—as expected—comes off as too convenient to be fully effective as a happily-ever-after ending.

And yet, despite the film's various shortcomings, Grosbard assembled a cast so incredible that the film is far better than it has any right to be. One would expect a 1984 film with the blasé title *Falling in Love*, written and directed by men with few significant credits behind them, to star a pair of B-list '80s actors like Harry Hamlin and Pia Zadora. Or maybe Richard Benjamin and Blair Brown? Instead, we get Meryl and De Niro, two of our finest actors.

But that's not where the greatness of this cast list ends: Harvey Keitel plays De Niro's best friend, and Dianne

Weist plays Meryl's best friend! Obviously the Keitel factor is a fascinating one, since he and De Niro shared the screen in the masterpieces *Mean Streets* and *Taxi Driver* (and later in the underrated *Cop Land*). What are they doing here, sitting in fine restaurants and chatting about their love lives? It seems so trivial compared to what these two have accomplished on-screen together before.

And then there's Meryl and Weist, so natural in their scenes, which mostly consists of them chatting about *their* love lives while walking along New York City sidewalks. Since the sight of Weist in any film, especially one made in the '80s, immediately brings to mind Woody Allen—she starred in four of his films between 1985 and 1987—these entertaining but fleeting moments in *Falling in Love* feel like deleted scenes from one of Allen's movies. One wishes that screenwriter Cristofer could have expanded on both of these friend roles more. (Also keep an eye out for a young Jesse Bradford, as Frank's son Joe, and *Six Feet Under*'s Frances Conroy, hilarious in a small bit as a waitress.)

Meryl appeared in eleven films between 1981 and 1989, and was nominated for an Academy Award for six of those performances. That means that she was nominated for more movies that she appeared in during this decade than films she *wasn't* nominated for. One could make a case for her being nominated for *Plenty* and *Heartburn*, but few would argue that *Falling in Love* is a film that ever warranted awards attention. She is fine in this movie, breathing much more life into Molly than surely there was on the page, but this is not among her more memorable performances.

There are some great quiet moments, like when she tells Frank the exact time she'll be on the train on Friday, and then stares out the window, slowly realizing what she's done. And a scene toward the end, where she finds herself stranded in front of railroad tracks, is an effective one. Mostly she succeeds here in that we don't come to hate her. She is, after all, agreeing to spend time with Frank when she knows he is married and has two little kids at home. In the hands of another actress, Molly might have been a character we turned against, but throughout the film she is always relatable and understandable in her actions. On the other hand, there is little for Meryl to play here, especially in relation to her other movies of the time, so it's hard to understand, besides the opportunity to act again with De Niro, what attracted her to this project.

And yet, with all its faults, *Falling in Love* is immensely watchable. As embarrassing as it might be to admit, I found myself more drawn into this film than I was with *The French Lieutenant's Woman*, *Sophie's Choice*, and *Silkwood*. Part of it may be that I had already seen those three films, and I had never watched this one before. Part of it may be the curiosity factor of watching such a simple romantic movie starring not just two but *four* of our great actors. Part of it may also be that this film doesn't overstay its welcome at 105 minutes, while *Sophie's Choice* and *Silkwood* in particular ran (arguably) a half-hour too long. While *Falling in Love* will never be remembered as one of Meryl's best movies or performances, there is an infectious charm to the film that keeps you watching all the way to the end, the same way a good book keeps you turning the pages.

AWARDS WATCH

Meryl won Best Foreign Actress at the David di Donatello Awards, and was nominated for Best Foreign Actress at the Sant Jordi Awards. She did not receive any wins or nominations for this film in the United States.

The only other award the film earned was Best Foreign Actor for De Niro at the Sant Jordi Awards.

FUN FACTS

This is one of the few films Meryl made in the 1980s not to receive any major awards or nominations. Only this film, *Still of the Night*, *Plenty*, *Heartburn*, and *She-Devil* were not recognized by at least one Academy Award nomination.

Meryl and De Niro agreed to do the film after they performed a reading of the screenplay together.

At the time that the film was made, both Meryl and De Niro had won two Oscars, one in the supporting category, and one in the lead category.

This movie is considered a modern version of 1945's *Brief Encounter*.

The next film Grosbard made after *Falling in Love* was 1995's *Georgia*.

WEEK 12
PLENTY (1985)

FILM FACTS

DISTRIBUTOR: 20th Century Fox
RELEASE DATE: September 20, 1985

DIRECTOR: Fred Schepisi
WRITER: David Hare (based on his play)
PRODUCERS: Joseph Papp, Edward R. Pressman
ALSO STARRING: Charles Dance, Tracey Ullman, John Gielgud, Sting, Ian McKellan, Sam Neill

REVIEW

Has Meryl ever made a boring movie? She has made the occasional lackluster drama over her long career, but she always manages to give even her lesser films her special spark. *Ironweed*, her 1987 period film with Jack Nicholson, is an example of a slow, rather uninvolving movie that still manages to entertain due to Meryl's amazing performance. Some more of her heavily flawed movies include *The House of the Spirits*, and *Lions for Lambs*, and even *The Iron Lady*, which despite Meryl's Oscar win is one of her most uneven films.

Whether uneven or well constructed, whether packed to the brim with action or loaded only with scenes of people talking, Meryl's films are almost always watchable. But *Plenty*, a serious drama from the play by David Hare, is one of her few anomalies. It's not a terrible movie. The performances are fine. Meryl does what she can. But I would argue that in a career of more than fifty films, the most boring of them would have to be *Plenty*.

1985 was a stellar year for Meryl. She was coming off of three back-to-back Academy Award nominations for Best Actress in a row, which included a win for *Sophie's Choice*, and she had not one but two films coming out. One was *Out of Africa*, the Sydney Pollack historical drama co-starring Robert Redford that went on to win the Oscar for Best Picture. And opening a few months before *Out of Africa* was the less popular but still well-reviewed historical drama, *Plenty*.

This is a film that was not brushed aside like her 1996 misfire *Before and After*, or the highly anticipated but quickly discarded 2007 disappointment *Rendition*. *Plenty* was given two thumbs up by Gene Siskel and Roger Ebert, it received a pair of BAFTA Award nominations, and the legendary John Gielgud was awarded two major honors, from the Los Angeles Film Critics and the National Society of Film Critics, for his brief but excellent supporting turn. It was essentially overshadowed that awards season, though, by *Out of Africa*, the same way Matthew McConaughey's turn in *Dallas Buyers Club* overshadowed his performance in *Mud* in 2013. And again, while it's well made and not completely lacking of merit, *Plenty* is definitely one of Meryl's least essential films.

Directed by Fred Schepisi, who also directed Meryl in 1988's *A Cry in the Dark*, and written by Hare, who adapted his award-winning play of the same name, *Plenty* stars Meryl as a young Englishwoman named Susan Traherne who spends twenty years trying to make a life for herself during post-World War II England. Yes, Meryl ages twenty years throughout the movie, and yes, she does so convincingly, living different kinds of lives with different kinds of men. As the film opens, she is irreparably altered by her experience as a fighter for the French Resistance, and after the war ends, she returns to England and tries to be someone she's not.

The main issue with *Plenty* is that it rarely comes to life, never drums up any energy. At two hours in length, it at times feels longer than the three-hour *Deer Hunter*. It doesn't help that Meryl plays a main character who is so unlikable, often reduced to scenes of bickering and shouting, shooting bullets at the wall, and making out and having sex with one man after another. When she romances a man named Lazar (Sam Neill) toward the beginning, their making out feels entirely warranted. However, when she's riding Sting's penis on a couch—definitely in the top three most awkward Meryl scenes ever—any good nature one might have had toward her character is tossed away for good.

The cast of *Plenty* is superb, and it's sad that the material doesn't live up to the great talent that was assembled. In supporting roles, some big and some small, Charles Dance,

Tracey Ullman, and Ian McKellan, as well as the aforementioned Gielgud, Sting, and Neill. Sting is surprisingly good, playing one of Susan's lovers Mick, and McKellan is so strong in a blink-and-you'll-miss-it scene that it's a shame his character wasn't utilized more. It is especially interesting to see Ullman in a rare dramatic role, one that she was given early in her career. But again, few of these actors make much of an impression, because the characters are given so little to do.

Meryl, in the lead, gets a *lot* to do, but even she feels lost at times. She has the occasional solid moment, like when she lashes out at her guests at a fancy dinner party, and when she runs away from one of her (many) lovers, only to treat the man's injury after he breaks his nose upon slamming it against a closed door. Her British accent is stellar, as expected, and she does feel like a different woman toward the end than she did at the beginning. She took over the role from Kate Nelligan, who originated the character on the stage in London in 1978. Who knows what Nelligan could have done with the part in the film, but ultimately this is one of the rare dramatic lead performances Meryl has given that leaves little of an impression.

Ultimately, *Plenty* lacks focus, and its ending, which leaves a luminous Meryl on an English countryside taking in a gorgeous view, feels like something out of a different movie. This might have been courageous and energetic and thought-provoking viewing on the stage, but as a film, most of the scenes feel stilted, like something is missing. *Plenty* offers another solid Meryl performance but in a career that includes such incredibly moving dramas as *Kramer vs.*

Kramer, *The Bridges of Madison County*, the underrated *Marvin's Room*, and *The Hours*, *Plenty* just doesn't make the cut.

AWARDS WATCH

Meryl received Best Foreign Actress at the Sant Jordi Awards, and won Best Actress for both *Plenty* and *Out of Africa* from the New York Film Critics.

Plenty earned two BAFTA Award nominations, for Gielgud in the Supporting Actor category and Ullman in the Supporting Actress category. Gielgud also won Best Supporting Actor from the Los Angeles Film Critics and the National Society of Film Critics.

FUN FACTS

Meryl would go on to collaborate with Schepisi and Neill in *A Cry in the Dark*. In 2002, she appeared in *The Hours*, also written by Hare. And she would co-star with Ullman in 2014's *Into the Woods* (as well as *Death Becomes Her*, in which Ullman's scenes were all deleted).

The original Broadway production of *Plenty* opened at the Plymouth Theater in New York in January 1983 and ran for ninety-two performances.

Hare re-wrote about sixty percent of the material from his play for the film.

WEEK 13
OUT OF AFRICA
(1985)

FILM FACTS

DISTRIBUTOR: Universal Pictures
RELEASE DATE: December 18, 1985

DIRECTOR: Sydney Pollack
WRITER: Kurt Luedtke (based on the book by Karen Blixen)
PRODUCER: Sydney Pollack
ALSO STARRING: Robert Redford, Klaus Maria Brandauer, Michael Kitchen, Michael Gough

REVIEW

Meryl is universally considered the greatest living actress currently working in film today, and she has spent nearly four decades proving her talent in movie after movie, now more than fifty in total. She has been nominated for nineteen Academy Awards—by far the record—with surely many more nominations in her future.

And yet it might be surprising to learn that of all the films she's made over the decades, and of all the acclaimed performances she's given, only a small handful of her movies have actually gone on to be acknowledged in the top categories at the Academy Awards. Her film debut *Julia*, in 1977, racked up a whopping eleven nominations, and two films she did soon after that won Best Picture—*The Deer Hunter* and *Kramer vs. Kramer*. But following that 1979 film, only two more of her films to date would go on to even be nominated for the big prize. *The Hours* was nominated, in 2003. The only other film she appeared in that was not only nominated but also won? 1985's *Out of Africa*.

Sydney Pollack's sweeping two-hour-and-forty-minute epic had all the makings of an award-friendly movie. It tells an epic true story, set in 1916 Africa, filled with warmth and heart and romance and tragedy. It paired two of our finest actors—Meryl and Robert Redford—in a film for the first and still only time (although Redford directed Meryl in his 2007 disappointment *Lions for Lambs*). It's the kind of film Academy members love, and it was honored with many of the top prizes, despite intense competition that year from other great films like *Prizzi's Honor*, *Kiss of the Spider Woman*, and *The Color Purple*, Spielberg's terrific achievement that scored eleven nominations but won nothing.

Out of Africa won seven Oscars, including Best Screenplay, Director for Pollack, and Picture. But is it one of Meryl's best movies? Has it held up well all these years later? While there is more interest to be found here than in the somber, slow-moving *Plenty*, *Out of Africa* remains one of Meryl's most overrated films.

She plays Karen Blixen, a Danish baroness who establishes a plantation in 1916 Kenya, Africa. Like in

Plenty, she is torn between more than one man—in this case, there's the husband Bror (Klaus Maria Brandauer, in an Oscar-nominated supporting role) who she married out of convenience, and the valiant, free-spirited hunter Denys (played by Redford). Based on the writings of Blixen herself (published under the pen name Isak Dinesen), *Out of Africa* shows in great detail the many ups and downs of Karen's complicated life, like troubles on the plantations, war, schooling of the natives, and catching syphilis from her husband, which nearly takes her life and prevents her from ever being able to bear children. But then there's Denys, who ultimately changes her life for the better. Will the two walk hand-in-hand into the sunset together? Or will their love end in tragedy?

Director Pollack initially didn't even consider Meryl for the part of Karen. He thought she wasn't sexy enough to play the character, and probably assumed she wouldn't have the right chemistry with the handsome leading man Redford. Meryl, who has fought hard for more roles than one might think, went to a meeting with Pollack wearing a low-cut blouse and a push-up bra—and the rest is history. Even though she never comes across as all that sexy in *Out of Africa*, she does give the richer, fuller performance in the movie, and while both stars are top billed, this is definitely more Meryl's movie than it is Redford's. Those who haven't seen it in awhile might be surprised to see Redford missing for most of the film's first half, a clever tactic used by Pollack and screenwriter Kurt Luedtke to keep them from getting involved romantically for as long as possible.

Of course Redford sticks out like a sore thumb in this period movie—Gene Siskel in his television review rightly says that Redford never manages to create a character here we think of as anything but himself—but Meryl is her typical transformative best. Nominated for her sixth Academy Award in just eight years, she sports brown curly hair and a realistic as usual accent, this time Danish. While *Plenty* provided a rare character she didn't really disappear into that much, she plays the kind of character in *Out of Africa* that yet again makes us forget we're watching Meryl up there on the screen. She shows pain and sadness, love and longing, and in one of the film's most memorable scenes, pure unadulterated terror, when a lion approaches her on dangerous terrain. And the reaction she displays upon learning of the film's closing tragedy is subtle and effective.

However, too much of the film, same as in *Plenty*, drones on and on. Let's consider 1985 as the year of the overindulgent Meryl. *Plenty* and *Out of Africa* both have a few terrific moments, but if it weren't for her stellar performances, these movies would register hardly at all. *Out of Africa* includes sumptuous cinematography by David Watkin, incredible views of the African countryside, but to what end? The film is too episodic in its first half, with endless scenes of strained dialogue, and by the time we arrive to the central relationship between Meryl and Redford it comes off as more awkward than tender—not as awkward as Meryl and Sting's relationship in *Plenty*, but awkward nonetheless. While Meryl and Redford probably would have made a great couple in a traditional 1980s romance, they never quite gel here.

While Meryl would go on later in her career to branch off into different genres, budgets and scopes in her work, she focused arguably too much in the 1980s on important, slow-moving historical dramas, many of which netted her Oscar nominations, but few of which offer emotionally involving experiences. Even *Sophie's Choice*, probably her best of the '80s period films, is flawed, and a bit on the long side. She would go on to make *Ironweed* and *A Cry in the Dark* but finally took a break from dramas to make a string of four light-hearted comedies in a row. In 1985 Meryl was considered one of the best, but audiences had no idea just what she was capable of.

AWARDS WATCH

Meryl received her sixth Academy Award nomination, for Best Actress. She also got a Golden Globe nomination for Best Actress – Drama and a BAFTA Award nomination for Best Actress. In addition, she won Best Foreign Actress at the David di Donatello Awards, and Best Actress from the Kansas City Film Critics and Los Angeles Film Critics.

Out of Africa earned eleven Academy Award nominations and won seven—Best Music, Sound, Art Direction-Set Decoration, Cinematography, Adapted Screenplay, Director, and Picture. It was also nominated for Best Film Editing, Costume Design, Supporting Actor for Brandauer, and Actress for Meryl. The film won Best Picture – Drama at the Golden Globes, as well as Supporting Actor for Brandauer, and won Best Adapted Screenplay at the BAFTA Awards. In addition, Pollack received a DGA Award nomination, and Luedtke received a WGA Award nomination.

FUN FACTS

Meryl was promised that the lion in the attack scene would be tethered by its back leg so it couldn't get too close. When the scene was shot, the lion had no restraints, and the lion got closer than Meryl anticipated, making the fear on her face completely real.

She developed her accent by listening to recordings of Karen Blixen reading her works.

Out of Africa was shot on location, but laws prohibited the use of wild animals in film. Trained lions were thus imported from California.

Audrey Hepburn was offered the role of Karen Blixen. Also, at one point, the story was planned as a project for Greta Garbo.

Redford intended to play Denys as an Englishman, but Pollack decided his accent would be too distracting for audiences.

WEEK 14
HEARTBURN (1986)

FILM FACTS

DISTRIBUTOR: Paramount Pictures
RELEASE DATE: July 25, 1986

DIRECTOR: Mike Nichols
WRITER: Nora Ephron
PRODUCERS: Mike Nichols, Robert Greenhut
ALSO STARRING: Jack Nicholson, Jeff Daniels, Maureen Stapleton, Milos Forman, Catherine O'Hara, Kevin Spacey

REVIEW

Sandwiched in between her serious, occasionally effective dramatic work—1985's *Plenty* and *Out of Africa*, and *Ironweed* and *A Cry in the Dark*, released in 1987 and 1988, respectively—was a lighter piece of entertainment directed by Mike Nichols and written by Nora Ephron, based on her novel. Nichols, Ephron, and Meryl had collaborated on *Silkwood* three years prior, and this time the gang came together to tell a much more personal story to Ephron, as well as to see if sparks would be captured on screen when Meryl played off Jack Nicholson on screen for the first time. What *Heartburn* ultimately turned into was a film that marked one of Meryl's few critical duds of the 1980s, a movie deemed a major disappointment by Gene Siskel and Roger Ebert, and one of the few films Meryl made in this decade that didn't receive a single major awards nomination.

Having sat through the slow-moving, more Oscar-friendly *Plenty* and *Out of Africa* in the last two weeks, I was more than happy to settle in for a less important and immensely watchable Ephron-scripted comedy with Meryl and Nicholson. And for the first hour, *Heartburn* is a winner, an episodic but engaging examination of two intelligent, hardworking New Yorkers who meet, fall in love, get married, and have children. Sure, there's nothing entirely original about the proceedings, but there is an instant chemistry between Meryl and Nicholson, and any scenes in the movie that has the two of them just sitting and talking to each other work wonders. A kiss they share on a New York sidewalk is so romantic in its simplicity, and the moment that follows—the two eating pasta in bed—is wonderfully tender, especially considering that two characters just spent their first night together. Another director might just have shown us the sex; Nichols, rightly so, was more interested in showing us the after-sex conversation.

Meryl plays Rachel Samstat and Nicholson plays Mark Forman, and only a few more minutes of the movie pass before the two are getting married. Rachel lays on her bed, curled in a ball, knowing full well that since her first marriage didn't last, this second one probably won't either.

But she finally commits to the man she's had a whirlwind romance with, and it's not soon after that they're buying a house, getting pregnant with girl number one, and then girl number two. But the movie eventually has to go somewhere, I guess, and so Rachel discovers that Mark is cheating on her with another woman, while Rachel is still seven months pregnant with her second child. The scene where Rachel stomps out of the bathroom, throws a drawer against the floor, and lashes out at Mark for his infidelity is a memorable Meryl moment.

Unfortunately, the rest of *Heartburn* isn't nearly as fun. Rachel heads home to stay with her father for awhile, and while there are still a few exciting moments in the later half of the movie—a thief (Kevin Spacey, in his film debut) robs Rachel and her friends, and even takes her wedding ring—the film eventually starts to feel like Ephron ran out of ideas for where to take the narrative. It's not a secret that her novel and later screenplay were based on true life experiences—Ephron said at Meryl's 2004 AFI Lifetime Achievement Award ceremony, "the true stretch (for Meryl), if I do say so, was playing me, in *Heartburn*." Sometimes writers are able to infuse even more honesty into their work when the experiences of the narrative come from their own lives, but other times, writers get so close to the real events that they struggle to give the story personality, or any surprises. *Heartburn* is a case in which another ten years might have given Ephron distance to write a more biting, satirical story. As it plays now, it's like a roller coaster that climbs and climbs but never descends.

This is not to suggest that I think Ephron is a lackluster writer. She's one of my all-time favorites, actually. *When Harry Met Sally* is my favorite romantic comedy of all time, and I have great affection for *Sleepless in Seattle* and *You've Got Mail*. Her non-fiction writing is laugh-out-loud hilarious, especially the last two books published before her untimely death in 2012—*I Feel Bad About My Neck*, and *I Remember Nothing*. And of course both *Silkwood* and *Julie & Julia*, which she made with Meryl, are solid. But *Heartburn*—both her screenplay and the novel, which I also read—misses the mark. The novel is written mostly in ranting big block paragraphs, with occasional recipes featured in the narrative, and at just over 100 pages (in *The Most of Nora Ephron* edition), it doesn't leave a lot of room for character growth.

The film is the same way. Rachel is in a different place in her life at the end of *Heartburn* than she was at the beginning, but Ephron nor Nichols ever give us a reason to care. Is a pie in Mark's face in the film's conclusion supposed to make us laugh? Make us cheer for Rachel? It's too ambiguous. But nothing in the film is worse than the last scene, with Rachel singing "Itsy Bitsy Spider" with her daughter, the plane they're on zooming up toward the sky. It's a non-ending on the level of 2013's disappointing *August: Osage County*, the kind that doesn't leave the viewer fulfilled (although the closing song "Coming Around Again," sung by Carly Simon, is quite nice).

With all its flaws, though, *Heartburn* is in no way a waste of time. As stated before, the first hour is engrossing, in both the big and small details. The first half-hour is involving because Nichols allows us to watch two of our finest actors simply *be* together on screen, sometimes in scenes that play out in one long take. Two successive scenes in which Rachel and Mark sing all the songs they can think of about babies are examples of spontaneous moments I wish there had been more of; the second scene that has Mark belting out another song to Rachel while she's trying to sleep marks Nicholson's most charming minute in the movie. But, then again, Mark isn't supposed to be charming. The film is told from Rachel's perspective, so once she discovers his infidelity, we follow her to a different city, and Nicholson's screen-time, sadly, dissipates for the remainder of the running time.

 Nichols always assembles stellar casts for his movies—just look at *The Birdcage*, or *Primary Colors*, or the stunning ensemble of *Catch-22*—and *Heartburn*, his second of four collaborations with Meryl (and his third of four with Nicholson), plays out like a who's-who of great actors. It's always fun to go back to movies made thirty years ago, and see major talents now who were given smaller parts then. Jeff Daniels, Maureen Stapleton, Richard Masur, Stockard Channing, Milos Forman (the director of *Amadeus*), and the great Catherine O'Hara all pop up in supporting roles. Daniels is particularly charming in an underwritten role (his lack of interest in the wedding while Stapleton cries in front of him is one of the film's funniest shots), while O'Hara does what she can with a somewhat air-brained character. Natasha Lyonne and Tony Shalhoub were both uncredited in bit parts, and then there's Spacey's slightly humorous two-scene role that literally steals the show.

But in the end, this is Meryl's film all the way, much more than it is Nicholson's, and she's, as always, able to elevate mediocre material into a movie that is always entertaining, even when the narrative seems to have no idea where it's headed. In the beginning, she wears her hair brown and short (the way she wears it in 2004's *The Manchurian Candidate*), and is instantly believable in the affection she has for Nicholson's Mark. Whenever the film makes big jumps in time, Meryl plays the character more assured, more confident, and it's only when the discovery of the infidelity unravels everything she thought to be true that we see the flailing, vulnerable side of Rachel. The long shot that slowly zooms in on her face in the hair salon is an example of her brilliance, the way she can slowly transition from lighthearted banter with her hair stylist to the horrifying realization about the man she loves.

Meryl is so strong in *Heartburn* that it's a shame a more focused, sharply plotted narrative isn't allowed to unfold. By 1986, Meryl had proven that not only was she one of our finest actresses, and not only was she able to effortlessly jump back and forth between historical and modern films, but that she was also able to elevate routine, sometimes unremarkable material that in the hands of another actress wouldn't have made a single impression. Even in her lesser movies, Meryl commands the screen like no other actress of her generation, so when she's in something great, there really is no telling the magic that can be made.

AWARDS WATCH

The film received one lone award—Best Actress for Meryl, at the Valladolid International Film Festival.

FUN FACTS

Meryl's daughter Mamie Gummer, now an actress herself, plays her baby daughter, Annie. Meryl's mother Mary and her brother Dana also play dinner party guests.

The movie is based on Ephron's marriage to, and divorce from, Carl Bernstein. The woman he had an affair with was Margaret Jay, who became a Baroness in 1992.

In real life, Ephron was so upset by her husband's infidelity that she went into labor prematurely.

Dustin Hoffman turned down the role of Mark. If he had accepted, the film would have been a *Kramer vs. Kramer* reunion, and he would have played a fictionalized version of a man he played once before, in *All the President's Men*.

Mandy Patinkin was originally cast as Mark, but he was replaced two days into shooting when Nichols realized he had no chemistry with Meryl.

WEEK 15
IRONWEED (1987)

FILM FACTS

DISTRIBUTOR: TriStar Pictures
RELEASE DATE: December 18, 1987

DIRECTOR: Hector Babenco
WRITER: William Kennedy (based on his novel)
PRODUCERS: Keith Barish, Marcia Nasatir
ALSO STARRING: Jack Nicholson, Carroll Baker, Michael O'Keefe, Diane Venora, Tom Waits, Nathan Lane

REVIEW

If *Plenty* was slow, *Out of Africa* was overlong, and *Heartburn* was disappointing, *Ironweed* has to be considered one of the most downbeat and depressing films of Meryl's career. Though well-acted by Meryl and especially Jack Nicholson, in a rare non-showy starring role, *Ironweed* is a miserable viewing experience—slow, overlong, and disappointing, all in the same movie. While the film received acclaim upon its release in 1987—Meryl and Nicholson both received Academy Award nominations (her seventh, his ninth)—it is ultimately a head-scratchingly dull experience with only the occasional fleeting moment that draws you in.

Unlike their previous film *Heartburn*, *Ironweed* is much more Nicholson's movie than it is Meryl's. It opens on an impressive long shot of Nicholson's character Francis Phelan walking down a dirt road, in 1938 New York. He's a bum, always dirty, wearing the same clothes day in and day out and sporting a large hat that covers most of his face. He digs graves at the local cemetery, and entertains himself at night by going out drinking at the local bar, where he meets the pale and sickly Helen Archer (Meryl). Francis eventually tracks down his wife and children, and, for the first time, meets his grandson. He's also haunted by ghosts (one played by a creepy Nathan Lane). Any of this making sense yet? The film is sprawling in its ambition but unfortunately plays out like paint drying on a stretch of fence five miles long.

Ironweed marked a sweet occasion, two major films stars reuniting for a second film. Everyone knows the winning pairing of Tom Hanks and Meg Ryan in films like *Sleepless in Seattle* and *You've Got Mail*, as well as Richard Gere and Julia Roberts, who teamed up in *Pretty Woman* and *Runaway Bride*. There's Keanu Reeves and Sandra Bullock in *Speed* and *The Lake House*, too, but looking further back in history you have a pair like Spencer Tracy and Katharine Hepburn, who appeared in nine movies together over the course of twenty-five years. What's significant about Nicholson and Meryl's pairing is that they teamed up in 1986's *Heartburn* and 1987's *Ironweed*, but never before or since. Also, the genres of their two films are so different—one a modern comedy-drama with flourishes of romance, and the other a historical, more downbeat drama that never puts the two in a romantic relationship. Despite the flaws in *Heartburn* and *Ironweed*, the two are always magnetic together on-screen, and it's too bad in their long, eventful careers they never were able to find the right project to do together.

Nicholson is so often over-the-top in his movies—he followed *Ironweed* with his most energetic performance ever in Tim Burton's *Batman*—that it's refreshing to see him play a calm, beaten-down individual who only rarely breaks a smile. While the 1970s saw the best acting Nicholson ever did, in films like *Five Easy Pieces*, *Chinatown*, and *One Flew Over the Cuckoo's Nest*, his output in his later career was always best when he played subtle, like in his last great performance in Alexander Payne's *About Schmidt*. In *Ironweed* he never gets a storyline truly worthy of the acting prowess, but he tries his best to give the character humanity and dimensionality in a movie that always feels like it's making things up as it goes along.

Meryl is brilliant at what she does with an underwritten role, showing us in just a look and a tiny grin the kind of person she's playing. She spends most of the film sporting the same outfit, a large green jacket and bowl-shaped red hat that covers messily cut blonde hair. Her face is robbed of any make-up, her teeth are dark yellow, and she talks in a realistic Irish-American accent. Meryl is known to disappear into her roles and in the case of *Ironweed*, she disappears so deeply that at times you're rising up out of your chair to get a closer look at the screen, just to try to see Meryl's face! If the film revolved around Helen and spent more time dramatizing her plight, *Ironweed* might have been a better film. But unfortunately the screenwriter William Kennedy (*The Cotton Club*) and director Hector Babenco (*Kiss of the Spider Woman*) yank her character out of the narrative so often that we're never able to truly care about her. The tragic end to her character, for example, is too little, too late.

The best scene in *Ironweed* takes place about thirty-eight minutes in, when Helen takes the stage to sing "He's Me Pal." Up until now, the film has been told from Francis's perspective, but here we get to spend a few minutes in Helen's subconscious, as she sings the song to a large crowd at the bar. It's always a pleasure to hear Meryl sing in a movie, accent or not, and her shining moment here is the emotionally draining rendition of a song that is usually more hopeful. She finishes on a tremendous note, everyone claps, and Helen and Francis share a kiss, in a moment that seems like it may signify a positive change for the two main characters. But then Babenco cuts back to the stage, where Helen finishes singing the song, for real this time, with the pitch way off, and with barely a single clap in the audience when she finishes. This five-minute scene is extraordinary, and the best example of her unrivaled talent in the movie.

Meryl might have been hitting Oscar-drama fatigue with *Ironweed* because after her next film, *A Cry in the Dark*, she broke off in a new direction, by appearing in four back-to-back comedies. Doing heavy drama has to be difficult for any actor; doing several back to back, with Meryl having to adopt different accents for each character, had to have eventually taken its toll on her. While *Ironweed* is one of

Meryl's lesser movies, and easily one of the least fun to watch, Meryl did receive another Oscar nomination and added yet another stunning and original character to her growing mantle of memorable screen creations.

AWARDS WATCH

Meryl received her seventh Academy Award nomination, for Best Actress. To date, this is the only film she earned an Oscar nomination for without getting a Golden Globe nomination for the same performance.

Jack Nicholson received an Academy Award nomination, as well as a Golden Globe nomination. He also won Best Actor for this film and for *The Witches of Eastwick* from the Los Angeles Film Critics and the New York Film Critics.

FUN FACTS

This is the only film for which Meryl received an Academy Award nomination and no win or nomination from anywhere else.

Nicholson's contract included a clause that allowed him to leave shooting to attend the Los Angeles Lakers basketball games.

Paul Newman, Robert De Niro, Gene Hackman, and Jason Robards all expressed interest in playing Francis, before Nicholson was chosen.

Nicholson wanted his son Caleb to play Francis as a boy, but Caleb himself turned the role down.

In The Bird in a Gilded Gage, where Meryl sings, the then Mayor of Albany, Tom Whalen, played an extra.

WEEK 16
A CRY IN THE DARK (1988)

FILM FACTS

DISTRIBUTOR: Warner Bros.
RELEASE DATE: November 11, 1988

DIRECTOR: Fred Schepisi
WRITERS: Fred Schepisi, Robert Caswell (based on the novel by John Bryson)
PRODUCER: Verity Lambert
ALSO STARRING: Sam Neill, Ian Gilmour, Peter Flett, Kate Gorman

REVIEW

"The dingo took my baby!" Or "The dingo ate my baby!" as it's better known now, even though that second line is never actually uttered in the movie. How often have we heard these phrases? When I was an intern at a movie production company in 2006, I asked one of the executives why his AOL screen name was *thedingoatemybaby*. "If you have to ask," he said, "you don't deserve to know the answer."

Naturally I looked into the matter and discovered that the phrase stemmed from a real life tragedy that took place in Australia in August 1980. A nine-week-old girl, Azaria Chamberlain, was taken by a dingo near Ayers Rock and killed. Her mother Lindy was later wrongfully convicted of murder, and she served three years in jail. She was finally found innocent when the baby's jacket was found in a dingo den, and it wasn't until June 12, 2012, that the cause of Azaria's death was officially listed as a dingo attack. It's a sad event that unfortunately has turned into a funny one-liner over the years—even Nora Ephron cracked a joke about it at Meryl's AFI Lifetime Achievement ceremony—but it fortunately also spawned a compelling 1988 film, *A Cry in the Dark*, re-uniting Meryl with her *Plenty* director Fred Schepisi and co-star Sam Neill.

Despite my love for Meryl, before starting this project there had been a few of her movies that I'd missed, and one was *A Cry in the Dark* (also released as the awkwardly titled *Evil Angels* in Australia). Therefore, it was a thrill to finally check it out, the last of the films that Meryl received an Oscar nomination for that I hadn't seen. Despite some slow stretches, and a few overlong court scenes, *A Cry in the Dark* is the most engaging of the four dramas Meryl made between 1985 and 1988, with a true-life story that offers more questions than answers. Director Schepisi's matter-of-fact storytelling, which hindered the slowly-paced *Plenty*, works much better here, showing the ups and downs of two parents who not only have to deal with the loss of their young daughter, but untrue allegations made about them that ultimately land Lindy in prison.

At the start of the film, only smiles are to be had on the main characters' faces. Lindy (Meryl) and her husband

Michael (Neill) take a camping holiday in the Outback with their two young sons and their new baby girl. One night, the family is enjoying a barbecue, as the baby sleeps in the zipped-open tent. Lindy returns to the tent to see a dingo running out of it, with something in its mouth. When she discovers her baby girl missing, she screams the immortal line: "The dingo took my baby!" Everyone at the camp joins forces to search for the baby, to no success. Michael is a religious man, and that night he questions God's intentions, asking why he would bestow onto them the gift of a daughter, only to snatch her away weeks later.

As Lindy and Michael deal with their immense grief, the allegations begin: the story about the dingo is made-up, the last name Azaria means "sacrifice in the wilderness," the parents decapitated their baby with a pair of scissors as part of a religious rite. After initially being discharged of any wrongdoing, Lindy is pulled back into an investigation about Azaria's disappearance, and is eventually found guilty for her murder and sentenced to life imprisonment.

A Cry in the Dark is not as well shot as *Out of Africa* or has the attention to detail in the production design of *Ironweed*, but it is certainly the most riveting of these three films. Even though I was aware of the outcome of Lindy and Azaria's story upon sitting down to watch this movie, it still had me in its grip for most of the running time.

Neill is always excellent, and it was a joy to see him and Meryl together in a second project. His part is just as complex as Meryl's because he is playing a man totally committed to his religious faith, yet, like Mel Gibson's character in *Signs*, a tragedy occurs that makes him question his beliefs. His commitment to his wife, even in the most trying of times, is also a refreshing change of pace, considering that their marriage, for dramatic purposes, could have been played more strained and contentious.

One of the main joys of watching a Meryl movie week after week is seeing how she will surprise me next. She's so gifted at creating wholly original and three-dimensional characters on the screen (even in lesser material), and her performance as Lindy has to be considered one of her most astonishing. With her black bob of a haircut, she looks almost unrecognizable, and, even more impressive, her Australian accent is so spot-on that within minutes of the movie you naturally assume that's how she talks, no questions asked. Meryl is famous for her accents, and she delivers one of her best in *A Cry in the Dark*.

But going deeper than that, she hits so many notes with Lindy, playing hysterics, grief, anger, resentment. One of her best scenes comes toward the end, in her revealing courtroom scene, when she doesn't play on the jury's sympathy about the loss of her baby girl, but instead appears emotionless on the stand, tired of all the allegations and the rumors, and wanting nothing more than to get the trial over with. Courtroom scenes are so common in the movies, but Meryl manages to make this one an original and captivating moment.

A Cry in the Dark closed out a remarkable run in the 1980s of dramas that scored Meryl a whopping six Oscar nominations, her last of which pitted her up against Glenn Close for a second time, ultimately losing to Jodie Foster for *The Accused*. When the film was taken to the Cannes

Film Festival in May 1989, not only was it nominated for the prestigious Palme d'Or, but Meryl won the Best Actress award of the entire festival, six long months after *A Cry in the Dark*'s US release. By 1989, she had proven her worth to audiences all over the world, so maybe it was Meryl herself who decided to give some other actresses a shot at the limelight, while she concentrated on a brand new genre few ever expected her to tackle—comedies.

AWARDS WATCH

Meryl received her eighth Academy Award nomination, for Best Actress. She also earned a Golden Globe nomination for Best Actress – Drama, and won Best Actress from the Australian Film Institute, Cannes Film Festival, and New York Film Critics.

A Cry in the Dark earned four Golden Globe nominations, including Best Director and Best Motion Picture – Drama, and won five Australian Film Institute Awards, including Best Actor for Neill, Best Director, and Best Picture. The film was also nominated for the Palme d'Or at the Cannes Film Festival.

FUN FACTS

Meryl has never revealed her opinion publicly on whether or not Lindy Chamberlain was innocent.

The film is known as *Evil Angels* in Australia and New Zealand.

In 1986, Azaria's jacket was found in an area filled with dingos. The case was reopened, and in 1988 the Criminal Appeals Court overturned the convictions against the parents. In 1990, the parents received compensation for wrongful imprisonment.

The film was one of the most expensive ever shot in Australia, with a cast of 350 speaking roles and 4,000 extras.

WEEK 17
SHE-DEVIL (1989)

FILM FACTS

DISTRIBUTOR: Orion Pictures
RELEASE DATE: December 8, 1989

DIRECTOR: Susan Seidelman
WRITERS: Barry Strugatz, Mark R. Burns (based on the novel by Fay Weldon)
PRODUCERS: Jonathan Brett, Susan Seidelman
ALSO STARRING: Roseanne Barr, Ed Begley Jr., Linda Hunt, Sylvia Miles

REVIEW

Meryl started the 1980s by appearing in one acclaimed drama after another, like *The French Lieutenant's Woman*, *Sophie's Choice*, and *Silkwood*. By the end of the decade, she had racked up multiple Academy Award nominations, and was considered by many the most gifted actress of her generation. After her superb performances in *Ironweed* and *A Cry in the Dark*, there was little left for Meryl to prove. So what did she do? She signed on for a role in a film that no one, including probably her own agent, could have ever expected. Her last film of the decade was the comedy flop *She-Devil*, co-starring Roseanne Barr.

Meryl has never discussed her role in *She-Devil* in any interviews since the release of this film, but many would deem it obvious that she took her role of wealthy romance writer Mary Fisher not because she thought the script was brilliant or that director Susan Seidelman was particularly original or that Barr was the co-star she had been waiting for her entire career; she clearly wanted to go outside her comfort zone and attempt the comedy genre. She had some good comedic moments in *Manhattan*, *The Seduction of Joe Tynan*, and *Heartburn*, but up until 1989, she had never appeared in a full-fledged comedy. Just like director Sydney Pollack didn't find her sexy enough to be in *Out of Africa*—she famously proved him wrong in her audition—many filmmakers couldn't picture her in something funny. Of course, no one says no to Meryl, and if she wants to give a new genre a try, she finds a way.

She-Devil was my introduction to Meryl. I was five years old when it was released to video, and I have a clear memory of watching it at home at a young age in Roseville, California. I remember being revolted by the shot of a boy puking, and amazed by a shot of a woman walking out of an exploding house (this shot looks ludicrously fake today). I also have a clear memory of being instantly intrigued by the nutty, self-absorbed blonde lady on the screen. My introduction to Meryl was through her comedies, not her dramas—*Death Becomes Her* was my childhood favorite—and it's a genre that to this day she doesn't get enough credit for. Without *She-Devil*, there might not have been

Death Becomes Her. Hell, there might not have been that *other* devil comedy she's so well known for. *She-Devil* is a flawed movie, much slower and convoluted than I remembered from childhood, but no one can deny Meryl's hilarious, original performance, and her seamless transition into a genre few could have imagined her attempting.

Arguably the funniest element in watching *She-Devil* today is that it wouldn't even be discussed or even thought of anymore if it weren't for Meryl's participation in it. As iconic as the show *Roseanne* was, Barr's unremarkable film career is without a single winner. Her only other significant features are the 1990s stinkers *Even Cowgirls Get the Blues* and *Blue in the Face*, and a rare Disney animated disaster, 2004's *Home on the Range*. *She-Devil* offers her most well-developed character in a movie, but unfortunately, she's still not developed enough. The main flaw in *She-Devil* is that Barr's character of Ruth Patchett, who discovers her husband is cheating on her with a famous author and ultimately vows to take revenge on him, never becomes a character we root for, or care about, or laugh at, or ever truly *believe*. Barr looks a bit lost at times, and any time the film focuses on her for too long, the pacing noticeably slows down. Ed Begley Jr., as Ruth's husband Bob, is more effective than Barr, although he plays such a dweeb that it's hard to believe Meryl's Mary would fall in love with him so hard and so fast.

While Meryl's other comedies *Death Becomes Her* and especially *Defending Your Life* have sharp, imaginative screenplays, the script for *She-Devil* is fairly routine, offering few surprises, and only the occasional laugh throughout its brief running time. The reason it remains a cult classic to some, and the reason it continues to be screened and discussed more than twenty-five years later, is Meryl's performance, which is far better than the movie itself. It's a shame that she couldn't have picked a better script for her first foray into the comedy genre, but there's still a lot to admire here. Her intro scene, which Ruth watches on a monitor, is hilariously over-the-top, with Meryl pursing her lips and walking down a giant staircase like royalty. We know within ten seconds of seeing her that this is a side of Meryl that she had never shown in a movie before—one that doesn't take itself too seriously.

Another actress would have turned Mary into a one-dimensional joke, but Meryl makes an underwritten character both funny and sad at the same time—funny in her outrageous mannerisms and lines of dialogue, and sad in her loneliness and desire to be loved. When she yells at her literary agent about not publishing her new manuscript, and when she snaps at her mother for revealing her real age of forty-one, we laugh, but at the same time, feel sorry for the emptiness she clearly feels inside. While Ruth is the central character of the film, Meryl manages to make Mary a full-blown, memorable comic character who has an arc all her own. Lost in her own world for most of the running time, she in the end is in a much happier place, even when she signs an autograph for the conniving Ruth, a person who for weeks made her life a living hell.

It's worth noting that Meryl and Barr share very few minutes in the movie together. Aside from a brief conversation at a dinner party toward the beginning, and the aforementioned final scene, they co-exist in their own separate story lines most of the time. Barr was an up-and-coming comic at the time of this film's production, and Gene Siskel, in his televised review, was right in pointing out that one missed opportunity in *She-Devil* was not having these two uniquely different actresses spar with each other more often.

As a whole, this is not one of Meryl's better movies. The script doesn't take a lot of risks, and Barr always appears uncomfortable in her leading role. What this movie will best be known for is giving Meryl her first chance at a meaty comedic role, which she clearly bit into with great verve and relish. She would go on to make better comedies in the next few years, but *She-Devil* was the one she needed to show critics and audiences a brand new side of her evolving screen persona.

AWARDS WATCH

The lone nomination *She-Devil* earned was a Golden Globe nomination for Meryl, her eighth at that point, and her first in the Comedy/Musical category.

FUN FACTS

Before making this film, Meryl was criticized and questioned as to whether she could do a comedy.

Meryl was one of the first actresses to read the script because she and the director shared the same agent.

Barr's first film.

At one point, Meryl considered playing Barr's role, but due to conceptual similarity with her previous film, *A Cry in the Dark*, she decided to portray Mary instead.

Fay Weldon's novel was also made into a 1986 TV mini-series, *The Life and Loves of a She-Devil*.

Romance novelist Jackie Collins received a special thanks credit.

This was Meryl's first time working with a female director. She would work with many more in her career, including Nora Ephron, Nancy Meyers, and Phyllida Lloyd.

WEEK 18
POSTCARDS FROM THE EDGE (1990)

FILM FACTS

DISTRIBUTOR: Columbia Pictures
RELEASE DATE: September 14, 1990

DIRECTOR: Mike Nichols
WRITER: Carrie Fisher (based on her book)
PRODUCERS: Mike Nichols, John Calley
ALSO STARRING: Shirley MacLaine, Dennis Quaid, Gene Hackman, Richard Dreyfuss, Rob Reiner, Annette Bening

REVIEW

Sometimes even the most acclaimed dramatic actress in the world needs to relax, and have some fun. After appearing in her first comedy *She-Devil* in 1989, some may have expected Meryl to go back to what she's best known for—serious dramas. She eventually did, but not until 1993's *The House of the Spirits*. With three kids in tow and a fourth on the way, Meryl didn't want to make a movie on location far, far away, and chose between 1990 and 1992 to make films closer to home, in Los Angeles. Is it a coincidence that the three movies she made during this time were also comedies? Meryl had proven her worth by the end of the 1980s, and it was her right to make a few humorous films. Following *She-Devil*, she re-teamed with her beloved director Mike Nichols and starred alongside Shirley MacLaine in the entertaining, Hollywood-centric *Postcards From the Edge*.

Of the four comedies she made during this time, *Postcards From the Edge* is the one that's more serious, featuring plenty of powerful dramatic scenes. It tells of a troubled, A-list actress named Suzanne (Meryl) who overdoses on pills and ends up in the hospital, then rehab. To get insurance on her next movie, she is forced into living with her drunk of a mother, Doris (MacLaine).

The two rarely see eye-to-eye, and so *Postcards From the Edge* scores with a ferocious bite when Meryl and MacLaine square off against each other. The script was written by Carrie Fisher, based on her novel, which has, she has even admitted, similarities to her own life with her actress-mother, Debbie Reynolds. Reynolds desperately wanted to play the role of Doris in the movie, but director Nichols had his eye on MacLaine from the start.

Meryl has often said that Nichols was one of her favorite directors to work with. They first collaborated on *Silkwood* in 1983, and then again on *Heartburn* in 1986. This would be their last motion picture together (they worked together one final time on the HBO mini-series *Angels in America*, in 2003), and once again, Nichols was able to bring out sides of Meryl that she had never shown before. As ridiculous as it may seem, up until 1990 Meryl had neglected showing herself on film simply as a modern-day American that much, and it's refreshing to see that simple side of her in *Postcards From the Edge*. She has her addiction problems, her turmoil with her over-protective mother, but she also lets loose, enjoying romantic flings with a handsome young producer (Dennis Quaid) and goofing around on movie sets—the shot of her pretending to hang off a high-rise balcony is a great one. She may not be playing Australian or Polish or British here, but what Meryl does is just as difficult, portraying a sexy, vibrant woman whose emotional battles are not yet won.

The film itself is, like Meryl's previous collaboration with Nichols, a mixed bag. Like *Heartburn*, *Postcards From the Edge* is made up of only a few good scenes. The opening sequence before the title cards may be its best; it features a long shot of Suzanne, acting within the movie, ruining a long take, taking a quick break to get her drug fix, and getting screamed at by her director (Gene Hackman, fantastic in a small part) for something no one on the set pretends is a secret. These first few minutes set up what could have been a more biting satirical film about Hollywood, but the tone of the movie fluctuates time and time again, going from straight comedy to intense drama to a romantic subplot that heads nowhere. There's one great ferocious fight between Suzanne and Doris on a staircase that revs up the energy, but like *Heartburn*, *Postcards From the Edge* rarely offers much tension, and starts to burn out in its second half, ultimately giving us a phony happy ending (with singing!) that feels like something out of a different movie.

Despite some flaws, one element that is always exciting in Nichols' films is the superb casts he assembles, and *Postcards From the Edge* is no different. Meryl could be the sole actor in a movie, a la Robert Redford in *All is Lost*, and it would still be fascinating, but she is always at her best when she has other great actors to play off of, and she has many here. MacLaine was an inspired choice to play her mother, and she often gets the best lines. While Meryl received another Academy Award nomination for her performance, MacLaine was snubbed in the Supporting category, despite her being a worthy contender. Quaid does his best with an underwritten role, while Hackman is so superb playing a controlling film director that the character's screen-time should have been doubled. Richard Dreyfuss, Rob Reiner, and the delightful Mary Wickes pop up in small roles, and Annette Bening, whose career was about to explode, makes an impression in just a single scene, playing an air-headed, gun-smacking actress who sleeps around and isn't afraid to admit it.

One of the great pleasures of *Postcards From the Edge* is watching Meryl belt out a few songs. While the only musicals she has played significant parts in are 2008's *Mamma Mia* and 2014's *Into the Woods*, she has sung in a few other movies, including *The Deer Hunter*, *Ironweed*, *Death Becomes Her*, and *A Prairie Home Companion*. Her singing voice is lovely, and it's always a treat when we get to hear it. While her ending song in the movie is a show-stopper, her quieter rendition of Ray Charles' "You Don't Know Me," which her character sings under pressure from her mother, is hauntingly beautiful. While *Postcards From the Edge* never quite connects as a satisfying whole, it features a dazzling performance by MacLaine and yet another rich and complex performance by Meryl, who received her ninth Oscar nomination. While she wouldn't receive her tenth for five more years, that's not to say she next appeared in a series of clunkers. No, her next movie, one of the most underrated of her entire career, is my favorite Meryl movie of all.

AWARDS WATCH

Meryl received her ninth Academy Award nomination, for Best Actress. She also earned a Golden Globe nomination for Best Actress in a Comedy/Musical, and won Funniest Actress in a Motion Picture at the American Comedy Awards.

Postcards from the Edge also received an Academy Award nomination for Best Original Song, Shel Silverstein's "I'm Checkin' Out." In addition, the film earned a Golden Globe nomination for MacLaine, for Best Supporting Actress, and three BAFTA Award nominations, including Best Adapted Screenplay, and Best Actress, not for Meryl, but for MacLaine.

FUN FACTS

Meryl did all her own singing.

John Cusack and Jerry Orbach both filmed scenes, but they were later cut.

Janet Leigh wanted to play the role of Doris, with her daughter Jamie Lee Curtis as Suzanne.

Gene Hackman based his performance on director Richard Donner, who he worked with on *Superman*.

The band accompanying Meryl at the end of the film is Blue Rodeo, one of the most popular rock groups in Canada at the time.

Meryl and MacLaine play mother and daughter, but are only fifteen years apart in age.

The only Academy Awards ceremony in which Meryl was nominated that she did *not* attend was the 1991 ceremony, when she was nominated for *Postcards from the Edge*. She was resting at home, about to give birth to her fourth child.

WEEK 19
DEFENDING YOUR LIFE (1991)

FILM FACTS

DISTRIBUTOR: Warner Bros.
RELEASE DATE: Marsh 22, 1991

DIRECTOR: Albert Brooks
WRITER: Albert Brooks
PRODUCER: Michael Grillo
ALSO STARRING: Albert Brooks, Rip Torn, Lee Grant, Buck Henry

REVIEW

Meryl has appeared in so many great movies that it can be hard to pick a favorite. Many would make a case for *Sophie's Choice*, or *Out of Africa*, or *Kramer vs. Kramer*. *Death Becomes Her* has its rabid fans, and *The Devil Wears Prada* is a modern comedy classic. Meryl's performances have been nominated for Academy Awards in nineteen movies, so you might assume my favorite would be one of those. You might also assume, at the very least, that my favorite film of hers would feature her in the lead role. These assumptions couldn't be further from the truth: my all-time favorite Meryl movie is one of her lesser-known works, one she didn't win any awards for, and one in which she plays a supporting role. Albert Brooks' *Defending Your Life* is an enchanting motion picture that also happens to be my favorite comedy of all time.

Brooks plays Daniel Miller, a thirty-something advertising executive who on his birthday dies when his car crashes into a bus. He wakes up in a place called Judgment City, a sort-of purgatory where everyone who passes away goes to defend his or her life, in a trial-like setting. The place looks a lot like Earth, with its high-rise buildings, sushi restaurants, and championship golf courses. But it's not Earth; in Judgment City, the life you just led is examined by a defender, a prosecutor, and two judges, to determine if you are ready to move on to the next higher stage of life, or if you need to go back and try again. For four days, you sit in a revolving chair and watch clips from your life, some of which show examples of your fear, and some that show examples of your courage. Did Daniel have enough courage? Or was he afraid, all the way to the end?

A story like this could have been told with a harder edge—Woody Allen, for example, probably would have gone for the jugular more often in his punch-lines—but it's the film's sweetness that makes it truly winning, especially when Meryl pops up about a half-hour into the picture. She plays Julia, a mother of two who died when she tripped and drowned in a pool. She has an instant chemistry with Daniel, after they meet at a comedy club, and even though they only have four days together in this alternate universe, they immediately fall in love. Daniel never found true love on Earth but he immediately feels a connection with this woman, who is intelligent, likable, and funny, and who led a mostly fearless life. She's obviously going to move on to the next stage—but is he?

Defending Your Life is a subtle film. There is nothing particularly special about any of the performances, or the cinematography, or the production design. The jokes more often put a smile on your face than they make you laugh out loud. At the heart of the film is a tender romance, with the required Meet Cute, the first tender kiss, the obligatory happy ending. The premise is a great one, and Brooks' screenplay is extremely clever, but there's nothing especially *extraordinary* about the movie from a filmmaking standpoint. So why then is this my favorite Meryl movie, and my favorite comedy ever?

Few movies, especially comedies, make you think differently about the world, but *Defending Your Life* truly transformed me when I saw it in high school. I had few friends at the time, and was always scared of social situations. I didn't have a phobia by any means, but fear seemed to cloud up my head every day in each endeavor I took on. Watching *Defending Your Life* for the first time not only entertained me to no end, with its witty one-liners and philosophical ideas and shades of romance, but it also woke me up to the fears that had been plaguing me year after year. At one point, a character says, "[People] can't get through that fog [of fear]. But you get through it, and baby, you're in for the ride of your life." *Defending Your Life* is about a lot of things, but mostly it's about conquering all that frightens you, and living a life in truth. This film is a whole lot more than a comedy. It's one of those rare movies that can change your life for the better; it certainly did mine.

The film is packed with one memorable scene after another. You can eat whatever you want to your heart's content without gaining weight in Judgment City, and so this concept plays a big role in the film. Judgment City has a Past Lives Pavilion, where you can see the people you've been in previous lives; the scene that takes the viewer into this Disneyland-like attraction offers some of the film's biggest laughs (and features Shirley MacLaine, Meryl's *Postcards from the Edge* co-star, in an unbilled role). Merely the way Brooks starts the film is ingenious, not rushing to the first punch-line, but instead giving us about ten minutes with Daniel as he goes about his day, chatting with a friend, buying a new car, singing a Barbra Streisand song to his heart's content. For those not knowing what's coming, his death might seem a surprise, especially given that this is a comedy.

Can a comedy about death be funny, though? Allen's done it, in *Love & Death*, as well as Warren Beatty in *Heaven Can Wait* and Alfred Hitchcock in *The Trouble With Harry*. Brooks' film is the most effective of all because it's not overly surreal, and it doesn't have a dead person returning to Earth. Brooks treats his premise seriously, and one of the elements that works so well is that after awhile you begin to believe that heading to Judgment City and defending your own life is what actually happens to you when death rears its ugly head. And it's not a ridiculous notion! I have no idea what happens to us when we die, but in the fifteen years since I first saw this movie, I haven't been able to find a more sensible afterlife, albeit brief at only five days, than the one featured here.

Casting is critical to a movie, especially comedies, and in *Defending Your Life*, Brooks gathered the perfect group. Brooks stars in every film he directs, and he's a unique actor who always brings something unexpected and moving to each role he plays, whether it's broader comedies like his *Lost in America* and *Mother*, or in more serious fare like the 2011 thriller *Drive*. He has a lovable face that harbors what always looks to be a tortured soul. In *Defending Your Life*, he brings the necessary mix of dry humor and self-loathing to a role that could have come across much blander in the hands of a different actor. His Daniel is not afraid to admit his past mistakes, and he has a sweet, romantic side even he probably didn't know he was capable of. He can be silly at times, over-the-top in his mannerisms occasionally, but incredibly moving, too, especially in the speech he makes to Julia his final night in Judgment City, and in his defeated expression he displays when the devastating verdict comes in. Brooks has only been nominated for one Academy Award—Best Supporting Actor for 1987's *Broadcast News*—but he deserved a second nod for his stellar turn here.

The supporting cast was especially well chosen. Rip Torn has rarely been more effective in a comedy than he is in *Defending Your Life*, playing Daniel's defendant, Bob Diamond. His corny counterarguments in the courtroom, the way he laughs at his own terrible jokes, his insistence on calling humans who live on Earth "little brains." He is simply fantastic in this. Lee Grant is equally memorable, playing Lena Foster, otherwise known as the Dragon Lady.

She's Daniel's prosecutor, and, coming off a loss the previous Thursday, she is determined to prove that Daniel's fears should keep him from moving forward. Her icy demeanor makes for great sparring between her and Daniel, as well as her and Bob, especially toward the end.

Meryl is at her cheery, likable best in *Defending Your Life*, and while this is my favorite film of hers, it's probably her least remarkable performance in her entire career. Her character Julia has only a little backstory—her marriage had more bad times than good, and she loved her children—and all we come to really know about her is that she is a smarter, more heroic, more giving individual than Daniel. It's not hard to see why he's attracted to her; not only is Meryl absolutely luminous in this film, but she makes Daniel a better person.

Despite her limited screen-time and lack of any true character development, Meryl makes an indelible impression. While she played more selfish, borderline wicked characters in her other two broad comedies at the time—*She-Devil* and *Death Becomes Her*—she plays, more or less, the perfect woman in *Defending Your Life*. It was probably the concept of the movie and the chance to work with Brooks that attracted her to the project—even Meryl would have to admit this may have been her least challenging role as an actress in her entire career—but it probably didn't hurt that she got to play funny, and at the same time be endearing.

While Julia is only in small chunks of the movie, she becomes firmly swept up in Daniel's journey. When Daniel is sentenced to return to Earth to try again, it seems inevitable that these two characters are not meant to be. *Lost in America*, Brooks' previous film he wrote and directed before this, is a 1980s comedy classic, but top critics at the time, including Roger Ebert, criticized the film for having a weak ending. Brooks must have learned his lesson because the ending to *Defending Your Life* couldn't be more perfect. Not only does it have a happy ending, with Daniel reuniting with his beloved Julia, but it is an *earned* happy ending, one that forces Daniel to prove his courage once and for all.

Released quietly in the spring of 1991, *Defending Your Life* did mediocre box office, stunningly, and made little impression on audiences. However, more than any movie Meryl has made, this film has grown in stature over the years through word of mouth, more than anything. Unlike so many movies that leave your mind when the credits start rolling, Brooks' film sticks with you, not just for days, but for years. It's one of those rare movies I own that I'll pop in to my DVD player once in a while, because it makes me think about where I am in my life and how I'm going to proceed from here. Fear robs us from what we can accomplish, from experiences we wouldn't otherwise be able to enjoy. When I have a moment of panic, or try to avoid a situation that might make me step out of my comfort zone, I think about this film. What would my prosecutor in Judgment City say if I said no to an opportunity because I was afraid? This is a very deep movie, especially for a comedy. Most films in this genre make you laugh. *Defending Your Life* has the ability to transform you, in every aspect of your life.

Best of all, this movie makes me happy. My favorite films include *Sunset Boulevard*, *The Truman Show*, *Mulholland Drive*, *Halloween*. All very different, all special to me for different reasons. These are timeless movies to me, the kind that never get old and actually seem to improve each time I watch them. *Defending Your Life* is the same way. It may not feature Meryl's most extraordinary performance—not by a long shot—but it's certainly an extraordinary film, one I will treasure for the rest of my life.

AWARDS WATCH

Meryl received a Saturn Award nomination for Best Actress at the Academy of Science Fiction, Fantasy & Horror Films, as well as a nomination for Funniest Actress in a Motion Picture at the American Comedy Awards.

Defending Your Life also earned Saturn Award nominations at the Academy of Science Fiction, Fantasy & Horror Films for Best Writing and Best Fantasy Film.

FUN FACTS

The trams used throughout the film are old ones from Universal Studios Hollywood.

The Hall of Past Lives is actually the old Fluor Daniel building in Irvine, California.

Feature film debut of Ethan Embry.

Buck Henry, who plays Bob's temporary replacement Dick Stanley, previously co-directed *Heaven Can Wait*, also about the afterlife.

The poster's tagline was "The first true story of what happens after you die."

WEEK 20
DEATH BECOMES HER (1992)

FILM FACTS

DISTRIBUTOR: Universal Pictures
RELEASE DATE: July 31, 1992

DIRECTOR: Robert Zemeckis
WRITERS: Martin Donovan, David Koepp
PRODUCERS: Robert Zemeckis, Steve Starkey
ALSO STARRING: Goldie Hawn, Bruce Willis, Isabella Rossellini, Jonathan Silverman, Fabio

REVIEW

"Meryl, you *are* a special effect," Goldie Hawn said at Meryl's 2004 AFI Lifetime Achievement ceremony, and while the line got a laugh, some might argue that what Hawn said is true. Meryl has appeared in, on average, at least one film per year, and decade after decade she continues to impress us with her incredible transformations. Best of all, she continues to surprise us, not just in her choice of roles, but in her choice of genres. In the late 1980s and early 1990s she moved away from dramas to have a bit more fun, in four comedies ranging in scope and broadness. Her fourth and final comedy for a long while—she wouldn't return to anything close to the genre until 2002's *Adaptation*—is also the only film Meryl has made in her career until *Into the Woods* that relies heavily on special effects. The splendidly entertaining and endlessly imaginative *Death Becomes Her*, directed by Robert Zemeckis (*Forrest Gump*), may not be one of Meryl's most important films, but it's easily one of my top three favorites she has ever appeared in.

More than any movie I'm discussing in this series, *Death Becomes Her* is the one I have a long history with, and such great affection for. It is the first Meryl film I ever saw in a theater, at the United Artists Sunrise Mall in Roseville, California. Why my mom thought I, at seven years old, would enjoy a black comedy about youth, beauty, and death, I'll never know, but I have a clear memory of sitting in the theater enraptured in the film from beginning to end. I spent many hours the rest of that year writing my own version of the story down on paper, as well as a sequel starring myself and two of my best friends called *Death Becomes Him*. When the movie was released on VHS, my mom bought me a copy for Christmas, and for the next year, I played it over and over again. I remember as late as high school bringing friends over to screen the film—"You haven't seen *Death Becomes Her*? Your life is not complete. Sit down!" was basically my pitch—but when I screened it again for this series, it had been at least ten years since I had watched it.

So being such a rabid fan more than twenty years ago, how does *Death Becomes Her* hold up after all this time? It is definitely an uneven film, and, I'm sad to say, some of the special effects, so revolutionary at the time—they won the Oscar that year—look a bit phony. The scene of Madeline talking to Ernest after her fall down the stairs looks particularly dated. What hasn't aged, and what still puts a smile on my face, is the sharp script by Martin Donovan and David Koepp, and the memorable comic performances by Goldie Hawn, Bruce Willis, and, of course, Meryl. Considering that Meryl had never worked closely with visual effects before, her turn here is particularly inspired, with her comfortable in the skin of one of her most self-obsessed and nasty characters this side of Miranda Priestley, and with her game for everything the special effects wizards throw at her.

The story begins in 1978, when a loving couple, Ernest Menville (Willis) and Helen Sharp (Hawn), go to see the latest Broadway production starring the critically panned Madeline Ashton (Meryl). Most of the audience walks out, but Ernest loves the show, and is delighted to meet Madeline backstage. Soon enough, Ernest and Madeline are married, and the scorned Helen spends the next seven years fattening herself up and hating Madeline. Another seven years pass, and Madeline is losing everything—her looks, her career, the love of her husband. So she turns to Lisle Von Rhuman (Isabella Rossellini), an eccentric but gorgeous woman living in a Vincent Price-esque castle who bestows onto Madeline a potion that promises beauty and immortality.

Madeline is delighted by her newfound youthful appearance; however, when Ernest pushes her down the stairs, causing her to break her neck, havoc ensues. She and Helen, who we also come to learn has been basking in the glory of the potion for years, can't die, so it's up to Ernest to ensure that these two diva broads will stay beautiful forever—unless, that is, he wants to find a way out.

It's interesting to note that Meryl preceded this film with Albert Brooks' *Defending Your Life* because it is another comedy, albeit more subtle, about death, and the ramifications of both good and bad decisions one makes in life. That's where the comparisons end, though; if one would describe *Defending Your Life* as a studious high school freshman, *Death Becomes Her* is like its nasty, constantly drunk, college-bound older brother. The film didn't do well at the time because black comedy has always been a hard sell, but anyone involved had to have known that it wouldn't appeal to everyone. None of the three main characters is likable. The movie touches on themes of fleeting beauty, wrecked marriages, animosity toward old friends, fat people as lazy and disgusting. The list goes on and on. This is not a movie your conservative grandmother will appreciate, but if you're in the right state of mind, it is one of Meryl's all-time most entertaining films.

When Meryl read the script, she originally thought director Zemeckis wanted her to play Helen, the intellectual writer, and was shocked when she discovered he wanted her for Madeline—watching the movie today, it's impossible to imagine the two actresses' roles flipped. Hawn's choice of material over the years was sometimes questionable—I can't imagine too many are revisiting *Bird on a Wire*, *Deceived*, or *Town & Country* these days—but *Death Becomes Her* offered her one of her most unique and inventive characters to play. The two transformations she has at the beginning of the movie are incredible by themselves, but when Helen finally goes mano a mano with Madeline's character at the mansion, Hawn revels in the outlandish qualities of her character. Willis was an unlikely choice at the time for Ernest, considering he was a huge box-office star in the *Die Hard* movies, and of the three leads, he might be the one who disappears into his character the most, playing a depressed alcoholic dweeb who looks so unlike the handsome Willis that it takes the viewer a few minutes to recognize that it's even him.

Meryl, however, looks to be having the most fun of all. She is the main character in the movie, a woman who obsesses over her image so much that she is incapable of feeling anything resembling love for her husband, and anything but animosity toward younger, more beautiful women. Meryl was, and still is, a stunningly gorgeous person, so the make-up artists had their work cut out for them when they needed to make her appear less than flattering in the two scenes that lead up to Madeline's taking of the potion.

Meryl is more known for her dramatic work than her comedic work, but her performance in *Death Becomes Her* has to be considered one of her most hysterically funny of her career, and absolutely worthy of her Golden Globe nomination she received in early 1993. The role allows her to play all sorts of different colors. She gets to sing and dance in the film's stupendous all-in-one-take opener. She gets one zinger after another, with many particularly memorable—just the way she says the line, "*Now a warning?*" is a classic. And she also had the opportunity, for the first time, to work with special effects. While Meryl commented in a later interview that she didn't enjoy working with all the innovative and time-staking effects in *Death Becomes Her*, it is a treat for the viewer to see Meryl, so known for her dramas, express great delight in surrounding herself with the most inventive special effects of the time.

There's not much left to say about this movie, except, where's the special edition Blu Ray? Zemeckis, whose celebrated films like *Back to the Future*, *Who Framed Roger Rabbit*, and *Forrest Gump* have all received special edition releases with generous supplements, has not yet contributed toward such a release for *Death Becomes Her*. And it's not to say there are no supplements in existence. There are surely many neat behind-the-scenes featurettes that could be made about the visual effects process, and even more enticing, in what is one of the holy grails of lost footage from a modern classic, the original ending was excised and a whole subplot involving Meryl's *Plenty* and *Into the Woods* co-star Tracey Ullman was completely removed (you can see hints of her character in the film's theatrical trailer). As of this writing, there is no special edition, no Blu Ray release, and only an old DVD release from January 1998 that offers merely a full frame presentation. Here's hoping Universal will eventually give fans of *Death Becomes Her* the release the film deserves.

Death Becomes Her marked the end of Meryl's momentary hibernation into the world of comedies. She returned the following year with the critically panned drama *The House of the Spirits*, and spent the rest of the 1990s appearing in more serious work, most of them acclaimed and well-respected. While it is easy to admire Meryl's work in a movie like *The Bridges of Madison County* or *One True Thing*, it's comedy that most actors say is the hardest of all, and what Meryl does in *Death Becomes Her* has to be considered one of her most challenging and groundbreaking performances of her entire career. She manages to make us sympathize with a mostly unsympathetic character, and gets us to laugh time after time, even though the material itself is extremely dark and frequently demented. *Death Becomes Her* is one of my all-time favorite guilty pleasures, a movie I can return to again and again. I'm already looking forward to the next time I give the disc a spin in my player, if only to hear Meryl one more time say the immortal line, "Ernest… my ass… I can see… my *ass*!"

AWARDS WATCH

Meryl was nominated for a Golden Globe for Best Actress in a Comedy/Musical. She also received a Saturn Award Best Actress nomination from the Academy of Science Fiction, Fantasy & Horror, and an American Comedy Award nomination for Funniest Actress in a Motion Picture.

Death Becomes Her won the Academy Award and the BAFTA Award for Best Visual Effects. It also received nine Saturn Award nominations from the Academy of Science Fiction, Fantasy & Horror, and won two, including Best Supporting Actress for Rossellini. In addition, Sydney Pollack, who directed Meryl in *Out of Africa*, won Best Supporting Actor from the Los Angeles Film Critics, for this film, as well as for *The Player* and *Husbands & Wives*.

FUN FACTS

Meryl accidentally scarred Hawn's cheek with a shovel during the fight scene.

In the opening scene, Madeline is starring in a musical version of *Sweet Bird of Youth*, about an aging actress who pines for her lost youth.

The date when Helen drinks the potion is the present date in Zemeckis' *Back to the Future*.

Kevin Kline, Meryl's *Sophie's Choice* co-star, was originally going to play Ernest, but he dropped out before filming began.

Catherine Bell (*JAG*) was Rossellini's nude body double.

The film went under major re-editing after a negative reaction at a test screening. The ending was re-shot, and the role played by Ullman was cut from the film completely.

WEEK 21
THE HOUSE OF THE SPIRITS (1993)

FILM FACTS

DISTRIBUTOR: Miramax
RELEASE DATE: April 1, 1994
(but premiered in Germany in 1993)

DIRECTOR: Billie August
WRITER: Billie August (based on the novel by Isabel Allende)
PRODUCER: Bernd Eichinger
ALSO STARRING: Jeremy Irons, Glenn Close, Winona Ryder, Vanessa Redgrave, Antonio Banderas, Vincent Gallo

REVIEW

Has Meryl appeared in any bad movies? She said in an interview with Andy Cohen that Robert Benton's *Still of the Night* is not one of her better efforts. Some may argue that *Heartburn* and *Ironweed* have major flaws and that the more recent *Lions for Lambs* and *Rendition* are snore-inducing borefests. *Before and After*, a 1996 bomb co-starring Liam Neeson, is probably her most critically ravished movie of all. But there was another 1990s movie, one released between her special effects extravaganza *Death Becomes Her* and her taut action thriller *The River Wild*, that also received a harsh beating from the critics. It has one of the most astonishing ensemble casts of any movie she's appeared in. It features splendid cinematography, superb editing, and an epic family story that spans decades. But with all its stellar attributes, *The House of the Spirits*, directed by Billie August (*Pelle the Conquerer*), may be Meryl's worst film of all, a bloated, never-ending mess that features one of her most phoned-in and least inspired performances.

I can almost hear the chat she had with her agent, probably sometime around 1992. Meryl had appeared in four comedies in a row, including a box office bomb with Roseanne Barr, and her agent likely wanted to get Meryl back into the business that wins her awards—dramatic work. I can see him waving the script for *The House of the Spirits* in her face, boasting about the acclaimed director, and the beloved novel, and the amazing cast that had already been assembled, insisting she sign on if she still wants to be considered a serious actress. While Meryl has often been smart and selective in her choosing of projects, bouncing around different genres and surprising us with new shades of what she's capable of, there is nothing fresh about *The House of the Spirits*. This feels all the way through like a movie made just to win its actors and craftsmen awards, not to tell a story anyone particularly cares about.

The cast is astonishing. Meryl, in a supporting role, is joined on-screen by such powerhouse actors as Jeremy Irons, Glenn Close, Winona Ryder, and Vanessa Redgrave, along with a young and pretty Antonio Banderas and a young and creepy Vincent Gallo. The pairings in the film are significant in a few ways. One, Meryl re-teamed with her *The French Lieutenant's Woman* co-star Irons and her *Julia* co-star Redgrave. Two, Close and Irons reteamed after their successful pairing in *Reversal of Fortune*, which won Irons an Academy Award. Lastly, and most interesting to Meryl fans, this is to date the only movie that she and Close have appeared in together (although they did have separate scenes in 2007's *Evening*). Often thought of as two of the finest actresses of their generation, and having competed for Best Actress in three Oscar races—in 1988, 1989, and 2012—they certainly have a history together. Therefore, it is unfortunate that they would only share screen-time in a dramatically inert movie like this one.

Meryl plays Clara, the wife of Esteban Trueba, a man who grows up poor but eventually becomes a powerful conservative in twentieth century Chile. She first appears about a half-hour into the movie, ages close to fifty years over the course of the narrative, then exits long before the film is over. Yes, this is one long movie. At about two hours and twenty minutes, *The House of the Spirits* feels an hour longer. It has scenes of joy, sadness, romance, and great tragedy—but *Titanic* this is not. When Close cries in a scene of grim truth-telling, no tears from the viewer are shed. When an older couple dies in an unlikely train collision, little care is expressed. A willing cast does what they can, but the story lacks depth and emotion, with only Ryder coming through in the end with a character that keeps us engaged. Meryl is given a rare role in her career that pretty much any actress her age could have played. She often appears bored, probably counting the days until she can leave the production and suit up for the more exciting and physically demanding *The River Wild*.

Not everyone is able to make a good movie each time out, not even Meryl. Classic stars like Bette Davis and Ingrid Bergman made the occasional flop, and even respected modern Oscar winners like Judi Dench and Cate Blanchett have made tired clunkers, some of which were never released to theaters. Meryl has appeared in more terrific films than any actress of her generation, so it's understood that once in awhile she may offer her talents to a film not worthy of her. Some may argue that *The House of the Spirits*, with its amazing cast and acclaimed source material, is nowhere near her worst movie, but if I had to pick one film she's ever starred in to never watch for the rest of my life, it's this one.

AWARDS WATCH

Meryl received zero wins or nominations for her performance, but *The House of the Spirits* won twelve awards at various international ceremonies, including Best Production at the Bavarian Film Awards, Best German Film at the Guild of German Art House Cinemas, and Best Film at the Robert Festival. Ryder also won a Jupiter Award for Best International Actress.

FUN FACTS

Annette Bening and Michelle Pfeiffer were considered for Meryl's role of Clara.

This is one of the only films Meryl has made that premiered overseas multiple months before its United States release. *The House of the Spirits* premiered in Germany in October 1993 but wasn't released in the US until April 1994.

William Hurt was the initial choice to play Esteban.

Julia Roberts turned down the role of Blanca, as did Kim Basinger.

The film debut of Grace Gummer, who would go on to appear with her mother in 2014's *The Homesman*.

WEEK 22
THE RIVER WILD (1994)

FILM FACTS

DISTRIBUTOR: Universal Pictures
RELEASE DATE: September 30, 1994

DIRECTOR: Curtis Hanson
WRITER: Denis O'Neill
PRODUCERS: David Foster, Lawrence Turman
ALSO STARRING: Kevin Bacon, David Strathairn, Joseph Mazzello, John C. Reilly, Benjamin Bratt

REVIEW

I miss the '90s. I miss Super Nintendo, and my best friend Brandon, and my second grade teacher Mrs. Uribe. I also miss that magical period when action blockbusters relied not on special effects but on actual suspense, and performances that delivered. 1994 was an excellent year for action movies, with *Speed* and *True Lies* making big impressions, and *The River Wild*, released that September, being one of the most exciting releases of all—and not just because visual effects don't drive the film. The film has a solid story, characters that make sense, and a breathless climax. It also remains the one and only action movie that Meryl has ever made.

Death Becomes Her had been Meryl's most surprising and daring film yet, but *The River Wild* was an even more unlikely choice, a project that allowed her to flex both her acting and physical muscles. Following in the footsteps of Sigourney Weaver and Linda Hamilton, Meryl took on an action movie with so much zeal and gusto that it's a shame she hasn't returned to the genre since. She commits one hundred percent to every character she takes on, so to play Gail Hartman, a skilled rafting expert, she trained for multiple weeks leading up to production, and got herself in the best physical shape of her adult life.

As the film opens, she is not in the best place. Her husband Tom (David Strathairn) is a workaholic who spends little time with the family, and so she doesn't expect him to tag along for a summer rafting trip. Therefore, Gail is stunned when he shows up to take the journey, and to save their crumbling marriage. The family adventure down the river begins calmly, with impressive views all around, but a trio of men in a separate raft begin impeding on the family's vacation almost immediately, saying a harmless hello at first but then asking for more help. Soon the trio is mysteriously cut down to two, and the more charismatic one—Wade, played by a chilling Kevin Bacon—convinces Gail and her family to let them board their boat. No movie like this exists without a villain, so Wade and his buddy Terry (John C. Reilly) eventually take the family hostage and demand that Gail bring them past the checkpoint and into the Gauntlet, a dangerous part of the river that has been off-limits to rafters for years.

Although Meryl and Bacon both received Golden Globe nominations for their performances, *The River Wild* was not well-received by some critics at the time. Gene Siskel and Roger Ebert gave the film two thumbs down on their show, neither one impressed by what they felt was a lackluster story that had a lack of surprises. While I agree that the story is a little thin, part of the charm of a movie like this—*Breakdown*, starring Kurt Russell, is another '90s movie that comes to mind—is a story stripped to the bare bones to offer the maximum suspense possible. Is *The River Wild* predictable at times? Does the good guy win and the bad guy lose in the end? This movie isn't trying to redefine a genre. As entertainment, it works, all the way through.

Curtis Hanson, who had previously directed the cheesy thriller *The Hand that Rocks the Cradle*, gives *The River Wild* just the right pacing. If Bacon's character went off the rails ten minutes in, half the fun would be lost. Anyone who's ever seen a movie before knows from his introductory scene that he is going to be bad, but the joy of the film's first half is watching and waiting for when he'll strike first. This is not an action-packed movie along the lines of *Speed* by any means, considering that the only true action sequence comes at the end, but the brewing tension that builds and builds is very effective. Take for instance the scene when Gail skinny dips, and discovers Wade watching her from up top the mountain. Or the extremely tense scene where Gail and Tom try to escape from Wade before he finds out what they're doing. As the viewer, you constantly put yourself in each scenario, wondering how you would handle it. Do the protagonists always make the right decisions? Not always. But again, that's the charm.

The River Wild is notable as one of the few movies my mother stayed in her seat all the way through the credits, and I'm guessing thousands of people did the same thing upon its release, not to find out what the character names were or to see who the second assistant director was, but to find out where the movie was shot. The film's cinematography by Robert Elswit (*There Will Be Blood*) is stunning, and no matter how wrapped up you get in the narrative, that burning question nags at you constantly: "Where was this *filmed*?" Most of the movie's whitewater scenes were filmed on the Kootenai River in Montana, while some additional photography was done on the Rogue River in Oregon. If shot today, the producers would probably cut corners and shoot bits and pieces on a water stage, or—gulp—use special effects water. But what you see in *The River Wild* is always real, and this element brings a much-needed sense of menace to the proceedings.

The performances are excellent all around. Meryl's *Plenty* and *A Cry in the Dark* co-star Sam Neill was asked to play her husband Tom—he turned the part down—but Strathairn (*Good Night and Good Luck*) was ultimately the best choice, a perfect mix of nerd and hero. Joseph Mazzello, as Gail's son Roarke, is not the typical annoying movie kid, and, the same way he did in the previous year's *Jurassic Park*, makes for a compelling character all his own. Reilly is the appropriate villainous sidekick, and Bacon, who up until 1994 was more known for playing a hero than a villain, was ingeniously cast against type in this as an unpredictable and threatening bad guy, to great effect. His intense chemistry with Meryl is one of the film's best qualities.

Many actresses at the time could have played the role of Gail—Julia Roberts, Geena Davis, and Sharon Stone were likely considered—and Meryl, despite all her Oscar nominations, probably wasn't an obvious choice. She had appeared in one suspense film before—the lame *Still of the Night*—but had never taken on a role in an action movie. Whether it was Meryl who pursued the project or Hanson who thought of her for the role, her casting in *The River Wild* was a masterstroke. It's always a thrill to see a strong, independent, capable woman on-screen, especially in a big-budget action movie, and Meryl makes what was already a solid project into something even greater. She had shown so many layers on screen before, but never had she displayed this tremendous of a physical side. Meryl did most of her own stunts throughout the movie, but what's most impressive of all is how she is able to balance humor, terror, and a love for her family with all the strenuous physicality.

The River Wild may be Meryl's one and only action movie, but at least we have the one—it's better than nothing. She would have looked silly in the '90s appearing in something like *Independence Day* or *Armageddon*, but *The River Wild* was the right choice for her, in a movie of this magnitude. It's one that tells an exciting, fast-paced story with tension and suspense, and that awesome finale that takes Gail and Co. down the Gauntlet. Unfortunately she must not have loved shooting this movie, since the following year she returned to drama with *The Bridges of Madison County* and stayed in the genre for the rest of the decade. Yes, any fun she showed, any big smiles or winks to the camera she displayed on screen between her risk-taking years of 1989 and 1994, were over—at least for a little while.

AWARDS WATCH

Meryl earned a Golden Globe nomination for Best Actress in a Motion Picture – Drama, as well as her first Screen Actors Guild Award nomination, for Female Actor in Leading Role. She also got her first Blockbuster Entertainment Award nomination, for Favorite Actress – Suspense.

The one other nomination *The River Wild* received was a Golden Globe nomination for Bacon, for Best Supporting Actor in a Motion Picture.

FUN FACTS

Meryl nearly drowned while filming an intense action scene. To make matters worse, a few minutes prior she had asked director Hanson if she could be done for the day due to exhaustion, but he insisted on one more take. When she returned to an apologetic Hanson, she told him to listen to her next time when she insists that she's done.

Meryl did almost all of her own stunts.

Carrie Fisher, who wrote *Postcards from the Edge*, did an uncredited script rewrite.

Oscar-winning composer Maurice Jarre wrote the film's score, but due to bad test screenings, his music was thrown out, and Jerry Goldsmith rescored the film.

The River Wild was one of Meryl's most successful films up to this point in her career, making nearly 100 million worldwide.

WEEK 23
THE BRIDGES OF MADISON COUNTY (1995)

FILM FACTS

PRODUCTION COMPANY: Warner Bros.
RELEASE DATE: June 2, 1995

DIRECTOR: Clint Eastwood
WRITER: Richard LaGravenese (based on the novel by Robert James Waller)
PRODUCERS: Clint Eastwood, Kathleen Kennedy
ALSO STARRING: Clint Eastwood, Annie Corley, Victor Slezak, Jim Haynie, Debra Monk

REVIEW

A quiet romantic film released in the midst of summer, starring, of all people, Clint Eastwood? *The Bridges of Madison County* was, like the runaway novel bestsellers like *The Da Vinci Code* and *The Help*, always going to be made into a movie—at one point Sydney Pollack circled the project with Robert Redford as his lead, and even Steven Spielberg briefly considered taking it on—but what kind of a movie was it going to be? Would it be too melodramatic? Would the two leads have any chemistry? When Eastwood—who in 1995 was most known for playing Dirty Harry, an action hero, and for directing *Unforgiven*, a dark western—was announced to be the co-actor and director of *The Bridges of Madison County*, there were likely more than a few eyebrows raised. Approaching age sixty-five, he was an unlikely romantic lead as the handsome photographer Robert Kincaid, but what's even more surprising is that the higher-ups at Warner Bros. wanted an actress far younger than what the part called for.

Many actresses could have played the pretty and complex Italian housewife Francesca Johnson, age forty-five. Jessica Lange and Isabella Rossellini were in contention for the lead, and the stunning French actress Catherine Deneuve (in her early fifties at the time) auditioned for the role. Younger actresses likely considered were Michelle Pfeiffer, Demi Moore, Rene Russo, and Kim Basinger, but Eastwood didn't want to hear any of it. He made one phone call, to a beloved actress who hadn't had a role this layered and deep since playing Lindy Chamberlain in *A Cry in the Dark*.

Meryl didn't so much care for the book, but she loved the script and she signed on immediately, making *The Bridges of Madison County* her first significant role in a drama in seven years. And while she's been nominated for an Academy Award nineteen times and counting, her Oscar-nominated performance as Francesca is easily one of her five greatest performances in her illustrious career. She is so quietly heartbreaking in this that she basically overshadows everything else in a flawed but effective film, one of Eastwood's best.

    The story is simple. Living in small-town Iowa, Francesca has a rare four days to herself, when her husband and two children leave to attend the Illinois State Fair. On day one, an attractive photographer arrives at her doorstep, asking for directions to a nearby bridge he has been commissioned to take pictures of. She shows him how to get to his destination, and from that moment on, they start spending more time together. They have dinner and drive to more bridges and talk about their histories and potential futures. By day two, it's clear that Robert and Francesca are smitten with each other, but is it possible that they have a happily ever after? Francesca has a life in Iowa, while Robert is constantly on the move, never settling in one place. In the end, he asks her to come away with him, and be the adventurous woman her current husband never allowed her to be. The decision she finally makes, in the film's haunting and most famous scene, is one that resonates with the viewer for days.

    Eastwood supplies *The Bridges of Madison County* with just the right tone. The same leisurely way he paced his Oscar-winning *Million Dollar Baby*, he gives this film a quiet authenticity that keeps it from ever becoming too heavy-handed. Another director might have filmed too many scenes of Robert and Francesca gazing into each other's eyes while the music swells and the camera spins around them so many times you get dizzy. There is a tender scene where the two just stare at each other for a moment, but it's done in a subtle, non-cheesy manner, with the music coming from the nearby radio. And while the two fall in love in a mere two days, the slow pacing allows the viewer to buy that these lost souls could fall for each other so fast. The pairing of Meryl and Eastwood seems like an unlikely one, especially for a romance, but their chemistry is electric, the kind that is rarely seen in movies. Unlike so many forced romantic pairings, they actually feel right together, and their attractions for each other from the get-go feel earned.

One of the great surprises of the movie is Eastwood's performance. While it's difficult to watch him in any movie and forget you're watching Clint Eastwood—unlike Meryl, who so easily disappears into each role she plays—he shows a different, more vulnerable side to his personality in *The Bridges of Madison County*. This is probably his sweetest performance ever captured on screen, and one of his most natural. Not too many actors could say the line "This kind of certainty comes but just once in a lifetime" with a straight face, let alone pull it off as an authentic movie moment, but somehow, he does. In addition, the image of Eastwood standing in the rain at the end, forever alone, clinging onto a false hope that Francesca will run away with him, is a beauty.

But as fine as Eastwood is, he as the director wisely made this Francesca's story, and Meryl's movie. *The Bridges of Madison County* is easily Meryl's most stellar dramatic performance of the 1990s. Every choice she makes is a good one, both the big and the small. Her Italian accent is without fault, but Meryl went much farther to bring this character to life. She reportedly gained fifteen to twenty pounds, which gives the character a specific look, one of a woman who, while pretty, has been beaten down a bit by a sedentary life. Just the way she walks, the way she holds herself, suggests a person who rarely feels joy. But when Robert comes around, her body language changes. She moves quicker, with more jubilance in her step. One of my favorite gestures Meryl makes in the whole movie is when she claps her hands together, after Francesca agrees to meet with Robert to go sightseeing. It's a lovely moment that tells so much with so little.

The role has endless layers. She gets to play goofy, sad, lonely, in love, desperate, at peace. Almost every scene gives Meryl a new note to play. Just the way she laughs in a handful of scenes—especially the one in which Francesca jokes that the flowers Robert gives her are poisonous—is perfectly modulated. She's great all the way through, but it's the hauntingly constructed scene at the end, in the truck, in the rain, that pulls at the viewer's heartstrings the most. She doesn't just long for Robert. She has an out-of-body experience as she tugs on that door handle. She knows in her heart she can't go, but she still doesn't want to give up the dream. With no words spoken, Meryl tells us in her eyes exactly what she's feeling. It's a marvelously acted scene that is probably one of the most famous moments of any romance film ever made. Meryl was rightly nominated for her tenth Academy Award for her performance, but she lost to Susan Sarandon, for *Dead Man Walking*; in a less competitive year, she likely would have won her third Oscar.

The Bridges of Madison County is not without its flaws. The awkward wrap-around story is too amateurishly acted, and the scene in the truck at the end is so powerful that the final ten minutes, which shows Francesca at an older age, seem unnecessary. But overall, it's grand entertainment, the kind of film Hollywood used to make all the time in the '30s and '40s but rarely in the '90s. The book, written by Robert James Waller, might not have been the finest piece of literature ever written, but Eastwood was able to translate these two unique characters and winning themes into a movie that works far better than it should have. Best of all, Meryl, after a seven-year hiatus from leading roles in dramas, rose to the challenge of playing a rich, complex character: a housewife in her forties who still has dreams and ambitions that go beyond her tiny farm in Iowa.

AWARDS DAILY

Meryl received her tenth Academy Award nomination, for Best Actress. She also earned a Golden Globe nomination for Best Actress in a Motion Picture – Drama, and a SAG Award nomination for Female Actor in a Leading Role. She also got Best Actress nominations from the Blockbuster Entertainment Awards, Chicago Film Critics, Dallas-Fort Worth Film Critics, National Society of Film Critics, and New York Film Critics.

The Bridges of Madison County earned a Golden Globe nomination for Best Motion Picture – Drama. It also won

Best Foreign Film at both Fotogramas de Plata and Mainichi Film Concours.

FUN FACTS

The idea to cast Meryl reportedly came from not just Eastwood, but also his mother.

The movie was filmed in sequence.

One of the few PG-13 rated movies to use the word "fuck" in a sexual context. The MPAA first rated it R because of the one line, but Eastwood appealed them to re-rate it.

Francesca's House was burned down in an arson fire in 2003, a year after the Cedar Bridge was destroyed.

Bruce Beresford (*Driving Miss Daisy*) was chosen as the director before Eastwood, but he wanted to make the character of Francesca English. When this was not accepted, he dropped out.

WEEK 24
BEFORE AND AFTER (1996)

FILM FACTS

DISTRIBUTOR: Hollywood Pictures
RELEASE DATE: February 23, 1996

DIRECTOR: Barbet Schroeder
WRITER: Ted Tally (based on the book by Rosellen Brown)
PRODUCERS: Barbet Schroeder, Susan Hoffman
ALSO STARRING: Liam Neeson, Edward Furlong, Julia Weldon, Alfred Molina, John Heard

REVIEW

Not every actor makes perfect choices in his or her career, not even Meryl, and *Before and After*, a somber, mostly dull drama that offers few surprises, was one of her most peculiar choices of all. Released quietly in February 1996, *Before and After* died a quick death at the box office and was quickly dismissed by most major film critics. The film is competently made, watchable, includes a few interesting scenes. But what about the mediocre screenplay attracted Meryl to this project? After a rare misstep with the dreadful *The House of the Spirits*, Meryl conquered action in

The River Wild and a hauntingly beautiful love story in *The Bridges of Madison County*. She was at the height of her dramatic power in the mid-1990s, and *Before and After*, while not a terrible movie, is never worthy of Meryl's talent.

The film plays out like a slow, dreary Lifetime TV-movie, the kind that would feature someone like Roma Downey in the mother role, not a ten-time-Oscar-nominated actress of Meryl's stature. She plays a small town doctor who has what she thinks is a simple, normal life, with a loving husband (Liam Neeson) and two kids at home. But everything changes one fateful day when a teenage girl turns up dead in the snow and her own son is accused of killing her. The film paints the son (Edward Furlong) as being guilty from the get-go, since he doesn't show up until well into the movie's second act. But did he actually kill her on purpose? And how will his parents react to the sentence their son is bound to receive in court?

These questions are meant to keep us engaged all the way through the movie, but they do only to a certain point. While the movie has plenty of explosive acting scenes to keep the viewer interested in the story, the movie ultimately flounders. The script could have been tighter and more focused, with fewer scenes that ramble on and on. The direction by Barbet Schroeder is serviceable and yet without any interesting visual flourishes or passion on his part that shows he really cared about telling this story. Nominated for an Oscar for the fantastic *Reversal of Fortune*, from 1990, Schroeder spent most of his later career making B-list thrillers like *Single White Female*, *Desperate Measures*, and the Sandra Bullock-starrer *Murder by Numbers*, to date his final

American film. He shoots *Before and After* like he's a director-for-hire, almost as if he's counting the days until he can move on to another project.

There never seems to be much interest in telling this story from the actors either. Neeson reportedly apologized to Gene Siskel at the 1996 Academy Awards for being in *Before and After*, which seems like a radical thing for an actor of his caliber to do—that is, until you watch this movie. He seems totally lost, almost always in a bad mood, sometimes for sensible reasons, and other times inexplicably. He also has no chemistry with Meryl and seems often like her mentally unstable younger brother, not her husband (making their unexpected sex scene halfway through the movie one of Meryl's most awkward moments on-screen). Alfred Molina hams it up as the son's smarmy lawyer (he even sports a thick, villain-like moustache) and Furlong, so great in *Terminator 2: Judgment Day* and *American History X*, appears so distant in the pivotal role of the son that sometimes it seems like he's reading off cue cards.

Meryl does what she can with a routine, underwritten role. This is not one of her most inspired performances; actually, this is one of her rare roles that could have been played by any other actress of her generation, maybe even better. Meryl has such an intelligent, vibrant face that watching her dour expressions throughout this movie, listening to her utter one inane line of dialogue after another, becomes trying after awhile. A mother of four at this point in her life, she might have been intrigued to play the mother of a child accused of murder, but the script and direction ultimately let her down. Her son is missing for days, she doesn't know if he's alive or dead, and yet there never seems to be enough worry on her character's part. Her profession in the film never rings true either, nor her relationship with her husband, nor the feeling ever that she is actually the mother of this unusual boy who trashes his room on a daily basis and hides secrets from everybody close to him. A decision the character makes to tell the truth late in the movie also doesn't feel earned, so in the end, you're left with Meryl doing all she can with a part that is one of her weakest ever.

This is not to say that the film is completely without merit. Meryl does have a few good moments, like when she defends her son to the sleazeball lawyer, and when she apologizes to the mother of the girl who died. It's Meryl—she's going to infuse even the most routine of scenes with authentic emotion and the utmost humanity. Unlike the unbearable *The House of the Spirits*, *Before and After* is never boring, with an early sequence involving Neeson burning evidence that does have a bit of tension. But unless you're a diehard Meryl fan, or are revisiting some older Neeson movies, or are the one person left who still has a mad crush on Furlong (don't be ashamed), this one is easy to skip. Meryl made much better movies in the '90s, even in the same year this film was released. If you want to see a great 1996 Meryl drama, pass on *Before and After*, and look no further than the funny and moving *Marvin's Room*.

AWARDS WATCH

Like her 2005 comedy *Prime*, *Before and After* received no nominations or awards of any kind.

FUN FACTS

Future Oscar nominee Paul Giamatti played an extra in a courtroom scene.

Meryl reportedly found the filming experience a difficult one because director Schroeder wouldn't let the actors' dialogue overlap.

The film is one of her most disliked, with a low 32% rating on Rotten Tomatoes, and one of her biggest flops, making just $8.8 million nationwide on a $35 million-dollar budget.

WEEK 25
MARVIN'S ROOM
(1996)

FILM FACTS

DISTRIBUTOR: Miramax
RELEASE DATE: December 18, 1996

DIRECTOR: Jerry Zaks
WRITER: Scott McPherson (based on his play)
PRODUCERS: Robert De Niro, Jane Rosenthal, Scott Rudin
ALSO STARRING: Diane Keaton, Leonardo DiCaprio, Hume Cronyn, Robert De Niro, Gwen Verdon, Hal Scardino

REVIEW

If there's one drama Meryl made that she didn't receive an Oscar nomination for, but one I feel she absolutely *deserved* one for, it's *Marvin's Room*. Released at the end of 1996 to mostly great acclaim by critics, this endlessly absorbing film unfortunately stalled at the box office and received only a few significant awards nominations. While Meryl received yet another Golden Globe nomination for her performance, she was passed over at the Academy Awards in favor of Diane Keaton, who earned a nomination in Meryl's place. There might have been some confusion as to whether Meryl should have been submitted in the Lead or Supporting Actress category, but no matter—her performance as Lee in *Marvin's Room* is one of her best of the 1990s, and certainly one of her most entertainingly vitriolic. The film is also a real winner, one of my favorites of her entire career.

Meryl originally didn't want to play Lee. At her friend Robert De Niro's request, she went to see the play by Scott McPherson in 1991, and instantly fell in love with the character of Bessie. The story of two estranged sisters who haven't talked in twenty years but who come together when one is diagnosed with leukemia, *Marvin's Room* features a terrific ensemble of characters, none more complex than the sick but eternally optimistic Bessie. The actress playing this part gets the most emotional scenes and the most heart-wrenching moments, but by the time the film finally went into pre-production in 1995, Meryl had played a string of proper, good-natured characters, and she wanted a change of pace with the bad-tempered, foul-mouthed, chain-smoking sister, Lee.

When we first meet her, Lee is trying to get her life on track, the best way she can. She's divorced and his two kids, including Hank (Leonardo DiCaprio), a troublemaker who burns down their house and enters a psychiatric ward for observation. However, things are getting better for Lee—she is about to receive her degree in cosmetology—so when her sister Bessie (Diane Keaton) calls to ask her if she and her two boys will come down to Florida to be tested for a possible bone marrow transplant, she isn't exactly thrilled to go. She's more nervous than excited to see Bessie after all these years, and she's equally concerned at how well Hank will fit in with a house full of strangers. When she first arrives, there's instant tension between her and her sister, but as the film goes on, and as Bessie becomes sicker, a bond forms between them that neither one could have expected.

The film's premise and differing personalities of the central characters give a wealth of complex scenes for the actors to play. While she shares about the same amount of screen-time with Meryl, Keaton is the heart and soul of the film. The beloved Oscar-winning actress had won over critics and audiences in *The Godfather*, *Annie Hall*, and *Reds*, but Keaton hadn't received a real juicy dramatic role in more than ten years when *Marvin's Room* came along. Any actress can go over-the-top when playing a character who's dying of cancer, and the beauty of Keaton's performance is that it is always understated, never going for that big showy moment. She is terrific throughout.

Equally impressive is DiCaprio, in his last major screen role before he made the fateful trip aboard *Titanic*. Wonderfully crazed and manic in the first act, his character has many layers throughout, too, with an earned transformation toward the end. De Niro, who also produced the film and developed it for many years from the stage to the screen, is hilarious as Bessie's local doctor, and Gwen Verdon, in one of her last film roles, is a hoot as Bessie and Lee's eccentric Aunt Ruth. Hume Cronyn, in his final theatrical film role, is quietly haunting as the film's title character, saying so much by never uttering a word.

Meryl hadn't ripped into a showy, angry, resentful character like Lee since she played Madeline in *Death Becomes Her*. After a string of quieter dramatic roles, her best being Francesca in *The Bridges of Madison County*, Meryl probably had a blast inhabiting a showy role like Lee, one who provides some funny moments, as well as unexpectedly emotional ones in the third act. Her interaction with Hank's therapist, Dr. Charlotte (Margo Martindale) is borderline goofy, and her initial interactions with Bessie feature awkward lines and moments that make the viewer laugh. But as the center core of her character comes through toward the end of the movie, the laughs drain away, and the true heart to her character finally starts beating. Just the way she hugs her sister in the final scene is enough to send any viewer into a crying fit. This is one of Meryl's most unexpected performances, and also one of her most affecting.

The beauty of *Marvin's Room* is the way that it treads the line between comedy and drama all the way through, and, somehow, almost impossibly, manages to succeed in both. Scott McPherson finished the screenplay mere weeks before he died (in November 1992, four years before the movie was released) and he clearly infused it with as much honesty and humanity as he could muster. The film is significant for featuring Keaton and De Niro in their first movie together since *The Godfather Part II*, and re-teaming Meryl and De Niro for the third (and to date, final) time, after *The Deer Hunter* and *Falling in Love*. It also is significant for being, like *On Golden Pond* and *Driving Miss Daisy*, one of the better modern stage-to-film adaptations made by a major studio.

Marvin's Room tells somewhat of a familiar story, but it remains one of my favorite Meryl movies. It teams half a dozen acting legends in one special film, and while Keaton ultimately received the Academy Award nomination for Best Actress, Meryl, in yet another standout performance, was equally as deserving.

AWARDS WATCH

Meryl received a Golden Globe nomination for Best Actress in a Motion Picture – Drama. She earned a Blockbuster Entertainment Award nomination for Favorite Actress – Drama, and also shared a SAG Award nomination for Outstanding Performance by a Cast. In addition, she got a Chlotrudis Award nomination not for Lead Actress, but for Supporting Actress.

Keaton received an Academy Award nomination for Best Actress. She also got a SAG Award nomination for Female Actor in a Leading Role. Verdon earned a SAG Award nomination for Female Actor in a Supporting Role, and DiCaprio won the Chlotrudis Award for Best Supporting Actor. In addition, director Zaks won the Golden St. George Award at the Moscow International Film Festival, and the film won Special Recognition for excellence in filmmaking at the National Board of Review.

FUN FACTS

Sigourney Weaver, Kathleen Turner, and Anjelica Huston were considered for the role of Bessie.

Carly Simon wrote and performed the theme song, "Two Little Sisters," for which Meryl added background vocals. You can see her singing with Simon in a short documentary on the film's Blu Ray release.

Everyone on board wanted Meryl to play Bessie, but it was her decision late in the game to switch to Lee. She then recommended Keaton to the producers for the role of Bessie.

WEEK 26
...FIRST DO NO HARM (1997)

TV MOVIE FACTS

DISTRIBUTOR: ABC
PREMIERE DATE: February 16, 1997

DIRECTOR: Jim Abrahams
WRITER: Ann Beckett
PRODUCER: Jim Abrahams
ALSO STARRING: Fred Ward, Allison Janney, Seth Adkins, Margo Martindale

REVIEW

Meryl has always been prolific in her career, often making one or two movies a year (sometimes even more), but she was really cranking films out in the second half of the 1990s, appearing in no less than seven in the span of just four years, between 1995's *The Bridges of Madison County* and 1999's *Music of the Heart*. While *Before and After* disappointed with critics, and *Dancing at Lughnasa* bombed at the box office, the film she made during this time that probably perplexed the most people was *...First Do Harm*, to date her one and only made-for-TV movie.

It's not that Meryl always shied away from television. She appeared in a significant role in the epic 1978 mini-series for NBC, *Holocaust*, as well the acclaimed 2003 HBO mini-series *Angels in America*, which won her an Emmy. But for her to appear in a lowly TV movie, one directed by the mastermind behind comedy spoofs like *Airplane* and who had never attempted drama before, seemed a bit of a head-scratcher to people. But don't let the fact that this isn't some big Hollywood production deter you; ...*First Do No Harm* is a riveting, first-rate film with excellent performances and a strong message about doing what's right for your health, no matter the opposition. Sure, it's a little rough around the edges, with cinematography that can be wanting (too much shaky-cam at times) and a sometimes obnoxious musical score (especially when something really, really *bad* happens). But if you're a Meryl fan, you owe it to yourself to seek this one out.

Lori (Meryl) is happily married to Dave (Fred Ward), a truck driver, and is the mother to three children. She seems to have the ideal, stress-free life, when her youngest son Robbie (Seth Atkins) falls in the front yard and experiences a seizure. At the hospital he is diagnosed with epilepsy, and is immediately put on a variety of drugs, including phenobarbital, phenytoin, and carbamazepine. But the drugs only make him worse, to the point that he's completely bed-ridden and dependent and suffering at least 100 seizures a day. When the doctors can't seem to solve Robbie's problem, Lori starts researching epilepsy herself, and discovers a natural remedy and sometimes cure called the ketogenic diet that hasn't even been brought up by the doctors as a potential option. Despite the misgivings of her doctor (Allison Janney), Lori stops at nothing to put her son on the diet, and stop his epilepsy for good.

Jim Abrahams, known for directing the two *Hot Shots* comedy spoofs, had never come close to stepping over into drama, but *...First Do No Harm* was a story he simply had to tell. Abrahams' own son Charlie suffered from severe seizures and was cured after going on the ketogenic diet. Upset that the diet had never been presented as a possible treatment, Abrahams created the Charlie Foundation to promote it, and he directed and produced this film. His strong tie to the story probably had something to do with Meryl coming on board, given that this was a movie produced for ABC TV and not for cinemas; it's not every day that a ten-time Oscar nominee headlines a project for the small screen. However, while many TV movies of the 1990s are practically unwatchable today—check out *She Cried No*, with Candace Cameron, for a hilarious example—*...First Do No Harm* is compelling, important entertainment, no matter the medium it was made for.

Abrahams assembled a stellar cast for this project, which includes faces still well known today. Ward is always a welcome presence in any movie, and he has powerful chemistry with Meryl, playing a man who loves his sick son but rarely knows what to do to make things right with his family. Margo Martindale plays Lori's compassionate friend Marjean, making this one of a few times she has appeared in a Meryl movie (they share scenes in *Marvin's Room* and *August: Osage County*, as well as both appear in *The Hours*). Janney wasn't that well known in 1997, and this was one of her first substantial roles (later that same year she made impressions in *Private Parts* and *The Ice Storm*, on her way to *The West Wing*). Her performance as the boy's stone-faced but sympathetic doctor is a standout. Also terrific is Seth Adkins, six years old when he played Robbie. His performance as the epileptic child is wholly convincing all the way through, and he rightly deserved his Young Artist Award for Best Performance in a TV Movie.

Of course, Meryl, who received Golden Globe and Emmy nominations for her performance as Lori, is as good here as she always is, and her stellar work raised the bar for acting in made-for-TV films. While she might have played one too many moms in the 1990s (in pretty much everything besides *Death Becomes Her*), she obviously believed in this project from the get-go and committed to a multi-layered character who does anything she can to save her child, including removing him from the hospital illegally and standing up to the narrow-minded authority. Scenes of her crying in desperation when she feels she's out of options rip your heart out, and scenes toward the end when she discovers her son might actually pull through returns your heart to its proper place. She's in almost every scene of the two-hour movie, and her performance makes an occasionally uneven film an absolute must-see. ...*First Do No Harm* is proof that old TV movies aren't necessarily lesser experiences than their theatrically released counterparts—but it also doesn't hurt to have Meryl in the lead.

AWARDS WATCH

Meryl earned a Golden Globe nomination for Best Actress in a Mini-Series or Motion Picture Made for TV, and an Emmy nomination for Lead Actress in a Mini-Series or a Special. She was also nominated for an OFTA Television Award and a Golden Satellite Award.

...*First Do No Harm* won Best Family TV Movie and Performance in a TV Movie for Adkins, at the Young Artist Awards. The film was also nominated for a Humanitas Prize.

FUN FACTS

To date, Meryl's only TV movie.

Director Abrahams helped set up the Charlie Foundation, an institution that spreads the word about the ketogenic diet to paediatric neurological centers.

Abrahams' son Charlie went from having ninety epileptic seizures a day to none after going on the ketogenic diet. He makes a brief appearance in the movie as Robbie Reimuller's playmate.

"First, do no harm" is from the Latin phrase that means, *prinum non nocere*. It reminds health care providers to always consider the possible harm that any intervention might do.

WEEK 27
ONE TRUE THING (1998)

FILM FACTS

DISTRIBUTOR: Universal Pictures
RELEASE DATE: December 18, 1998

DIRECTOR: Carl Franklin
WRITER: Karen Croner (based on the novel by Anna Quindlen)
PRODUCERS: Jesse Beaton, Harry J. Ufland
ALSO STARRING: Renee Zellweger, William Hurt, Tom Everett Scott, Lauren Graham

REVIEW

One True Thing completed an unofficial Meryl trilogy of disease movies that started with 1996's *Marvin's Room* and continued into 1997's *...First Do No Harm*. It is probably a coincidence that Meryl made three movies in a row with a sick character at the forefront (with only *...First Do No Harm* having an uplifting ending), but it's worth noting, especially given that this period in the late 1990s featured the most serious projects of her career. From 1993 to 1999 she made eight dramas, many of which are about families, so maybe being a mother of four attracted her to this kind of material. It wouldn't be until 2002's *Adaptation* that she would lighten up and have some fun.

This is not to suggest that *One True Thing*, one of her two fall 1998 releases, is a bad film. While it's certainly one of her most downbeat productions—you spend most of the two-hour-plus running time watching Meryl's character Kate slowly die—it's compelling all the way through, with three outstanding performances. While the more comedic *Marvin's Room* typically shied away from showing the horror that cancer wreaks on one's body, *One True Thing* shows the viewer every sad detail, not just in the physical realm, but in the mental one as well. When we first see Meryl, she is luminous, wearing a Dorothy Gale costume from head to toe, her hair in pigtails, her feet sporting ruby red slippers. By the end of the movie, she has withered away to almost nothing, a skeletal frame that houses only pain and anguish. *One True Thing* shows Meryl's most astonishing transformation on film since *Sophie's Choice*.

As great as Meryl is, though, she isn't technically the lead of this film. The story is told not from Kate's perspective, but from her daughter Ellen, played by Renee Zellweger. Ellen has no knowledge that her mother is ill; a busy, ambitious journalist, she is only heading home for the weekend to celebrate her novelist father George's birthday. But when it is discovered that Kate has cancer, George asks Ellen to move home and help take care of her mother. Ellen always got along more with her father, with their shared writing interests, and she from an early age thought her mother's decision to be a homemaker to be outdated. Kate's terminal illness, however, finally brings mother and daughter together, and shows Ellen the kind of her person she never thought she could be.

I saw this movie on opening weekend with my mom and aunt when I was thirteen, and I still remember the loud sniffles coming from all the women who surrounded me. *One True Thing*, after all, is a film designed to tug on your heartstrings and make you cry. Sometimes a tearjerker drama can feel manipulative, and there are moments in *One True Thing*, with the occasionally sappy music, and happy holiday settings, that hover right on the edge. Screenwriter Karen Croner adapted Anna Quindlen's beloved 1995 novel a bit too faithfully, and director Carl Franklin, the man behind the crime thrillers *One False Move* and *Devil in a Blue Dress*, doesn't paint the sad moments with any unique colors.

What saves certain scenes from turning too maudlin are the performances. This is the kind of movie that lives or dies by its actors, and with a different cast, the results might have been different. But with the three actors chosen, magic occurs. William Hurt has excelled in one role after another for nearly forty years, and while his character of George isn't a big stretch for the actor, he imbues the man with the perfect balance of love for his family and disgust in watching his wife waste away. The character borders on being unsympathetic at times, but his humanity creeps in at just the right moments. Zellweger has rarely been more natural in a movie; while Hollywood gave her award after award for her flashier performances in *Chicago* and *Cold Mountain*, it's her quiet, genuine performance in *One True Thing* that should have received more attention. The restraint she often shows elevates the movie considerably, like when her character rests her head on her mother's shoulder as a group of carolers sing "Silent Night" and the heartbreaking moment when George finds his daughter holding Kate's hand on a tragic morning, her face not red with tears, but with a removed kind of numbness.

And then there's Meryl, who, after watching Diane Keaton get sick in *Marvin's Room* and little Seth Adkins get even sicker in ...*First Do No Harm*, finally got to be sick herself as the dying central character in *One True Thing*. Meryl said in an interview that when she heard that the book was being made into a movie, she immediately contacted her agent to see if she could be a part of it. There's no mystery in why she wanted to play Kate; this role is an actor's dream. She's full of life in the beginning, but then slowly disintegrates as cancer wreaks havoc on her mind and body. She has one emotional moment after another in the film's final act, and one particular scene, where she tells her daughter that she's sad because she won't be able to help plan her wedding, is Meryl at her absolute devastating best. Here's a long monologue that could have felt overwritten or schmaltzy with another actress, but Meryl nails every beat, every gesture. This is the clip that was shown from the film at her AFI Lifetime Achievement ceremony, and it's likely the one that netted Meryl her eleventh Oscar nomination.

By 1998 Meryl had little more to prove in her acting brilliance, but *One True Thing* showed yet another side to her artistry. While the film isn't always an easy watch, one superb element is that it doesn't shy away in showing the painful realities of how cancer can attack a beloved member of your family. Meryl has never been one to turn against roles that show the not-so-pretty side of herself in movies—think her characters in *Ironweed* and *August: Osage County*—and in *One True Thing* she allowed viewers to see one of her saddest, most vulnerable sides of all. While the film has its flaws, Meryl's ingenious performance stands out as one of her best of the 1990s.

AWARDS WATCH

Meryl earned her eleventh Academy Award nomination, for Best Actress. She also received Golden Globe and SAG Award nominations for her performance. In addition, she was nominated at the Blockbuster Entertainment Awards, the Awards Circuit Community Awards, and the Satellite Awards.

Zellweger also earned a second place Best Actress award from the New York Film Critics.

FUN FACTS

The only time Meryl has worked with an African-American director.

Julianne Nicholson, who would go on to play one of Meryl's daughters in *August: Osage County*, appears in this film as an unnamed college student.

Bette Midler sung the end credits song, "My One True Friend."

All three of the lead actors have won Academy Awards, Hurt for *Kiss of the Spider Woman*, and Zellweger for *Cold Mountain*.

WEEK 28
DANCING AT LUGHNASA (1998)

FILM FACTS

DISTRIBUTOR: Sony Pictures Classics
RELEASE DATE: November 13, 1998

DIRECTOR: Pat O'Connor
WRITER: Frank McGuinness (based on the play by Brian Friel)
PRODUCER: Noel Pearson
ALSO STARRING: Michael Gambon, Catherine McCormack, Kathy Burke, Sophie Thompson, Brid Brennan, Rhys Ifans

REVIEW

When I began My Year With Meryl Streep, I was excited to watch a select few of her movies that I hadn't yet seen. There was *The Seduction of Joe Tynan*, *The French Lieutenant's Woman*, *Heartburn*, and *Before and After*, as well as her television mini-series, *Holocaust*. My favorite by far of the ones I hadn't seen is *A Cry in the Dark*, the fascinating, heartbreaking story of a woman accused of murdering her child. Now we arrive at 1998's *Dancing at Lughnasa*, officially the *last* of her movies I hadn't watched, and it's one that up until now I knew next to nothing about. When it came to this production, I was only aware of two things—Meryl sports an Irish accent, and she dances around with gusto at some point during the movie.

Unfortunately, now having watched the movie, I struggle to explain much more that I know about it apart from those two aforementioned nuggets. Meryl has appeared in more than fifty films, and *Dancing at Lughnasa*, adapted by Frank McGuinness and directed by Pat O'Connor (*Inventing the Abbots*), is one of her most inconsequential. It has some nice cinematography, solid performances, and Meryl once again sporting a truly remarkable accent. But there is little to maintain your interest here. When the most excitement in a movie comes when a man rocks a rowboat back and forth, you know something is off. It's not just that this film is unbearably slow; the story lacks tension and is almost bereft of conflict. Watching *Dancing at Lughnasa* is equivalent to witnessing everyday life play out on-screen—in real time.

It explains a lot that the film is based on a beloved stage-play. Sometimes movies can seamlessly make the transition from stage to screen (Meryl's own *Marvin's Room* is a prime example), but other times the material never really pops when it's adapted for a major motion picture. The play by Brian Friel premiered in Dublin in 1990 and then ran on Broadway for more than a year, going on to win the 1992 Tony Award for Best Play. Watching the sisters interact on stage could potentially be an intimate and absorbing experience, but on film, the story never comes to life. Set in 1930s rural Ireland, *Dancing at Lughnasa* tells of five sisters (Catherine McCormack, Kathy Burke, Sophie Thompson, Brid Brennan, and Meryl) who live together and go through various ups and downs in their lives, including falling in love and spending time with their elderly brother, a priest played by Michael Gambon. The film is told from the perspective of one of the sister's young sons, a plot device that never amounts to much.

The most entertainment value in *Dancing at Lughnasa* comes from watching Meryl's magnificent performance, which deserves a better movie. With her short black-and-gray haircut, lack of make-up, and dowdy clothes, she disappears into yet another role from her first scene on. It would have been possible for her to be distracting in an ensemble film like this one, given that it features four lesser-known actresses playing her sisters. The viewer could have gotten swept up in the stories of the other performers but not in Meryl's, since she is American, not Irish, and she is a *movie star*. But these potential problems never come to pass, and Meryl makes her role of Kate Mundy, the stern older sister, her own.

The synopsis makes it look like Meryl would have a mere supporting role in this film the same way she plays small roles in other ensemble works like *A Prairie Home Companion*, *Evening*, and *The Giver* (not to mention her teeny-tiny part in *The Homesman*). But Meryl is front and center in a lot of *Dancing at Lughnasa*, and while the film rarely captivates, she has a few significant moments. One in which she stands in an empty classroom, grief-stricken at the possibility that she might never teach again, is the kind of tender acting moment that works beautifully on its own. And then there's the scene toward the end of the movie where the five sisters finally dance. There's nothing particularly special about the way this scene is shot or choreographed, but the one memorable aspect has to do with Meryl herself, the way she initially refuses to get up and take part in the joy. For so much of the movie she is the one in charge, ultra-serious, never to give in to frivolous pleasures. The way she starts tapping her feet against the floor, failing to hide her growing smile, only to then leap into the air and start dancing around the room like she has an hour left to live, is the key moment from *Dancing at Lughnasa* I will never forget.

I have now watched every Meryl movie released through the end of 2014 at least once. I have my favorites of those I've re-watched and written about, and my favorites of those I look forward to watching again soon. In the end, Meryl has been in a lot of great movies, time and time again, and only occasionally does she appear in a misfire. *Dancing at Lughnasa* is not poorly made, and it has the best of intentions, but it is not one of her more compelling works. She had two dramas released in 1998. The one worth watching is *One True Thing*.

AWARDS WATCH

Meryl was nominated for Best Actor in a Female Role at the Irish Film and Television Awards.

Dancing at Lughnasa received five nominations at the Irish Film and Television Awards, including Best Feature Film, and won Best Actor in a Female Role, for Brid Brennan. Director O'Connor was nominated for the Golden Lion at the Venice Film Festival, and the National Board of Review picked *Dancing at Lughnasa* as one of the year's Top Ten Films.

FUN FACTS

Frances McDormand and Kate Winslet were considered for roles in the movie.

Brennan won a Tony Award for her performance in the original Broadway play.

Mementos from the filming are on display at the St. Connell's Museum in Glenties.

One of the reasons Meryl reportedly signed on to the project was the opportunity to join a large ensemble.

WEEK 29
MUSIC OF THE HEART (1999)

FILM FACTS

DISTRIBUTOR: Miramax
RELEASE DATE: October 29, 1999

DIRECTOR: Wes Craven
WRITER: Pamela Gray
PRODUCERS: Marianne Maddalena, Susan Kaplan, Walter Scheuer
ALSO STARRING: Aidan Quinn, Gloria Estefan, Cloris Leachman, Angela Bassett

REVIEW

Meryl is usually the first choice for a movie, not a second or third. She usually has talented, seasoned actors sharing the screen with her, not a Latina pop star making her film debut. And throughout her long career, despite belting out some screams in the disappointing thriller *Still of the Night*, she hasn't come close to appearing in the kind of grisly horror films genre mastermind Wes Craven is so well known for. So what in the world is *Music of the Heart*?

Meryl's final movie of the twentieth century turned out to be a fairly standard biopic-drama, one that tells the inspirational true story of a violin teacher who changes the lives of her inner-city students. The film takes place in two time periods—1988 and 1998. In the first hour of the film, Roberta Guaspari is struggling as a single mother to two kids. Her husband has left her for another woman, and she takes a long-term substitute teacher position at a Harlem elementary school to make ends meet. Her positive influence on these kids—many from broken homes, most who live in less than ideal circumstances—is immediate, and violin playing gives them confidence and a new creative outlet. Roberta doesn't think she will make it through the first year, but a decade later she is still teaching, still inspiring the latest batch of young students. But when the school budget is slashed, and the violin program is eliminated, Roberta faces potential unemployment, and no musical outlet for kids who desperately need it. She and the community band together to save the problem, and change lives in the process.

Meryl initially didn't want to be in *Music of the Heart*. She probably didn't love the idea of stepping in after Madonna left due to creative differences with Craven—it's well known that Meryl really wanted to play Evita, a part that ultimately went to Madonna and earned the singer-actress a Golden Globe award—but instead Meryl didn't think she could learn how to play a new musical instrument in the short window she had before production commenced. Not only was she promoting her two fall 1998 releases—*One True Thing* and *Dancing at Lughnasa*—but she also had to train for hours every day to convincingly play a violin teacher. Craven wrote her a heartfelt letter that told for his passion of the project and his insistence that she be the perfect person to play the real-life Roberta. Meryl gave in.

A horror director since the 1970s, Craven had wanted to make a non-genre movie his entire career, with no one ever giving him a chance to do something different. The success of *Scream*, though, finally gave him the opportunity he was looking for, and he chose *Music of the Heart* as his prestige project that would break him away from all the things that go boo.

One of the best, and worst, elements of *Music of the Heart* is its simplicity. This is an engaging story, well told, with Meryl in top form, as always. It makes you feel good from beginning to end, and while the film is a tad long at more than two hours, it is never boring. At the same time, while Craven makes the transition into making a true-life drama with ease—he's a born storyteller, and could probably make a terrific film in any genre of his choosing—the complete lack of any directorial style or flourishes is a little disappointing. He didn't need flashes of his horror movie roots—a knife-wielding maniac chasing Meryl through the elementary school would have been out of place—but it's a shame that he couldn't make any significant mark, visually or otherwise. He stays out of the way in this one, and lets the story and Meryl's performance do the work.

Music of the Heart may not be one of Meryl's most memorable movies, but it's the best one she made between *Marvin's Room* and *Adaptation*, and she is certainly the best part about it. She is in almost every scene, commanding the screen by employing both her comedic and dramatic gifts, not to mention her musical chops. When she appeared on *Inside the Actor's Studio* with James Lipton, she said that if she hadn't become an actress, she would have loved to be a musician, and in *Music of the Heart* she got to finally show what she's made of. She is great in this movie, not just in portraying an emotionally distraught mother and a teacher who truly cares about her students, but as a failed musician who gets a second chance when she plays a sold-out concert in Carnegie Hall. Meryl is so convincing as a violin player that one would assume she had been practicing the instrument her entire life. Meryl received her twelfth Academy Award nomination in early 2000, closing out the century with one last magnificent screen performance.

1999 is often regarded as a significant year for movies, much like 1939, or any year of the 1970s, because modern classics like *Fight Club*, *Being John Malkovich*, *American Beauty*, *Three Kings*, and *Magnolia* all came out within three short months of each other. Released at the end of October (Halloween weekend, ironic given Craven's involvement), *Music of the Heart* may have been a little too ordinary to stand out from the crowd, but it holds up today as a terrific inspirational story, and an important reminder that music should never be dropped from a school's curriculum, no matter the economy's hardships. Music teaches kids how to work hard, to be strong and empathetic, and to achieve something much bigger than themselves. Roberta Guaspari, whose story was also captured in the documentary *Small Wonders*, gave her students a reason to dream when no one else could, and *Music of the Heart* beautifully captures this woman's stimulating journey. It also gave Meryl one more great character to play before she would take her first, and to date only, break from film acting. She wouldn't appear in another movie for three long years, but when she returned, she was ready to give us a new decade of brilliance that not even her biggest fans could have dreamed of.

AWARDS WATCH

Meryl received her twelfth Academy Award nomination, for Best Actress. She also earned Golden Globe and SAG Award nominations for her performance.

Music of the Heart also received an Academy Award nomination for Diane Warren for Best Original Song, "Music of My Heart." In addition, the song won at the ASCAP Film and Television Music Awards and Critics Choice Awards. Bassett won Outstanding Supporting Actress in a Motion Picture at the Image Awards, and the film won Best Family Feature Film – Drama at the Young Artist Awards.

FUN FACTS

Meryl learned to play the violin by practicing six hours a day for four weeks.

The original title of the film was *50 Violins*.

Screen debut of Estefan.

Aside from the short he contributed to *Paris, Je T'aime*, Craven's only non-genre film.

The only time Craven directed an actor to an Oscar nomination.

Craven said he would only direct *Scream 3* if he could direct this movie.

After Madonna dropped out of the project, Sandra Bullock and Meg Ryan were considered for Roberta.

Michael Angarano, who plays Meryl's older son, also learned to play the violin for his role, and he still plays today.

WEEK 30
ADAPTATION (2002)

FILM FACTS

DISTRIBUTOR: Columbia Pictures
RELEASE DATE: December 6, 2002

DIRECTOR: Spike Jonze
WRITERS: Charlie Kaufman, Donald Kaufman (based on the book by Susan Orlean)
PRODUCERS: Jonathan Demme, Vincent Landay, Edward Saxon
ALSO STARRING: Nicolas Cage, Chris Cooper, Tilda Swinton, Judy Greer, Maggie Gyllenhaal, Brian Cox

REVIEW

For the first time since she started making movies, Meryl took a hiatus from film acting. She wasn't gone too long—*Music of the Heart* opened in late 1999, and she shot *Adaptation* in early 2001, a year and a half before it was released—but any Meryl fan will tell you that a year without her in a movie is never a good one. Aside from a scene of voice-over work as Blue Mecha in *A.I. Artificial Intelligence* (surprisingly the only time in her entire career she's collaborated with director Steven Spielberg), she was absent from the screen for three whole years. Of course, she wasn't going to be away for that long without returning to the screen with something fantastic, and in December of 2002, her fans were treated to not just one, but two excellent new Meryl movies, two of the strongest she has ever been in.

The second film from the writing-directing team behind *Being John Malkovich* was up first. One of the best films of 2002, *Adaptation* is still one of the most unique American movies of the last twenty years. It tells of a screenwriter named Charlie Kaufman (Nicolas Cage) who receives quite the impossible task: adapt the acclaimed but mostly story-free book *The Orchid Thief*, by Susan Orlean (Meryl), about her adventures with a kooky orchid hunter (Chris Cooper). Wanting to break free from the absurdist tone of his first film *Being John Malkovich*, Charlie attempts to construct a script out of small moments and little conflict, but he struggles a great deal, especially when his cocky brother Donald (also Cage) starts writing a script of his own, a silly action thriller. With no clue how to proceed, Charlie injects himself into his screenplay, as he tries to locate the real Susan and John, as well as the perfect ending for his movie.

It's interesting to note that the real Charlie Kaufman actually did receive the assignment to adapt Orlean's book into a screenplay, and it's remarkable that the endlessly creative, wholly unique script that came out of it actually became a major Hollywood production, with three of the finest actors around. Adapting a book into a movie is a difficult, highly intuitive process that had rarely been a source for narrative in a film before, and *Adaptation* succeeds in going a step further by making wise commentary on the three-act structure itself: do we abandon all the elements that make up what most audiences would consider a satisfying movie, or do we embrace it? This film manages to do both, in a highly creative way. Most movies you walk into knowing exactly what to expect. You know where the necessary beats will be, what the twists will likely consist of. *Adaptation* loves surprising the viewer by taking him or her in different directions.

Most would agree that Meryl is one of our finest actors but some may also agree that she doesn't take many chances when it comes to her choices in director and material. Too often, especially in the late 1990s, she picked good character roles in so-so movies, the kinds of dramas that might have aired on the Hallmark Channel if an actress of her caliber had turned the producers down. And Meryl is such an iconic force to be reckoned with that maybe she makes an effort not to work with visionary directors (think Martin Scorsese, Quentin Tarantino, and Christopher Nolan) who might push her into realms we could never expect, and instead opts for the kinds of directors who stay out of the way (think David Frankel, John Wells, and Phyllida Lloyd) and let her do her thing. *Adaptation* was one of those rare occurrences where she teamed up with a young, creative team consisting of the great director Spike Jonze (who went on to win an Academy Award for writing *Her*) and the genius screenwriter Charlie Kaufman (who won his screenplay Oscar for the brilliant *Eternal Sunshine of the Spotless Mind*).

As great as Meryl was in her dramas of the 1980s and 1990s, *Adaptation* shows a whole new side to the accomplished actress. For the first time since *The Bridges of Madison County*, she is allowed to be sexy on-screen, and to shed all her inhibitions. In the early scenes, she is an unhappily married journalist, trying to find meaning in the story she's writing about the wacky orchid hunter, but when Kaufman's imagination kicks into overdrive, Susan Orlean becomes a different person entirely, a cocaine-snorting, profanity-dropping, sexually-ravenous being who will gladly murder the snooping screenwriter of her bestselling book if she absolutely has to. Probably Meryl's most famous and talked-about scene (one she has said in interviews she mostly improvised) takes place in a hotel room, when she takes one too many illegal substances and becomes obsessed with perfecting the sound of a dial tone. The light in her face, her complete freeness, is a delight to witness, and she has such fun with her character that it's a shame she doesn't get more screen-time.

This brings me to the other interesting element about Meryl's performance in *Adaptation*: it is very much a supporting one. The film is Cage's all the way through, with Meryl and Cooper standout featured players. She was the star of almost every film she made in the 1990s, but in the new decade she more often took smaller roles in bigger ensemble pieces, usually to great success. Films like *The Manchurian Candidate*, *Lemony Snicket's A Series of Unfortunate Events*, and *A Prairie Home Companion* allowed her to take on new dynamic characters without having to carry the weight of an entire film on her shoulders. All of the actors in

Adaptation are outstanding—Cooper won an Oscar for his performance, Cage is at the top of his form and hasn't been as good since, and Tilda Swinton and especially Brian Cox make memorable impressions—but it might have been Meryl who benefitted most of all for taking a chance on this unique and fascinating film.

AWARDS WATCH

Meryl earned her thirteenth Academy Award nomination, her first for Best Supporting Actress since *Kramer vs. Kramer*. She won the Golden Globe for Best Supporting Actress and received a BAFTA Award nomination. She also won Best Supporting Actress prizes from the Chicago Film Critics, Dallas-Forth Worth Film Critics, Florida Film Critics, Online Film & Television Association, Toronto Film Critics, and Utah Film Critics.

Adaptation won the Academy Award for Best Supporting Actor, for Cooper. It also earned Academy Award nominations for Best Adapted Screenplay and Actor, for Cage. It earned six Golden Globe nominations total, including Best Motion Picture – Musical or Comedy, and won a trophy for Cooper, who went on to earn multiple wins and nominations for his performance. The screenplay won at the BAFTA Awards, and the film received an Outstanding Cast nomination at the SAG Awards. In addition, *Adaptation* won the Jury Grand Prix at the Berlin International Film Festival and the Top Ten Films designation from the National Board of Review, and earned PGA and WGA Award nominations.

FUN FACTS

Curtis Hanson plays Meryl's husband. He previously directed her in *The River Wild*.

Meryl took a salary cut to be in the film.

Before the film was released, Susan Orlean was reportedly nervous that moviegoers would assume her depiction in the third act was true to life.

Donald Kaufman was nominated for an Academy Award, despite the fact that he's a fictional character.

Tom Hanks was the first choice for Charlie and Donald Kaufman.

Joaquin Phoenix was almost cast as John Laroche.

Robert McKee is a real script guru. He even suggested Cox play him in the film.

WEEK 31
THE HOURS (2002)

FILM FACTS

DISTRIBUTOR: Miramax
RELEASE DATE: December 25, 2002

DIRECTOR: Stephen Daldry
WRITER: David Hare (based on the novel by Michael Cunningham)
PRODUCERS: Robert Fox, Scott Rudin
ALSO STARRING: Nicole Kidman, Julianne Moore, Ed Harris, Toni Collette, Claire Danes, Allison Janney, John C. Reilly

REVIEW

One of the best films Meryl ever made that she received no Academy Award nomination for is Stephen Daldry's *The Hours*, a haunting, gorgeous movie about three women's lives that are intertwined despite the locations and decades between them. More accolades might have come Meryl's way for *The Hours*, but the film community chose to acknowledge her equally strong work in *Adaptation* that holiday season. After a three-year absence from the screen, Meryl had not one but two fantastic films released in the same month—December 2002—and both were highly creative endeavors that played with the expectations of narrative and told of the power of books and hypnosis of writing. Both also featured Meryl not in the lead role, but as part of an ensemble.

And quite the ensemble *The Hours* is. Featuring Julianne Moore and Nicole Kidman as the other two women, as well as a cast that includes Ed Harris, Miranda Richardson, Toni Collette, Jeff Daniels, and Claire Danes, among others, this film is a who's-who of great actors. In one of the two DVD audio commentaries, director Stephen Daldry (*Billy Elliot*, *The Reader*) said that he and the producers got their first choice for every single role, a rarity even in the most prestigious of Oscar-bait movies. It was producer Scott Rudin who suggested Meryl for the role of Clarissa, a woman living in 2001 New York who's in a strained lesbian relationship and spends most of her time caring for her dying ex-boyfriend Richard (Ed Harris). Meryl was aware of the material before being offered the film—she had previously read Michael Cunningham's Pulitzer-Prize-winning novel. Many deemed the book unfilmable, but screenwriter David Hare managed to translate much of the interior monologues into a highly cinematic experience.

The Hours is about three different women who all have the essence of one soul. The first woman is the famous, troubled writer Virginia Woolf, working on her books and fighting her bouts of depression in Essex, England, in 1923. The film uses a mix of Woolf's real words and Hare's manufactured ones to show a woman at the height of her creative powers. Nicole Kidman, a surprising choice for the real-life figure, won an Academy Award for her subtle, haunting work. With a fake nose and pale, almost lifeless cheeks, she completely disappears into the role like she has never done before or since in her long career. While it was purely a political move for Kidman to win her Oscar for Best Actress instead of Best Supporting Actress—with less than thirty minutes of screen-time in a two-hour movie, it's difficult to make the case for this being a lead performance—she delivers tremendous work for the little time she has.

Virginia Woolf wrote the beloved novel *Mrs. Dalloway*, which the film's second major character Laura Brown, a sad 1950s housewife, spends much of her time reading. Fighting the romantic feelings she has for another woman and weighing the pros and cons of abandoning her family for a better life, Laura is the most complex character in the film. Julianne Moore, who received an Academy Award nomination for her role and also starred as a '50s housewife that same year in the equally outstanding *Far From Heaven*, breathes life into a woman who has no life, who cares for her child when she barely cares *about* him at all. Of the three stories, this is one that could have existed as its own movie, but the way Laura's story is tied into Virginia's and Clarissa's makes the experience all the richer.

Clarissa, of the three central characters, has the most screen-time in the movie, at over forty minutes, but while Meryl gets a few great moments, her character is surprisingly the least interesting of the three women. Talented actors surround her all the way through, and this is a unique part in that it's to date only one of two gay characters she's played (the other being *Manhattan*).

However, unlike the other two lead characters, Clarissa seems to *react* more than *do*. In her two scenes with her dying friend Richard, Harris gets to chew the scenery (all the way to an Oscar nomination of his own), while she looks on. She reacts more than interacts with her partner Sally (Allison Janney) and daughter Julia (Claire Danes), and the film's mesmerizing final scene that brings Clarissa and Laura into the same space is almost completely guided by a verbose Moore, as a quiet Meryl looks on.

Usually Meryl is the star of a movie, taking charge of one scene after another, but *The Hours* makes for a rare scenario in which she takes a back seat to other more colorful characters. The one scene that does offer her a moment to shine takes place when she reunites with an old friend Louis, played by Jeff Daniels. She is put together at the beginning of their conversation, but then she has an emotional breakdown, right in front of him, one that sends her down to the floor and wrings out more than a few tears. In this scene—the longest in the movie, at almost nine minutes—Meryl commands the screen, showing the vulnerability of a woman who normally refuses to show a shred of it.

Meryl has said that the experience shooting *The Hours* was a lot different than shooting *Adaptation*. While the atmosphere on the set of *Adaptation* was usually light and fun, on *The Hours* it was more serious and difficult. The core trio joked later that the production should have been called *The Long Hours*. Daldry is one of the most acclaimed and sought-after filmmakers—the man received a Best Director nomination for each of his first three movies, a record—and with this kind of difficult subject matter, he needed to get the tone of his film just right. Casting great actors was only the first step; endless hours of rehearsal and long days on the set were the norm. Not that she was complaining about it, as Meryl said in one of the two DVD audio commentaries. She works extremely hard on each movie she makes, and she said that sometimes the movie works, and sometimes it doesn't. *The Hours* is one that really, really worked. Sometimes her performances are better than the movies they're featured in, but in 2002, Meryl made the rare feat of appearing in not just one but two excellent movies, and *The Hours*, to this day, remains one of her very best.

AWARDS WATCH

Meryl earned a Golden Globe nomination for Best Actress in a Motion Picture – Drama, and a BAFTA Award nomination for Best Actress in a Leading Role. She shared a SAG Award nomination for Best Ensemble Cast, as well as a Best Actress award with both Kidman and Moore at the Berlin International Film Festival. In addition, she won the Screen Idol Award for Best Actress at L.A. Outfest.

The Hours won the Academy Award for Best Actress, for Kidman. It received eight additional Oscar nominations—Best Picture, Supporting Actor for Harris, Supporting Actress for Moore, Director, Adapted Screenplay, Costume Design, Editing, and Score. The film won Best Motion Picture – Drama at the Golden Globes, as well as Best

Actress in a Motion Picture – Drama, for Kidman. It also earned eleven BAFTA Award nominations, including Best Film and Director, and won Best Actress, for Kidman, and Best Score. In addition, *The Hours* won Best Movie of the Year at the AFI Awards, Outstanding Film in Wide Release at the GLAAD Media Awards, Best Film at the National Board of Review, and the WGA Award for Adapted Screenplay.

FUN FACTS

Meryl didn't re-read *Mrs. Dalloway* in preparing for the film, as she felt her character would have read it in college and not have understood it then.

Meryl prepares for her characters by selecting a piece of music that she constantly listens to. Director Daldry loved her selection, "Four Last Songs," so much that he included it in the movie.

Kidman would often wear the prosthetic nose outside the set to evade the paparazzi.

Kidman learned to write with her right hand, as Virginia Woolf was right-handed.

Moore played her final scene as the older Laura a year after filming had wrapped. It took six hours to apply the make-up, and she was seven months pregnant at the time.

WEEK 32
ANGELS IN AMERICA (2003)

MINI-SERIES FACTS

DISTRIBUTOR: HBO
PREMIERE DATE: December 7, 2003

DIRECTOR: Mike Nichols
WRITER: Tony Kushner (based on his plays)
PRODUCER: Celia D. Costas
ALSO STARRING: Al Pacino, Emma Thompson, Mary-Louise Parker, Jeffrey Wright, Justin Kirk, Ben Shenkman, Patrick Wilson

REVIEW

After a somewhat stuffy dramatic period in her career in the late 1990s, Meryl came roaring back in 2002 with two of her freshest, most creative endeavors ever—*The Hours* and *Adaptation*. These movies showed audiences that Meryl was not interested in appearing in more mediocre dramas made better only by her participation. Instead, they showed that she was willing to take chances with a pair of unique scripts, and two young directors who wanted to push Meryl into exciting new territories. A spark of this creativity must have stayed with Meryl when she chose her next project, a magnificent achievement that marked her third gem in a row. The HBO mini-series *Angels in America*, which went on to win nearly every Emmy it was eligible for, is one of the most engrossing, fascinating, and important projects that Meryl has ever appeared in.

Before the project premiered on HBO—an event that spanned two Sunday nights that December—it was one of the most anticipated mini-series to have ever been produced. Tony Kushner had adapted his two incendiary plays, and Oscar-winning director Mike Nichols had assembled a brilliant cast of actors, both famous figures and brand new faces. Meryl was starring alongside the powerhouses Al Pacino and Emma Thompson, and she was reuniting with Nichols for the first time since 1990's *Postcards From the Edge*. Most exciting for Meryl fans, though, may have been that she wasn't playing just one role in *Angels in America*, but four! While none of the characters truly make up a lead performance, her range and talent shine all the way through this beautifully constructed and perfectly executed six-hour production.

Set in New York City in 1985, *Angels in America* has many characters, plot threads, and themes. Prior Walter (Justin Kirk) is a gay man dying of AIDS, and having visions of an angel (Emma Thompson) descending to his bedside. His boyfriend Louis (Ben Shenkman) abandons him, unable to deal with his illness, and begins a relationship with a closeted gay Mormon named Joe (Patrick Wilson). Joe works for a closeted gay lawyer Roy (Al Pacino), struggles making an emotional connection to his wife Harper (Mary-Louise Parker), and eventually comes out to his mother (Meryl). The mini-series blends reality with flights of fantasy, some wild, some lyrical, always hypnotic. The ghost of Ethel Rosenberg (also Meryl) visits the dying Roy in the hospital, an irate Harper at one point finds herself trudging through snow in Antarctica, and there's even a vision of Heaven (where Meryl plays yet another character).

Meryl is all over these six hours, popping up as one character you might expect, but also as three others you absolutely wouldn't. With her cropped gray hair and pale white skin, Joe's mother is the one who looks and feels closest to Meryl, although the arc this character goes on is one of the most moving in the entire mini-series. Without much to her in the beginning, other than traveling to New York to make amends with her adult son, she eventually transforms at the sight of something truly magical. Meryl is nearly unrecognizable as the ghost of Ethel Rosenberg, with her chubby cheeks and black, tight-fitted hair. These quiet, haunting scenes she shares with the great Pacino are electric. She is *literally* unrecognizable as a rabbi, who appears at the very beginning. Yes, after years of people probably making jokes about it, since many believe Meryl can play just about anyone or anything—she finally plays a man! More amazing, it doesn't feel like a gimmick, with her long soliloquy being so mesmerizing and truthful that you forget you're watching Meryl inhabiting an old bearded guy. Meryl lastly plays a character at the very end—The Angel Australia—and who knows? Maybe she's in more. Has anyone double-checked? No matter, she brings humanity and heart to each of the roles she plays, making this production one of the great tour-de-forces for an actress who has impressed us many times before.

Despite focusing on the AIDS epidemic and showing various men hiding their homosexuality and trying to come to terms with who they are, *Angels in America* is never a condemnation of gay men. Kushner's two plays, *Angels in America: Millennium Approaches* and *Angels in America: Perestroika*, were produced and performed in the early 1990s, long before the majority of Americans supported homosexuals in all ways of life, particularly when it came to gay marriage. Alongside other milestones like *The Normal Heart* and the 1990 film *Longtime Companion*, they broke new ground in showing that the love and heartache every gay person feels is just the same as anyone else, and that stories brimming with homosexual characters were just as compelling and important as any production featuring only straight ones. The mini-series itself premiered long before *Brokeback Mountain*, long before *Milk*. Receiving Emmy awards for Best Mini-Series, Best Director, and Best Screenplay (not to mention acting awards in all four of its categories, including a Best Actress statuette for Meryl), this adaptation of Kushner's beloved plays was another much-needed work of art that pushed the nation's acceptance of gay rights even further in the proper direction.

Angels in America actually marked the second project in a row for Meryl that dealt with gay themes. She even kisses a woman in both—Allison Janney in *The Hours*, and Thompson in this. It's great that at this point in her career, with thirteen Oscar nominations behind her and nothing left to prove, she would appear in two gay-themed stories before they were more commonly accepted. But what's truly remarkable about Meryl is her constant hunger for challenging herself as an actress, and appearing in projects that might not necessarily be fashionable or easy to digest. She has appeared in more than fifty productions and counting, but in the end, *Angels in America* will likely go down as one of the best decisions she ever made. It's not just an HBO mini-series. It's not just a great story well told. It is, and has been, a story that changes lives.

AWARDS WATCH

Meryl won the Emmy Award for Best Actress in a Mini-Series or TV Movie. She also won a Golden Globe and a SAG Award for her performance. In addition, she won Outstanding Female Lead in a Drama Special at the Gracie Allen Awards, as well as an OFTA Television Award and a Satellite Award.

Angels in America earned a whopping twenty-one Emmy nominations and won eleven, including Outstanding Directing, Writing, Supporting Actor for Wright, Supporting Actress for Parker, Lead Actor for Pacino, and Mini-Series. It also earned seven Golden Globe nominations and won five, including Best Mini-Series or TV Movie. *Angels in America* won the AFI Award for TV Program of the Year, the DGA Award, the GLAAD Media Award for Outstanding TV Mini-Series, the Humanitas Prize for Kushner, Best Mini-Series from the National Board of Review, the PGA Award, and the WGA Award.

FUN FACTS

The only time Meryl has played a man on film.

Angels in America was the most-watched cable show of the year.

Robert Altman and Neil LaBute were considered to direct.

Dustin Hoffman was considered for the role that went to Pacino.

Jodie Foster was considered for the role that went to Thompson.

Jeffrey Wright was the only member of the original Broadway cast to appear in the mini-series.

WEEK 33
THE MANCHURIAN CANDIDATE (2004)

FILM FACTS

DISTRIBUTOR: Paramount Pictures
RELEASE DATE: July 30, 2004

DIRECTOR: Jonathan Demme
WRITERS: Daniel Pyne, Dean Georgaris (based on Richard Condon's novel and George Axelrod's 1962 screenplay)
PRODUCERS: Jonathan Demme, Ilona Herzberg, Scott Rudin, Tina Sinatra
ALSO STARRING: Denzel Washington, Liev Schrieber, Jeffrey Wright, Kimberly Elise, Jon Voight

REVIEW

Everyone loves a good villain. Actors often say that it's boring to play the hero and that it's a lot more fun to be the bad guy—therefore it's surprising to note that in more than fifty motion pictures, Meryl has rarely played evil. She plays flawed characters each time out, but rarely the kind of person you run away from when you see her coming toward you. She has some nastiness in her in *Death Becomes Her*, and plays the boss from Hell in *The Devil Wears Prada*. She's horrible to her kids in *August: Osage County*, and plays a witch in *Into the Woods*. Arguably, however, the most villainous role that Meryl ever played is the Lady Macbeth-like Eleanor Shaw in *The Manchurian Candidate*.

Jonathan Demme's 2004 remake of the classic 1962 film—the older movie having been directed by John Frankenheimer and starring such legendary actors as Frank Sinatra and Janet Leigh—received criticism from movie fans before it even went into production. Remakes have always been a sore subject for people who love film because almost always, that original film shouldn't be touched, and doesn't need to be modernized. Demme had just directed another remake—the critically maligned box office bomb *The Truth About Charlie*, an update of 1963's *Charade*—and the original *The Manchurian Candidate* is so beloved than many were dumbfounded in how a remake could improve on it. Meryl must have agreed in some respect—to this day, this film remains her only remake—but the bigger-than-life character of Eleanor had to have been too hard to pass up.

It didn't hurt that Demme recruited several terrific actors. Denzel Washington came on board to play the lead character, Ben Marco, one of many soldiers in the Gulf War who were kidnapped and brainwashed to further the malevolent plans of others. He's magnetic in the film, as always, although it seems a missed opportunity to not have given one of our finest actors more screen-time with one of our finest actresses. Jeffrey Wright, Meryl's *Angels in America* co-star, plays a small but pivotal role as one of the other soldiers, and Jon Voight is effective as a senator who believes Ben's story and wants the truth to come out. Liev Schreiber was hand-picked by then Paramount Pictures CEO Sherry Lansing to play Eleanor's son, Raymond Shaw, an ambitious political figure, and Kimberly Elise is strong as Rosie, a potential love interest to Ben who turns out to be someone different than we thought. Demme also cast newbie actors in small roles who have gone on to do bigger and better things—Vera Farmiga, Pablo Schreiber, Ann Dowd, and Anthony Mackie, to name a few.

And then there's Meryl, in a supporting role that almost steals the movie. One might think that Angela Lansbury, who played Eleanor Shaw in the 1962 film, would have taken to the idea of an actress of Meryl's stature giving a new spin on her memorable character, but Lansbury reportedly had displeasure at the idea. Lansbury probably didn't believe that such a special film, one that earned her an Academy Award nomination and a Golden Globe award, should have been remade, but she also probably knew in her heart that Meryl was going to make the juicy character even harsher, meaner, and more memorable. And, yes, she would have been right. The 2004 remake is serviceable entertainment, a good but not great film, with plenty of suspense and fine acting throughout. It's Meryl's harrowing performance, though, that makes the movie stand out.

She said in an interview that she never saw Eleanor as a villain. Really, how could she? An actor will be one-note on screen if he or she plays a character as purely *evil*. Every character, good or bad, has a motivation, something he or she believes in, and Meryl viewed Eleanor as someone who is strong and passionate about her wants and needs, especially when they come to her son. She modeled the character after several major political figures (but not Hillary Clinton, according to Meryl), and she watched hours of talking-head political commentary. She had been so reserved and soft-spoken in many of her films at the time (*The Hours*, in particular), and *The Manchurian Candidate* shows a delectably sinister side to Meryl that is sometimes funny, sometimes sad, but most often chilling.

Her screen-time is limited, but she makes the most of every scene. Her first thirty seconds on screen immediately tell the viewer the kind of woman she is—that layered brown hair, the lime green business suit, those awful pearls hanging around her neck. Her constantly on-the-move body language is feisty and uncompromising, and the way she shoots a glare at her son gives the viewer an immediate sense of unease. Her monologue to a room full of political figures early in the film is the kind of awe-inspiring moment that wins awards. It's a little calculated to be sure, but it's also Meryl at her commanding best. Toward the end of the movie, the way she stops Raymond from walking out of the room is probably the scariest Meryl moment ever captured on film, and the ensuing disturbing kiss she shares with her son just might be the runner-up. Meryl is such a sweet person in real life, but in *The Manchurian Candidate*, she's the opposite: a tyrannical mother who will let nothing and nobody stand in her way.

Meryl won the AFI Lifetime Achievement award in the summer of 2004. It's an award that had been previously bestowed on people like Bette Davis, Alfred Hitchcock, and John Ford: actors and directors at the end of their career with little else to offer audiences worldwide. Of course, in 2004, Meryl wasn't near the end at all—she was just getting started, with dozens more movies still to come, starting with *The Manchurian Candidate*. While the film might not be one of Meryl's best, she soars, in her most villainous role to date.

AWARDS WATCH

Meryl received Golden Globe and BAFTA Award nominations for Best Supporting Actress. In addition, she earned a Saturn Award nomination at the Academy of Science Fiction, Fantasy & Horror Films.

The Manchurian Candidate won Costume Designer of the Year for Albert Wolsky at the Hollywood Film Awards. It also earned Black Reel nominations for Wright and Elise, and a Best Action/Adventure/Thriller Film Saturn Award nomination at the Academy of Science Fiction, Fantasy & Horror Films.

FUN FACTS

To prepare for her role, Meryl watched political talk shows with Peggy Noonan and Karen Hughes. She also cited Condoleezza Rice and Dick Cheney as inspirations.

Meryl didn't watch the 1962 original until after filming wrapped.

Meryl's *Julia* co-star Jane Fonda turned down the role of Eleanor because she didn't want her film comeback role to be a villain.

Frank Sinatra's daughter Tina was instrumental in getting the remake off the ground after she inherited the production rights.

Brian De Palma and Neil Jordan were considered to direct the film.

WEEK 34
LEMONY SNICKET'S A SERIES OF UNFORTUNATE EVENTS (2004)

FILM FACTS

DISTRIBUTOR: Paramount Pictures
RELEASE DATE: December 17, 2004

DIRECTOR: Brad Silberling
WRITER: Robert Gordon (based on the books by Daniel Handler)
PRODUCER: Laurie MacDonald, Walter F. Parkes, Jim Van Wyck
ALSO STARRING: Jim Carrey, Liam Aiken, Emily Browning, Timothy Spall, Catherine O'Hara, Jude Law

REVIEW

When Meryl received the 2004 AFI Lifetime Achievement Award, a who's-who of acclaimed Academy Award-winning dramatic actors took to the stage to honor her, including Jack Nicholson, Diane Keaton, Robert De Niro, and Clint Eastwood. The actor who kicked off the show, however, was more known for comedy than for drama, and to many, he might have seemed an unlikely choice to even be in the building, let alone begin the ceremony. That night Jim Carrey gave one of the funniest, and most heartfelt, opening speeches ever at an AFI Lifetime Achievement event, but he wasn't just there to provide laughs. Carrey had recently wrapped his newest movie, one that teamed him for the first time with Meryl herself. Yes, one of the most unlikeliest cinematic pairings ever can be seen in Brad Silberling's *Lemony Snicket's A Series of Unfortunate Events*.

That is not to say that Carrey isn't worthy of starring alongside Meryl in a movie. Known for talking out of his ass in *Ace Ventura: Pet Detective* for much of the 1990s, he came into his own as a dramatic actor later in the decade in *The Truman Show* and *Man on the Moon*. Like Robin Williams before him, Carrey became one of those rare actors who could bounce back and forth between broad comedies and complex dramas with ease. The same year that *A Series of Unfortunate Events* was released, Carrey gave what many consider his best dramatic performance in Michel Gondry's fantastic, similarly long-titled *Eternal Sunshine of the Spotless Mind*. He was at the peak of his career when he chose to play the cartoonish and most certainly villainous Count Olaf, an opportunity that allowed him to play two scenes with Meryl, in one of her goofiest performances to date.

A Series of Unfortunate Events is based on the first three books of Lemony Snicket's beloved children's series. The Nickelodeon-produced film, directed by Silberling (*Casper*) and written by Robert Gordon (*Galaxy Quest*), tells of three young siblings—Violet (Emily Browning), Klaus (Liam Aiken), and baby Sunny (Kara and Shelby Hoffman)—who become orphans when a fire kills their parents, and then are sent to live with the mysterious Count Olaf, an eccentric distant relative only interested in inheriting the kids' money. When Olaf unsuccessfully tries to have them murdered, the kids momentarily go to stay with their odd uncle (Billy Connolly), then their agoraphobic aunt (Meryl). But Olaf arrives and steals the kids back, leaving their quirky Aunt Josephine to be eaten by leeches (this is one of the few movies that Meryl perishes in, albeit off-screen). In the end, Olaf tries to marry young Violet to get the kids' money for good.

Parents were reportedly mortified by this film upon its release, given the dark elements of the story and the vindictive nature of Count Olaf. This is a bad, bad man who makes Carrey's previous larger-than-life villains The Riddler and The Grinch look like Mother Theresa. The film performed okay but not great at the box office, making a little over 200 million dollars worldwide off a 140 million dollar budget, but it's not the Tim Burton-like approach that keeps the movie from ever soaring. Carrey does what he can with his juicy role, and the art direction and make-up (the latter of which won an Academy Award) are outstanding. The main problem with *A Series of Unfortunate Events* is that it never fully engages the viewer with a worthwhile story. So much of it comes off flat, with set piece after set piece that slows down the narrative rather than speeds it up. Also, unlike the *Harry Potter* series, which this film was obviously trying to emulate in some respects, the two main kids come off rather dull.

Meryl has fun with her small part of Aunt Josephine. She's in so little of the movie that her role barely registers as a glorified cameo—she has only a few more minutes of screen-time in this than she had in the previous year's *Stuck on You*, in which she played herself—but her participation in *A Series of Unfortunate Events* is interesting for a few reasons. One, she gets a couple of scenes with Carrey, an actor that few would have expected her to ever share screen-time with. Two, it remains the only live-action children's film she's ever appeared in; besides voicing characters in *The Ant Bully* and *Fantastic Mr. Fox*, and providing narration for other short animated works, she has stuck to adult fare. Three, she has rarely played a character as loony and off-the-wall than the one here. Aunt Josephine looks ridiculous, with her huge ruffled shoulders, tiny glasses, and poofy blonde hair. She is also incredibly stupid, a quality Meryl almost never plays. Whether she's screaming at the local realtor (an uncredited Jane Lynch) or being seduced by a disguised Count Olaf, Aunt Josephine is a wild, unusual character that many would have pegged someone like Joan Cusack or Helena Bonham Carter to play. But Meryl has a blast, clearly relishing the opportunity to break out of her comfort zone.

Lemony Snicket's A Series of Unfortunate Events will not be remembered as one of Meryl's most memorable movies. While all the elements are there, particularly an inspired performance by Carrey, the film never comes to life the way the viewer hopes. Most disappointing of all, Meryl is in so little of the movie that if you blink, you'll miss her. While she didn't need to be the star, it would have been nice for the screenwriter to incorporate her character a little more into the narrative. Meryl proved in 2004 that she could play supporting characters in two very different kinds of movies and still, with far less screen-time than the movie-star protagonist, steal the show. While her chilling performance in *The Manchurian Candidate* is more impressive, Meryl's comical role in *A Series of Unfortunate Events* is a wonderfully goofy lark the actress rarely takes.

AWARDS WATCH

Meryl didn't receive any awards or nominations for her performance, but the movie earned some love, including four Academy Award nominations—Best Original Score, Costume Design, Art Direction, and Makeup, the latter of which won. It also won Best Period or Fantasy Film at the Art Directors Guild, Best Actress for Browning from the Australian Film Institute, Excellence in Period/Fantasy Film at the Costume Designers Guild Awards, Composer of the Year for Thomas Newman at the Hollywood Film Awards, and Choice Movie Bad Guy for Carrey at the Teen Choice Awards. Carrey was also nominated for Best Villain at the MTV Movie Awards and Favorite Movie Actor at the Kids' Choice Awards.

FUN FACTS

Tim Burton was initially attached to direct, with Johnny Depp playing Count Olaf and Glenn Close playing Aunt

Josephine. When Silberling came on board, he replaced Close with Meryl, feeling she was better suited for the role.

Meryl accepted the role of Aunt Josephine upon the request of one of her daughters, who was a huge fan of the books.

This is the first Nickelodeon movie to win an Academy Award.

Liam Aiken grew four and a half inches while filming the movie.

Carrey's make-up and hair took three hours to finish each day.

The movie was filmed entirely on soundstages, even the scenes set outside.

Helena Bonham Carter appears uncredited as Beatrice Baudelaire.

WEEK 35
PRIME (2005)

FILM FACTS

DISTRIBUTOR: Universal Pictures
RELEASE DATE: October 28, 2005

DIRECTOR: Ben Younger
WRITER: Ben Younger
PRODUCERS: Jennifer Todd, Suzanne Todd
ALSO STARRING: Uma Thurman, Bryan Greenberg, Jon Abrahams, Jerry Adler

REVIEW

Meryl has made a lot more great movies than she has bad ones. For every *Kramer vs. Kramer* and *The Hours*, there's only the occasional mess like *The House of the Spirits*. In 2007 she had a string of bad films—*Rendition* probably being the worst—and her Oscar-winning *The Iron Lady* has its haters. Arguably the most *forgettable* movie she's made in her long list of credits, though, is the 2005 comedy *Prime*. Here is a film with a decent premise and two strong female leads that starts off okay but then goes nowhere. More than maybe any project she's appeared in, *Prime* has the feeling of something she did for a paycheck, or because she had a free chunk of time and simply wanted to work. This is not to say that the movie is a boring, joyless experience. It's totally watchable, with a few moments of tension and some funny Meryl lines. As a whole, though, the film doesn't add up to much.

Prime blends comedy, drama, and romance in a story of missed connections and ironies that Woody Allen probably could have done more with. Uma Thurman, fresh off her performance in *Kill Bill* (and taking over a role that Sandra Bullock dropped out of when the director refused to make script changes) plays Rafi, a career woman who's been unlucky in love. She meets regularly with a psychoanalyst Lisa (Meryl), who is the person Rafi feels most comfortable discussing her sexual escapades with. She meets a cute younger man David (Bryan Greenberg) at a film event, and the two begin dating. Even though she is thirty-seven and he is twenty-three (both prime numbers! a coincidence?), they connect in a genuine way and he soon moves into her apartment. Rafi shares every intimate detail of David with her psychoanalyst Lisa, but here's the catch: Lisa is David's mother! What will happen when Lisa finds out that Rafi's dating her son? Will their therapy-patient relationship continue? Will Rafi and David be able to stay together? Do we care?

The best scenes in the movie are the therapy sessions, when the camera is locked off and allows us to just observe Thurman and Meryl playing off each other. There are at least five of these scenes, and it's during these moments that the narrative kicks into gear, especially once Lisa knows her patient is dating her son. But when these two aren't sharing the same frame together, the movie suffers.

Ben Younger wrote and directed *Prime*, his second theatrical film, and to date his *last* theatrical film. His first movie *Boiler Room* was a top-notch corporate thriller with Giovanni Ribisi riveting in the lead role, Vin Diesel before *The Fast and the Furious*, and Ben Affleck in a memorable supporting turn. *Prime* is of a different genre and style, and it just doesn't suit him. He says in the behind-the-scenes DVD documentary that the story was inspired by real life circumstances; maybe he should have gone deeper into his imagination, to pull out something more original. While the Meet Cute between David and Rafi in the beginning is nice, their relationship, especially the growing amount of bickering, soon becomes tiresome, and it's only the fleeting moments of Meryl in the second half that gives the film any life.

One of the main problems with the movie is Bryan Greenberg, an actor with little charisma. While he is pretty to look at, and would be at home in an ensemble on, say, a CBS TV series, he lacks the star power necessary to carry a whole film. He tries to hold his own with Thurman and Meryl, and while he doesn't give a bad performance, he never pops off the screen. There's no chemistry between him and Thurman (their kissing scenes are so intense it's weird to think what Sandra Bullock in Thurman's role would have been like), and he often looks lost in the scenes he shares with Meryl, like he was doing everything in his power to not blow his lines in front of an acting icon.

The movie is predictable and calculated all the way through, with an ending that the director might have thought of as daring, when in reality it can be seen a mile away. The film lacks energy, in a story that very much needs it. There's too much emphasis on quickly cut flashbacks. Even the title is odd. There's nothing in *Prime* one hasn't seen before, so it's difficult to see what attracted Meryl to the project. In the behind-the-scenes documentary, she says that the script made her laugh. That's as good a reason as any, I guess, but one would hope she has a bit higher standards for the projects she commits to be in, especially at this point in her career. Thankfully she would shoot *The Devil Wears Prada* less than a year later, and all is right with the world.

The story of *Prime* had the makings of an interesting comedy romance, but it got boggled in the process, with the wrong storyteller, a miscast male lead, and a tone that never strikes the right balance. Meryl creates an amusing character, a psychoanalyst with bushy brown hair and a no-nonsense voice who has neuroses all her own. Her facial expressions as Rafi talks about David's perfect penis get some laughs, and a sitcom-y moment when Lisa pulls her husband down to the ground in a furniture store is entertaining. Meryl does the best she can with a script that is often more tired than inspired. In the end, *Prime* is proof that even the finest of actors can't save every movie they're in, even when they have the best of intentions.

AWARDS WATCH

Like her 1996 drama *Before and After*, *Prime* received no nominations or awards of any kind.

FUN FACTS

Sandra Bullock was originally set to play Rafi, and even completed rehearsals with Younger and Greenberg, but pulled out soon thereafter. Thurman stepped in to replace her a mere two weeks before filming commenced.

The film was originally rated R by the MPAA, but it was re-rated PG-13 on appeal.

The dog sitting at Meryl's feet as she is eating the pastrami sandwich with her husband is her own dog, Digby.

Like his character David, Greenberg was born to psychologists.

Greenberg's trip to New York to make this movie was documented as part of HBO's semi-reality series, *Unscripted*.

WEEK 36
A PRAIRIE HOME COMPANION (2006)

FILM FACTS

DISTRIBUTOR: Picturehouse
RELEASE DATE: June 9, 2006

DIRECTOR: Robert Altman
WRITER: Garrison Keillor (based on his radio program)
PRODUCERS: Robert Altman, Wren Arthur, Joshua Astrachan, Tony Judge, David Levy
ALSO STARRING: Woody Harrelson, Tommy Lee Jones, Garrison Keillor, Kevin Kline, Lindsay Lohan, Virginia Madsen, John C. Reilly, Maya Rudolph, Lily Tomlin

REVIEW

Meryl singing—it makes any movie she's in better. Her show-stopping number in *Ironweed* is that film's best scene, *Death Becomes Her* has an awesome Broadway-style opener, and *Postcards from the Edge* ends with a truly grand finale. When most people think of Meryl singing, they think of *Mamma Mia* or *Into the Woods*, but probably half of her entire performance in *A Prairie Home Companion*, the final film by legendary director Robert Altman, is comprised of Meryl belting out songs, often with her on-screen sister, the great Lily Tomlin. While the film hasn't much of a plot, the entertainment in this movie comes from watching terrific actors sing their hearts out, in the final film of one of the most important film directors of the twentieth century.

A Prairie Home Companion has been a live radio variety show hosted by Garrison Keillor since 1974, and, as of 2015, it still runs every Saturday. Music is the main feature of the show, typically American folk music that includes country, blues, and gospel. The film shows a look behind-the-scenes at the famous radio show, albeit a fictionalized one. For example, the radio broadcast in the movie is the long-running public radio show's last, despite the fact that in real life it's still going strong. And while major musical talents have appeared on the show, no celebrities on the level of Kevin Kline or Tommy Lee Jones—both of whom have starred with Meryl, in *Sophie's Choice* and *Hope Springs*, respectively—have lent their talents to the actual broadcast (although Meryl herself once appeared in an episode, in character from the movie!). The film is faithful to the show, however, with it given a slow, thoughtful pacing by Altman that suits this material well.

The film takes place over one night, before, during, and after the final broadcast. Keillor, the show's creator, appears as himself, while many great film actors play fictionalized roles. Almost every Robert Altman film has an amazing ensemble—even a clunker like *Dr T. and the Women* got an astonishing cast—and *A Prairie Home Companion* is no different, with actors like Woody Harrelson, Kevin Kline, Maya Rudolph, Lily Tomlin (who appeared in his masterpiece *Nashville* three decades earlier), John C. Reilly, Tommy Lee Jones, and Meryl, in her first and only performance in an Altman movie. Lindsay Lohan, playing Meryl's daughter Lola, is miscast, with a character who's given way too much emphasis in the finale, and Virginia Madsen, hot off her Oscar nomination for *Sideways*, plays a strange character called the Dangerous Woman that doesn't add much to the narrative. The joy in this movie comes when Keillor, who wrote the screenplay, stops trying to give the story emotional weight and conflict, and allows these fine actors to talk about their lives and sing their favorite songs.

Altman is known for making movies that ramble, and feel true to life. *Gosford Park*, the last movie to net him an Oscar nomination for Best Director, is a mystery set in a large country house that plays out like few mysteries do, and his classics *MASH* and *Nashville* amaze with the way multiple characters and storylines overlap with one another. *A Prairie Home Companion* has the feel of his classic films, and it is in every way the appropriate swan song for Altman, who shows the kind of sweetness and care he brought to all his movies. In a career that spanned more than fifty years, it's astonishing that he and Meryl never worked together up until his last movie. She reportedly jumped at the chance to work with Altman, and, just like how the late-in-their-careers Henry Fonda and Katharine Hepburn created magic in *On Golden Pond*, two great artists coming together once is always better than nothing.

Meryl plays Yolanda Johnson, one half of a sister singing team from Wisconsin. They are the last remaining duo from a famous country music act, bound and determined to keep singing long into the radio show's final broadcast. Tomlin plays her sister Rhonda, and the chemistry between these two pop off the screen from their first moment they share backstage. Despite the ten-year age difference between the actresses in real life, they feel like sisters from the get-go, finishing each other's sentences, cracking up at each other's jokes even before the other completes the telling of it. While *A Prairie Home Companion* is a true ensemble piece, Meryl gets plenty of moments to shine as this plucky, tender, loving mother (a total opposite from her other major role in a film that came out the same month—*The Devil Wears Prada*).

Her songs are definitely the highlights of the movie. One fantastic moment takes Meryl from backstage to the microphone all in one take, before she starts on one of her songs. She sings a goofy duet with Keillor about rhubarb pie and takes the stage with most of the cast at the end to sing a farewell ballad, but it's the two main songs she sings with Tomlin that bring out the best in her. "My Minnesota Home" is a gem, with Altman keeping the camera floating back and forth between Meryl and Tomlin's faces as they belt out the nostalgic lyrics. And then there's "Goodbye to My Mama," which was so moving to Tomlin, who lost her mother soon before shooting this movie, that it didn't take much for her tears to start flowing. This is probably the most devastating song in the film, one that Altman plays out in mostly one long take, and it's a treat to hear Meryl sing the lyrics.

In Meryl's career, the year 2006 will likely most be remembered for her ingenious turn in David Frankel's *The Devil Wears Prada*, a movie that still remains one of her great entertainments. It's the film she received an Academy Award nomination for that year, and it's the Meryl movie you're most likely to find playing on cable. But she also made a worthwhile ensemble movie that year, one that is wholesome and sweet and feels like few films that get made anymore. *A Prairie Home Companion* doesn't have a complicated plot or much tension, but that's okay. This is the kind of film you let wash over you with its myriad of small delights.

AWARDS WATCH

Meryl won Best Supporting Actress, for this film and for *The Devil Wears Prada*, at the National Society of Film Critics. She also won a second place ICS Award for Best Supporting Actress at the International Cinephile Society Awards. In addition, she shared in Best Ensemble Cast nominations at the Critics Choice Awards and the Gotham Awards.

Robert Altman, who passed away in late 2006, received a posthumous Independent Spirit Award nomination for Best Director. He also won Best Foreign Film at the Hochi Film Awards, and was nominated for the Golden Berlin Bear at the Berlin International Film Festival. Also, Tomlin was nominated for Best Supporting Actress and Keillor was nominated for Best Adapted Screenplay at the Satellite Awards.

FUN FACTS

Altman's final film.

Meryl accepted her role right away, as it has been her career-long ambition to make a film with Altman.

Meryl's mother-in-law helped her practice the Midwestern accent necessary for her role.

Altman remarked that Meryl was twenty-five percent above anyone else.

For insurance purposes, in the event that Altman was unable to finish the film, Paul Thomas Anderson (*Magnolia*) was employed as a standby director.

Anderson's real-life wife Maya Rudolph, who plays the pregnant character Molly, was actually pregnant during filming.

All of the music was recorded live.

George Clooney was offered the role of Guy Noir, but was forced to turn it down due to scheduling conflicts.

Michelle Pfeiffer, Tom Waits, and Lyle Lovett were also offered parts in the film.

When Kline's character pops the cork off a bottle of champagne, the cork shot off-camera and hit director Altman on the forehead. A cry of "Ow!" can be heard, and Kline says, "Sorry!" without breaking character.

WEEK 37
THE DEVIL WEARS PRADA (2006)

FILM FACTS

DISTRIBUTOR: 20th Century Fox
RELEASE DATE: June 30, 2006

DIRECTOR: David Frankel
WRITER: Aline Brosh McKenna (based on the novel by Lauren Weisberger)
PRODUCER: Wendy Finerman
ALSO STARRING: Anne Hathaway, Emily Blunt, Stanley Tucci, Simon Baker, Adrian Grenier

REVIEW

When people think of movies that gross big bucks in the summer time, they'll often think of action films, sequels, bloated studio tentpoles that cost 200 million dollars or more; most people don't think of movies made for a female audience, and they certainly don't assume a film with a lead actress who's—yikes—older than *fifty* could possibly star in a movie that makes money. Studio executives have been known, now more than ever before, to make their summer movies for a specific demographic—teen boys—and any movie aimed at women that happens to earn a few dollars is typically regarded as a fluke. In the summer of 2006, when blockbusters like *Poseidon* and *Superman Returns* were failing, a sharp, clever, exceedingly funny film broke through and became a modern comedy classic. *The Devil Wears Prada* is not only one of Meryl's most entertaining films but it was also her first true blockbuster.

Meryl has had a few noteworthy stages in her career. In the late 1970s, she was a supporting actress, appearing in small roles in five films and one mini-series that started to get her noticed. Throughout the 1980s, she appeared in one heavy drama after another, in complex roles that netted her a whopping six Academy Award nominations for Best Actress in a span of just seven years. From 1989 to 1992 she stretched her comedic muscles by making four comedies in a row. She moved into action with *The River Wild*, gave a startling performance in *The Bridges of Madison County*, then played it sort of safe for the rest of the 1990s with a series of mediocre dramas. In the first half of the 2000s she made a few memorable turns in *Adaptation* and *Angels in America*, and started becoming more unpredictable with her choices. And then in the second half of the 2000s she became something truly unexpected, probably by no one more than Meryl herself—a box office superstar.

She made *The Devil Wears Prada* when she was fifty-six years old, an age when most actresses have been relegated to the role of the supportive mother or the wise schoolteacher. Women in their fifties almost never receive exciting lead roles in movies, and it's practically unheard of for a woman in that age bracket to be able to open a movie. So when *The Devil Wears Prada* opened to twenty-seven million dollars and went on to earn 125 million in the United States alone, more than a few people turned their heads. The only movie Meryl was a lead in prior that even came close to such a mammoth box office take was *Out of Africa*, in 1985, with eighty-seven million—and that won Best Picture. Many assumed *The Devil Wears Prada*'s high gross was a rare success story, but then it kept happening. Two years later, Meryl's female-driven *Mamma Mia* opened on the same weekend as *The Dark Knight*, and still made 144 million nationwide (and 610 million worldwide!), her highest film gross to date. A year later *Julie & Julia* soared to ninety-four million, and *It's Complicated* topped out at 113 million. Even 2012's *Hope Springs*, a low-key relationship dramedy, made sixty-four million. For the last few years, Meryl has enjoyed a fascinating new stage of her career, and it all started with *The Devil Wears Prada*.

Meryl's 2006 blockbuster is not a perfect film by any means. It's predictable most of the way through, and while Anne Hathaway, Stanley Tucci, and especially Emily Blunt shine in their roles, the movie would not work nearly as well without Meryl's memorable portrayal of the boss from Hell. Hathaway, who received a major career boost of her own with this project, plays Andy Sachs, a recent college graduate who comes to New York to be a famous journalist and ends up working as second assistant to Miranda Priestley (Meryl), one of the most important and notorious fashion magazine editors in town. Working alongside first assistant Emily (the hilarious Blunt), Andy tries to survive under the dictatorship of her maniacal boss who expects everything and more from those who work for her. Miranda barks seventeen orders at Andy, then changes them, then demands her to find an unpublished *Harry Potter* manuscript in a matter of hours. It at times gets to be too much for Andy, especially as she tries to make a relationship work with her boyfriend Nate (Adrian Grenier). As the year goes on, however, she hits her stride at work and becomes Miranda's most trusted assistant. Will Andy ultimately become the next Miranda Priestley and abandon the person she used to be, or will she get out before it's too late?

David Frankel, who had previously directed episodes of *Sex and the City* and *Entourage*, made *The Devil Wears Prada* colorful and fun, with a brisk pacing that almost never falters. From the quick-moving opening titles to the various fashion montages to an ending that wraps things up fast and satisfactorily, this is not a slow-moving drama that takes its time. *The Devil Wears Prada* is meant to be a crowd-pleaser from beginning to end, and on that level, it shines. It's a movie that knows what it wants to be but at the same time never panders to its audience. The screenplay by Aline Brosh McKenna, which was adapted from Lauren Weisberger's popular novel, has a familiar structure, but it's the dialogue throughout that makes this film stand out from others. Miranda's vicious speeches and outrageous demands always yield laughs, and Emily's put-downs to Andy might be the funniest of all. Many movies in this genre can feel too pedestrian, too manipulative at times, but such is never the case with *The Devil Wears Prada*.

Casting always makes or breaks a film, and in this case, the casting of the four major characters is perfect. While Andy's boyfriend Nate could have been played by anyone—Grenier is OK but doesn't have a lot to work with—and Simon Baker is adequate but nothing special in the role of the scheming Christian, the four leads all leave memorable impressions. Hathaway was most known for playing a Disney princess before this movie (Meryl was reportedly skeptical of Hathaway's casting in the beginning), but it was her charming performance in *The Devil Wears Prada* that signified a new chapter to her blossoming career. She is appropriately dowdy in the beginning, wearing awkward sweaters and eating onion bagels, and as well as her outer transformation into the more fashionable Andy works, it's the change on the inside that pops off the screen. Hathaway holds her own against Meryl all the way through.

Blunt was plucked from near obscurity for this movie—she had mostly acted in British television productions before—and was an inspired choice for the smart-mouthed, hot-tempered Emily. "I'm one stomach flu away from my goal weight" is probably the line people remember the most but she has plenty of great zingers. Tucci, who went on to play Meryl's loving husband in *Julie & Julia*, makes the role of Miranda's right hand man Nigel an original and ultimately endearing character, when he could have been played more selfish and stereotypical by another actor. He is at his best here, too.

Meryl received yet another Academy Award nomination for *The Devil Wears Prada*, one of the few she has nabbed for a comedic film, and she, more than any other actor in the film, takes a role that could have easily—*very* easily—been one-note and obvious, and yet makes it three-dimensional in every way. Remarkably, Meryl gets us to care about Miranda by the end of the movie, no small feat. When we are first introduced to her, she is the tyrannical boss who trudges down her office hallway like a Tyrannosaurus Rex willing to squash anyone who gets in her way. The early scenes where she spits out one venomous line of dialogue after another give the film some of its best entertainment value, and the monologues when she voices her disappointment in Andy are always shockingly vitriolic.

Despite her being the villain of the movie, Miranda can't always be a hateful witch, and no one knows that better than Meryl herself. Occasionally we see traces of Miranda's personal life at home, but it's in a heartbreaking scene in a Paris hotel room, when Meryl wears no make-up and trembles as she talks about the break-up of her marriage, that shows more than anything else Meryl's mastery. She finds just the right balance of Miranda's vulnerability and still brewing cynicism in this moment, the scene that made Meryl want to do the movie, and probably the scene that netted her the well-deserved Oscar nomination.

The Devil Wears Prada will never be viewed on the same level as Meryl's brilliant *Kramer vs. Kramer*, and in a career that has seen two comedic gems—*Defending Your Life* and *Death Becomes Her*—this film might not even be considered her great comedy achievement. But in the year since its successful release, it has become one of Meryl's most beloved movies and features what will always be one of her most memorable performances. Meryl could have played the role of Miranda as a superficial villain but instead infused in her just enough humanity to show why she became this way and what she really wants out of her life and career. *The Devil Wears Prada* is grand entertainment every step of the way, and it remains one of my all-time favorite Meryl movies.

AWARDS WATCH

Meryl received her fourteenth Academy Award nomination, for Best Actress. She won the Golden Globe for Best Actress in a Motion Picture – Comedy or Musical, and earned BAFTA Award, Critics Choice Award, and SAG Award nominations for her performance. She won the EDA Award for Best Actress in a Comedic Performance from the Alliance of Women Film Journalists, the ALFS Award for Actress of the Year from the London Critics, and Best Comedic Performance from the Women Film Critics. In addition, she received an MTV Movie Award nomination for Best Villain and a Teen Choice Award nomination for Choice Sleazebag.

In addition to Meryl's Best Actress nomination, *The Devil Wears Prada* earned an Oscar nomination for Best Costume Design. The film was nominated for Best Motion Picture – Comedy or Musical, and Supporting Actress, for Blunt, at the Golden Globes. It also earned five BAFTA Award nominations, including Best Screenplay, and a nomination for Best Comedy Movie at the Critics Choice Awards. Blunt also won British Supporting Actress of the Year from the London Critics and a Breakthrough Performance nomination at the MTV Movie Awards. In addition, the film was nominated for a WGA Award, and it was picked as one of the Top Ten Films by the National Board of Review.

FUN FACTS

Meryl donated all of her wardrobe to a charity auction.

On the first day of filming, Meryl told Hathaway that she was perfect for the role and was happy to be working with her, but then added that was the last nice thing she'd say to her until the end of filming.

The idea of having Miranda appear without make-up in the film's memorable later scene was Meryl's.

The original line in the limo at the end was, "Everyone wants to be me." Meryl did not like this line, finding it too self-involved. She later changed it to "Everyone wants to be us."

Meryl's daughter Mamie Gummer, who appeared in *Evening* the following year, played a Starbucks clerk, but her scene was deleted.

Anna Wintour, editor of *Vogue*, was the rumored inspiration for Miranda Priestley.

Kim Basinger and Helen Mirren were considered for the role of Miranda.

Tucci was cast right before filming started. Thomas Lennon turned down the role of Nigel because of scheduling conflicts with *Reno 911!*

Hathaway prepared for her role by volunteering for a week as an assistant at an auction house.

WEEK 38
EVENING (2007)

FILM FACTS

DISTRIBUTOR: Focus Features
RELEASE DATE: June 29, 2007

DIRECTOR: Lajos Koltai
WRITERS: Susan Minot, Michael Cunningham (based on Minot's novel)
PRODUCER: Jeffrey Sharp
ALSO STARRING: Claire Danes, Toni Collette, Vanessa Redgrave, Natasha Richardson, Patrick Wilson, Hugh Dancy, Mamie Gummer, Eileen Atkins, Glenn Close

REVIEW

2007 was a strange year for Meryl. After the stellar summer of 2006, when *A Prairie Home Companion* opened to glowing reviews and *The Devil Wears Prada* became an unexpected smash at the box office, Meryl became busier than ever, shooting various projects with stellar casts and acclaimed directors. In one of her most prolific years since 1979, when *Manhattan*, *The Seduction of Joe Tynan*, and *Kramer vs. Kramer* were all released, 2007 gave us a Meryl movie seemingly every few weeks. Her underrated and mostly forgotten *Dark Matter* played at the 2007 Sundance Film Festival (but wasn't officially released until early 2008), *Evening* came out in the summer, *Rendition* opened in October, and *Lions for Lambs* was released in November, as Oscar season was heating up. She seemed to be everywhere that year, but what made 2007 particularly strange was not that she was in a lot of movies, but that she appeared in a lot of *bad* movies. *Rendition* falls flat, *Lions for Lambs* is a complete disaster, and *Evening*, the first of her three official 2007 films, is a major disappointment.

All of the elements are in place for *Evening* to be a great movie. Michael Cunningham, whose novel *The Hours* became the Academy Award-winning 2002 film with Meryl, co-wrote the screenplay to *Evening* with the author of the bestselling novel, Susan Minot. The Oscar-nominated director Lajos Koltai was coming off an acclaimed foreign film, *Fateless*. The ensemble cast is one of the most impressive to have ever been assembled—Claire Danes, Toni Collette, Vanessa Redgrave, Patrick Wilson, Hugh Dancy, Eileen Atkins, Glenn Close, and Natasha Richardson, in her final dramatic role. Meryl's daughter Mamie Gummer appeared in her second major film role (after 2006's *The Hoax*), playing the younger version of Meryl's character Lila. Everything about this movie screamed success.

Two storylines are featured, one set close to present day, the other in the 1950s. The present day storyline is by far the weaker of the two. Redgrave plays Ann, who is spending her last dying days withering away in an upstairs bedroom. Her two adult children (Collette and Richardson, the latter of whom was Redgrave's real life daughter) are spending time with her at the home, wanting to bond with their mother in the little time they still have. Ann speaks of a special time in her life, when she was in her twenties and attended the wedding of her friend, Lila. Danes plays the younger Ann, and during the course of a few memorable days, Ann pursues the gorgeous Harris (Wilson) while the quirky Buddy (Dancy) falls for her. When a tragedy occurs, nothing ever stays the same for Ann.

Evening is the sad case of a movie where everyone involved surely thought it was going to be a winner, but little about it works. Dancy is the one member of the cast who creates an intriguing character, a guy with inner demons who could have been the focus of a film all his own. Danes is solid as usual, and it's especially bittersweet to watch Redgrave and Richardson share a tender moment on screen, when Richardson was two years away from her untimely death. However, most of the film lays inert on the screen. Little tension is ever established, and most awkward of all is the cutting back and forth between storylines. Just when the 1950s narrative starts to get interesting, the director cuts back to the present day narrative, often not for just a minute or two, but for a long, unnecessary stretch of time. More effective would have been to open and end with the present day storyline, and allow the 1950s storyline to encompass the majority of the screen-time. Two or three scenes of Redgrave rotting away in a bed is sad; fifteen scenes of it is monotonous.

As dull and uneventful as the movie turned out to be, there are many parallels to previous Meryl movies worth noting for trivia buffs. As previously mentioned, this was Meryl's second collaboration with Pulitzer Prize winner Michael Cunningham. Of all films she has made, *Evening* is very much like *The Hours*; both films deal with multiple narratives, both have a significant storyline set in the 1950s, and both star Meryl, Collette, and Danes. Meryl's first film *Julia*, from 1977, won Vanessa Redgrave a Best Supporting Actress Oscar, and here, the two actresses got to have their first, and to date only, scene on film together. This movie marked the first time Meryl and her daughter Mamie appeared in the same project, and it was the second time for Meryl and her good friend Glenn Close (although never in the same scene, unlike in *The House of the Spirits*).

Meryl doesn't actually appear in *Evening* until the third act, about ninety minutes in. In what amounts to little more than a cameo, Meryl, playing the older Lila, arrives at the home, walks upstairs, reminisces with Ann, shares a tender moment with Ann's daughter Nina (Collette), and leaves; that's about it. Meryl looks extremely old in *Evening*, with credible and unflattering make-up, and she does her best with a mostly nothing role that she probably took because she felt she had to. The film had stellar talent in front of and behind the scenes, and her daughter Mamie was actually cast first—everyone on the crew therefore must have thought it pretty obvious to cast Meryl as the older version of her for the film's conclusion. She gives the present day narrative a jolt of energy it desperately needs, and while it's nowhere near her finest moment on screen, there's a fascination in watching two pros like Meryl and Redgrave play a scene together, even if only for a few minutes.

Overall, *Evening* is a film that should have been great but rarely delivers. It bombed with most critics, was a clunker at the summer box office, and did not receive any year-end awards nominations that many involved likely expected. The film was a disappointment for Meryl, but most shocking of all, the lame *Evening* would actually be the best of her three 2007 films.

AWARDS WATCH

The lone, awkward nomination this film received was Movie You Wanted to Love But Just Couldn't, at the Alliance of Women Film Journalists.

FUN FACTS

Along with *The Homesman*, this includes one of Meryl's smallest roles in a movie.

Gummer plays the younger version of her real-life mother Meryl, while Richardson plays daughter to her real-life mother, Redgrave.

Keira Knightley was considered for young Ann, but she was busy shooting *Pirates of the Caribbean: At World's End* and *Atonement*.

Ellen Burstyn was considered for older Ann.

Spouses-to-be Danes and Dancy met on this film.

WEEK 39
RENDITION (2007)

FILM FACTS

DISTRIBUTOR: New Line Cinema
RELEASE DATE: October 19, 2007

DIRECTOR: Gavin Hood
WRITER: Kelley Sane
PRODUCERS: Steve Golin, Marcus Viscidi
ALSO STARRING: Jake Gyllenhaal, Reese Witherspoon, Alan Arkin, Peter Sarsgaard, J.K. Simmons

REVIEW

The line of disappointing 2007 films continued for Meryl with the release of *Rendition*, even though, like *Evening*, it had the makings of a stellar achievement. It paired Meryl with a superb group of actors, many of whom had recently won or been nominated for Academy Awards. Reese Witherspoon was coming off her Oscar for *Walk the Line*, Alan Arkin had just won for *Little Miss Sunshine*, and Jake Gyllenhaal had been nominated for *Brokeback Mountain*. The director Gavin Hood had directed the acclaimed South African movie *Tsotsi*, the winner of the

2005 Academy Award for Best Foreign Film. *Rendition* told an important topical story that featured multiple narratives and scenes of shocking violence and potentially heart-wrenching emotion. When it premiered at the Toronto Film Festival, early word was solid, and the great Roger Ebert even considered it perfect.

But everything changed when the movie opened in late October. Audiences stayed away, and most who showed up walked away disappointed. Topping out at less than ten million nationwide, *Rendition* was a flop that was essentially pulled from theaters by the time Meryl's next flop, *Lions for Lambs*, opened in November. It has some good performances and a couple of scenes that work, but for the most part, this film is cold, uninvolving, and extremely slow. Meryl is barely in it, and worst of all, she plays a role that literally any woman in Hollywood age fifty to sixty could have played with ease. Susan Sarandon, Jessica Lange, Kathy Bates—all of these actresses would have been equally fine in the part. Meryl does a serviceable job in this one, but nothing more, and certainly nothing extraordinary.

Rendition is a two-hour drama with too much talk and too little drama. At the beginning of the movie, a terrorist bombing kills an American in Africa, and an investigation leads to an Egyptian man Anwar El-Ibrahimi (Omar Metwally) who has lived in the United States for many years and who is married to an American woman, Isabella (Reese Witherspoon). He is apprehended when his plane lands and the U.S. sends him back to the country where the terrible incident occurred. A CIA operative Douglas Freeman (Jake Gyllenhaal) watches the torture of this man and debates whether to keep it going or not. The pregnant Isabella continues to ask about the whereabouts of her husband but nobody, despite her increasing frustration, gives her any information. Meryl plays Douglas' boss Corrine Whitman, who asks that the detention of Anwar continue, thinking that to set him free could put thousands of people in harm's way.

What drew Meryl to this project, and this banal character? She has said in interviews that the script got her heart racing and that she wasn't typically offered thrillers (although whether *Rendition* can be considered a thriller is up for debate). Her daughter Mamie played her younger self in *Evening*, so it made logical sense for Meryl to appear in that film. *Lions for Lambs* offered her the chance to act in scenes with Tom Cruise, as well as reunite with her *Out of Africa* co-star Robert Redford, albeit this time with her as the actress and him as the director. But besides the high wattage of star power and a director coming off a beloved foreign movie, *Rendition* must have simply read better on paper. Meryl has said that she likes playing the boss—*The Devil Wears Prada*, *The Iron Lady*, and *The Giver* are just a few of her recent films showing her in charge—so maybe the prospect of playing another powerful figure appealed to her. However the part must have looked in the screenplay, it doesn't give her much to play with, and the role has to be considered one of her weakest in her entire career.

The problem with *Rendition* is that despite all the talent involved, and all the ambition that went into the piece, little of it stays with the viewer once the end credits start rolling. It's one of those movies that has way too many narratives, to the point where none of them get enough screen-time to make any real impact. Witherspoon's storyline had the best chance for emotional resonance, but she's seen so infrequently that it's hard not to giggle when she screams at Meryl that immortal line, "Just tell me he's *okay!*" Gyllenhaal is one of our finest actors, but he basically just stands around and looks stoic; how many scenes are we supposed to watch of him brooding in a dark corner? Peter Sarsgaard plays a character he always seems to play, the fantastic JK Simmons appears in a small intimidating part that goes nowhere, and Arkin throws out a few snarky lines before he basically disappears for the rest of the movie.

Meryl has no more than ten scenes, most of which consist of her talking angrily into a phone or standing at an upscale party looking like Lady Macbeth, in a regal gown Miranda Priestly likely would have vomited on. Her first scene, waking up in bed at two in the morning, doesn't even allow her a memorable entrance; the camera just pans around the bed as she talks on the phone in the dark. You would think that she would have one explosive scene, or some kind of eye-popping moment that captures your attention. But aside from a short monologue she says to Sarsgaard, she doesn't even say much in her scenes. She stands around looking not like our finest living actress but like a movie star waiting to cash a check before she moves on to her next project. *Rendition* is an unsuccessful movie that commits the worst of crimes; it wastes Meryl's talent by giving her a totally unworthy character. Meryl is known for being offered the cream of the crop when it comes to film parts, but in a trio of movies in 2007, for some strange reason, she only seemed to be offered scraps.

AWARDS WATCH

Meryl did not receive any awards or nominations for her performance, but *Rendition* won Best Narrative Feature for director Hood at the Mill Valley Film Festival, and it received Teen Choice Award nominations for Choice Movie Actor: Drama, for Gyllenhaal, and Choice Movie Actress: Drama, for Witherspoon.

FUN FACTS

Hood said in interviews that his greatest privilege on *Rendition* was working with Meryl.

The film is based on the true story of Khalid El-Masri, a German citizen who was mistaken for Khalid al-Masri, who was rumored to have been involved with the September 11 terrorist attacks.

A similarly themed film called *Extraordinary Rendition* was released the same year.

In real life, Sarsgaard is married to Jake Gyllenhaal's sister, Maggie.

WEEK 40
LIONS FOR LAMBS (2007)

FILM FACTS

DISTRIBUTOR: MGM
RELEASE DATE: November 9, 2007

DIRECTOR: Robert Redford
WRITER: Matthew Michael Carnahan
PRODUCERS: Robert Redford, Matthew Michael Carnahan, Tracy Falco, Andrew Hauptman
ALSO STARRING: Robert Redford, Tom Cruise, Michael Pena, Andrew Garfield, Derek Luke, Peter Berg, Kevin Dunn

REVIEW

After the misfires of *Evening* and *Rendition*, Meryl's last major release of 2007 looked to be a slam dunk with audiences and critics, and potentially bring Meryl year-end nominations in the Supporting Actress category. *Lions for Lambs* was a topical film at the time, a serious examination of the Iraq war that received a major wide release and an awards-friendly November opening. The film marked Robert Redford's seventh film as director, and despite the 2000 bomb *The Legend of Bagger Vance*, Redford had achieved great success years earlier with *Quiz Show*, *A River Runs Through It*, and *Ordinary People*, the latter of which won Redford his first, and to date only, Academy Award. *Lions for Lambs* marked Andrew Garfield's feature film debut, and it gave Tom Cruise—coming off a record seven blockbusters in a row that all grossed more than 100 million—his first purely dramatic role since 1999's *Magnolia*. It re-teamed Redford and Meryl for the first time since *Out of Africa* (albeit never in the same scene), and best of all, it gave Meryl the most screen-time and juiciest character of any of her 2007 releases.

Evening and *Rendition* should have worked but didn't, and *Lions for Lambs* definitely should have been at the very least competent entertainment. That it bores the viewer senseless just as much as the other two is inexplicable. The film is about serious issues and it's got a variety of powerhouse actors, but while it starts strong, with nice tension developing, especially between Meryl and Cruise in their early scenes, the movie peters out around the halfway mark and ultimately doesn't go anywhere, even with its brief ninety-minute runtime. The biggest problem is that the film ultimately just becomes a series of talking heads, with little revealed about any of the characters and even less revealed that we as the audience didn't already know about the state of the world. Redford didn't need to make an action picture by any means, but *Lions for Lambs* at the time felt like too little too late, which is only made worse all these years later.

Like *Rendition*, which was released just three weeks prior, *Lions for Lambs* features multiple narratives that all deal with issues of international terrorism. It specifically has three stories: one about a Republican Senator named Jasper Irving (Cruise) who gives an hour-long interview regarding the war in Afghanistan to a jaded television reporter, Janine (Meryl), who praised the senator years ago but now feels he might be letting her down; one about a political science professor named Stephen Malley who holds an early morning meeting with a potentially brilliant student, Todd (Garfield), who rarely comes to class and never does the readings but who always has something profound to say; and one about two students-turned-soldiers, Ernest (Michael Pena) and Arian (Derek Luke), who fight for their lives against Taliban forces on an Afghani ridge. The stories come together in some predictable ways, but also in ways viewers may not expect.

Despite its problems, *Lions for Lambs*, as previously mentioned, maintains one's interest throughout most of its first half. Meryl and Cruise are two actors who are just naturally interesting to watch in whatever they do on-screen, so to see them debate each other back and forth for minutes on end commands the viewer's attention. When they start disagreeing and she asks increasingly difficult questions, his frustrated answers give the film its most harrowing moments. Cruise was actually perfect casting for this slick senator character, and despite the shortcomings of the screenplay by Matthew Michael Carnaham, he is particularly good, never going over-the-top with his mannerisms, always selling his ideas like any good politician would. Cruise plays smarmy well—*Magnolia* and *Collateral* come to mind—and he is at his smarmy best here.

These scenes with Cruise and Meryl are solid, if a bit longwinded by the time their chat finally wraps up; it's the other two storylines that bring the film down. Garfield is natural in his first big screen role as the intelligent pupil, but his scenes with Redford lack energy, and they become monotonous after awhile. If there was a worthwhile payoff regarding Todd's future, it might have worked, but since this story doesn't go anywhere, it doesn't belong in the film. Even worse is the story with Pena and Luke. The scene in the classroom where they explain their decisions to enlist in the military is a good one, but the actual combat scenes in Afghanistan, all done at night, feel like reused footage from other movies, and they're out of balance with all the other talking heads.

The scenes with Cruise and Meryl work the best, and in Janine, Meryl found her most complex and engaging character of her films released in 2007. So ruthless and powerful in her previous *The Devil Wears Prada* and *Rendition*, Meryl here plays an aging journalist who feels like she can no longer make any real impact on the world. You can always see her wanting to dig in to Cruise's character more and more as the film goes on, but she's clearly afraid of going too personal or accusatory, and she holds back. It's after she leaves the senator's office and endures a bitter meeting with her editor (Kevin Dunn) when Meryl delivers her best work in the movie. She's tired of all the bullshit and disappointed in what she's been force-fed, and while her boss demands her to get on with the story, she has a moment of clarity that changes everything.

While *Lions for Lambs* marked Meryl's third bomb in a row, one that only topped out at 15 million (about a third of what many of Cruise's previous films made in the opening weekends), she did get a few nice scenes to play, allowing her to create the kind of fully embodied character she didn't get in either *Evening* or *Rendition*. While one more obscure Meryl film awaited release in early 2008, thankfully she was not on the verge of appearing in a dozen more movies no one would care about. Instead, she was on the verge of a career renaissance that actresses half her age could only dream about. Yes, *Mamma Mia*, *Doubt*, and a third Academy Award, were all on the horizon.

AWARDS WATCH

The lone nomination *Lions for Lambs* received was the EDA Female Focus Award for Actress Defying Age and Ageism, for Meryl, from the Alliance of Women Film Journalists.

FUN FACTS

When Redford called Meryl to ask her if she'd be in the film, she told him if he was in, she was in.

The photo that Janine observes in Irving's office of him dressed as a young cadet is a still photo from Cruise's role in 1981's *Taps*.

Cruise said in interviews that he agreed to be in the film due to his deep respect for Redford.

This was the first Cruise/Wagner Productions film following Cruise's falling out with Paramount Pictures in 2006.

Release prints were delivered to theaters under the fake title, "Barrie."

WEEK 41
DARK MATTER (2008)

FILM FACTS

DISTRIBUTOR: Myriad Pictures
RELEASE DATE: April 11, 2008

DIRECTOR: Shi-Zheng Chen
WRITER: Billy Shebar
PRODUCERS: Andrea Miller, Mary Salter, Janet Yang
ALSO STARRING: Ye Liu, Peng Chi, Aidan Quinn, Blair Brown, Bill Irwin, Taylor Schilling

REVIEW

And now we've arrived at Meryl's most obscure film of all. Sure, she's made movies that didn't connect with audiences—*The House of the Spirits* and *Dancing at Lughnasa* come to mind—and she's made some that fell short at a dramatic level, like the lame *Still of the Night* and the bland *Before and After*. But if I had to pick the oddest title of all on Meryl's lengthy resume, it would be *Dark Matter*, which premiered at the Sundance Film Festival in January 2007 but wasn't officially released in the United States until April 2008, when it played in just a handful of theaters before it quickly disappeared (the film only made $30,000 in its initial run, easily an all-time low for Meryl). This is a quiet, mostly insignificant movie that few people know about, and the die-hard Meryl fans who do will be disappointed when they discover how short of screen-time she has.

Dark Matter is loosely based on the tragic shooting that took place at the University of Iowa in 1991, when a physicist named Gang Lu, who had recently received his PhD, shot and killed three of his former professors, as well as a school administrator. In the film, Liu Xing (Ye Liu) has moved from China to attend school in Salt Lake City as a graduate student in Cosmology. Liu pursues theories about dark matter for his dissertation, which his professor Jacob Reiser (Aidan Quinn) ultimately rejects, leaving Liu lost and without purpose. His benefactor Joanna Silver (Meryl) sees potential in him early on, but also recognizes a dark side to the young man—albeit a little too late. Blair Brown, Bill Irwin, and Taylor Schilling round out the ensemble cast.

This is not a bad movie, so much as it is a confused one. The story of a Chinese student trying to find his way in the American university system is a worthwhile one, and the frustrations that Liu goes through in the first hour of the movie make for compelling viewing. The initial complements he receives from Professor Reiser, who thinks he has the potential for greatness, only add to the disappointment later when Reiser disapproves of Liu's theories and asks him to pursue simpler, more factual territory. Director Shi-Zheng Chen, who made his debut here, and whose only other feature film to date is *Disney*

High School Musical: China, gives the film a unique, muted physical look.

However, while some of these scenes work well, the movie is all over the place in terms of its narrative structure, and at only eighty-five minutes, it's so short to barely have time to register for the viewer. There's a plot involving Liu's parents that never plays a strong enough role. There are interludes involving words like "fire" and "water" that add little to the movie's impact. Some of the music is tonally out of place, especially "This Land is Your Land," and the overly depressing conclusion comes so wildly out of left field that it's hard to get worked up about it. If a film is going to end on such a downbeat note, it needs to be earned, and *Dark Matter*'s finale isn't in the slightest. Liu is an effective screen presence, but there is little set-up, few clues ever given throughout the narrative, to show the darkness his character is capable of.

The biggest letdown of all, though, is that despite her large presence on many of the DVD covers, Meryl has just a tiny part in the movie, one that unfortunately doesn't add much to story. The director had never made a movie before, it's a small film with a downer ending, and her part is mostly without interest, so it's truly puzzling what made Meryl sign on to this project. She did get to act with her *Music of the Heart* co-star Quinn again, and working with a group of international actors might have peaked her interest. But, like in most of the movies she made around this time, her character is not given enough for an actress of her talent and caliber to do. She has more screen-time in this than in *Rendition* and *Evening*, but only a couple of her scenes resonate with the viewer. Weirdly, she's also never looked so pale and sickly in a movie since her Oscar-nominated role in *Ironweed*; it's almost as if following her role in *The Devil Wears Prada*, Meryl wanted to shed every ounce of her vanity for her next project.

Dark Matter actually opens on Meryl, as she performs tai chi in her backyard underneath a dark, cloudy sky. We are not formally introduced to her character for a long time after this, but if nothing else, this film provides one of the most haunting opening shots of Meryl in any of her movies. When she finally appears in a classroom scene, sporting a wild, curly hairdo and almost no make-up, excitement brews as to what kind role she will play. Will she get behind Liu and help him reach his lofty goals? Will she enter a scandalous romantic relationship with him? Unfortunately little comes of their strange friendship, and only one scene toward the end can be considered memorable. Liu arrives at Joanna's house unannounced, and when he drops to his knees and starts applying make-up first to her hand, then to her face, she stops him, the intimacy finally too much for her to bear. This effectively creepy moment between the two shows the only real foreshadowing of the horrors that are to come.

After a string of disappointing supporting roles in mostly forgettable movies, Meryl finally bounced back in 2008 to the mainstream consciousness in two massive hits, one a summer blockbuster, the other an awards-friendly darling. Meryl may have lost her way for a while, as all actors do from time to time, but following the mediocre

Dark Matter, it was pure bliss for Meryl fans in the years to come.

AWARDS WATCH

Meryl did not receive any awards or nominations for her performance, but *Dark Matter* did win the Alfred P. Sloan Feature Film Prize for director Chen and writer Shebar at the 2007 Sundance Film Festival.

FUN FACTS

Meryl's lowest grosser at the US box office. The film grossed only $30,000, a bit less than her next project, *Mamma Mia*, which grossed more than 600 million worldwide.

Meryl reportedly convinced Quinn to be a part of the film.

The release date was pushed back because the film's plot eerily resembled the events of the Virginia Tech massacre.

Val Kilmer was involved at one point, but he dropped out before filming began.

WEEK 42
MAMMA MIA (2008)

FILM FACTS

DISTRIBUTOR: Universal Pictures
RELEASE DATE: July 18, 2008

DIRECTOR: Phyllida Lloyd
WRITER: Catherine Johnson (based on her musical book)
PRODUCERS: Judy Craymer, Gary Goetzman
ALSO STARRING: Amanda Seyfried, Pierce Brosnan, Colin Firth, Stellan Skarsgard, Christine Baranski, Julie Walters, Dominic Cooper

REVIEW

One of the great joys in watching a new Meryl movie every week is seeing her take chances not just on daring projects and unique characters, but on new genres. So many actors unfortunately get typecast in certain kinds of movies, but Meryl continues to surprise with her genre choices. While drama is her number one genre of choice, she has not shied away from comedies, with *Defending Your Life*, *Death Becomes Her*, and *The Devil Wears Prada* being three of her best movies ever. In addition, she has appeared in a suspense film (*Still of the Night*), an action movie (*The River*

Wild), a children's film (*Lemony Snicket's A Series of Unfortunate Events*), animated movies (*The Ant Bully* and *Fantastic Mr. Fox*), and a western (*The Homesman*).

One of the last major genres she hadn't tackled before 2008 was the musical, which was odd given her beautiful singing voice. Meryl memorably sang in *Ironweed*, *Postcards from the Edge*, and *A Prairie Home Companion* but had never led an all-star musical. It was bound to happen sooner or later, and *Mamma Mia*, based on the award-winning musical that premiered in London in 1999 and went on to be one of Broadway's longest running hits, turned out to be the one that called her name. Meryl saw the musical in New York a few weeks after the September 11 terrorist attacks and wrote a letter to the show's producers telling them how thankful she was for their bringing much-needed happiness to theatergoers. Phyllida Lloyd, who directed the stageshow and was ultimately chosen to direct the film version, never forgot about that letter; her first and only choice for Donna in the movie was Meryl.

It would have been understandable for Meryl to say no to this project. Not only is this the kind of lightweight entertainment she hadn't pursued in many years; pulling off a movie musical is difficult—for every *Chicago*, there's *The Producers*—and singing ABBA songs, as any member in the cast can attest to, can be a challenge. But when she was offered the part, Meryl was initially shocked that she was even considered, and she agreed to star in the film without a moment's hesitation. She reportedly is never allowed to sing in her house around her son and daughters, so she must have decided to get her mini-revenge by leading a movie musical. Of course, the exotic location, amazing ensemble cast, catchy songs, and engaging story probably had something to do with her decision, too.

Mamma Mia tells of twenty-year-old Sophie (Amanda Seyfried), a young woman living in Greece who is about to marry her equally young Prince Charming named Sky (Dominic Cooper). Before her big day arrives, however, she sends out letters to her three potential dads, men her mother dated the one eventful summer she was conceived. They all unexpectedly show up, to Sophie's great joy, and her mother Donna's consternation. As the wedding ceremony draws near, Sophie questions if she wants to get married at all, and Donna wonders if she still has the capacity to fall in love again. This original story, written by Catherine Johnson for both the stage version and the film version, plays out with more than a dozen ABBA songs that fit seamlessly into the plot.

Viewed in the right frame of mind, *Mamma Mia* is grand entertainment from beginning to end, a movie that exists for no other reason to make the viewer smile and feel good. While at times the cinematography feels a little too glossy—much of the film was shot on the Pinewood Studios soundstages—and while there are a couple of musical numbers that slow down the film's pacing—as fun as "Does Your Mother Know" is, removing it would not affect the plot in any way—for the most part this movie works. There's one more key flaw—more on that in a moment—but overall, the film is loads of fun, with one delightful song after another ("Honey, Honey" and "Super Trouper" are two of the best) and lots of great actors clearly having a blast on-screen and not taking the cheesy story too seriously.

Pierce Brosnan reportedly signed on to the movie not even knowing what it was—only that it was being shot in Greece and that Meryl was set for the lead role. At this point in her career, Meryl had the power to attract terrific actors the world over to movies she was attached to, and *Mamma Mia* was no different. Playing Donna's best friends, Christine Baranski and Julie Walters were perfectly cast, making the life-long friendships between the three women believable; Walters is especially a hoot in the most comedic role in the movie. Seyfried is luminous, and Cooper is at his most handsome and charming. Colin Firth and Stellan Skarsgard joined Brosnan as Sophie's potential fathers, and all three actors brought welcome qualities to their roles, with Firth at his most confused and Skarsgard at his silliest. Brosnan is fine in his most high-profile role since he retired from the James Bond series, but the other huge flaw in the movie is his absolutely *godawful* singing voice, which is so bad that any emotion meant to be stirred up in the film's sappy conclusion is tempered. While one has to give Brosnan credit for really going for it—his Razzie Award for Worst Supporting Actress is undeserved—it's wise to assume he won't be singing on-screen anytime soon.

Meryl had played such dour and reserved characters in her previous films, like *Rendition* and *Lions for Lambs*, and even *The Devil Wears Prada* to some extent, that to watch her be sexy and kid-like and totally uninhibited in *Mamma Mia* is a great pleasure. This was one of her most physically demanding roles since *The River Wild*, so much so that the then fifty-eight-year-old had to train for three weeks to get in proper shape—climbing a tall ladder while singing "Mamma Mia" takes a little stamina—and her exuberance really comes through, particularly in her early scenes when she's dancing through the streets and doing cannonballs off piers. Meryl is absorbing in a central role that could have been one-note in the hands of a different actress. Despite the emphasis on entertaining musical numbers over moments of subtlety and character realizations, Meryl always finds time for genuine emotion, even when it's just a flirtatious look at Brosnan or a somber glimpse at Seyfried in the mirror.

But the greatest thrill of all in watching *Mamma Mia* is to finally hear Meryl belt out not just a couple of songs, which audience members had been privileged to hear in a few of her previous movies, but multiple ones, each with its own tempo and flavor. It's a little weird to watch someone of her stature sliding down a bannister and singing the silly but infectious "Dancing Queen," and she's unfortunately not given much help by Brosnan in the strained version of "S.O.S." Her best songs are "Mamma Mia," "Slipping Through My Fingers," and her big, emotional showstopper, "The Winner Takes It All," which allows her to just sing, without choreography, without any bells and whistles. If anything can prove that Meryl could record her own album and be taken seriously as a singer, it's her goosebumps-raising rendition of "The Winner Takes It All."

Mamma Mia opened on July 18, 2008, the same day as *The Dark Knight*, acting as the perfect counterprogramming to the Christopher Nolan juggernaut. *Mamma Mia*, while only making peanuts that weekend compared to the giant haul *The Dark Knight* pulled in, turned into a true blockbuster all its own, quickly besting *The Devil Wears Prada*'s stupendous box office take with 144 million nationwide and an astonishing 610 million worldwide. Given that Meryl doesn't star in a Marvel movie (she did tell Jimmy Kimmel that she wouldn't *not* consider being in a superhero film), *Mamma Mia* will likely stand as her all-time highest grosser. And after having made four disappointing bombs in a row, this musical, her only until 2014's *Into the Woods*, proved that Meryl was back on track.

AWARDS WATCH

Meryl received a Golden Globe nomination for Best Actress in a Motion Picture – Comedy or Musical. She won the National Movie Award for Best Performance – Female, Best International Actress at the Rembrandt Awards, Best Comedic Actress from the Women Film Critics, and Outstanding Actress in a Feature Film at the Women's Image Network Awards. She also earned Satellite Award and Jupiter Award nominations for her performance.

Mamma Mia earned a Golden Globe nomination for Best Motion Picture – Comedy or Musical. It received three BAFTA Award nominations, including the Alexander Korda Award for Best British Film. It won the Empire Award for Best Soundtrack, the People's Choice Award for Favorite Song—"Mamma Mia"—and the Rembrandt Award for Best International Film. *Mamma Mia* also received a few not-so-kind awards, including the Movie You Wanted to Love But Just Couldn't award from the Alliance of Women Film Journalists, the Oklahoma Film Critics Award for Not-So-Obviously Worst Film, and the Razzie Award for Worst Supporting Actor, for Brosnan.

FUN FACTS

To date, Meryl's highest grossing movie.

Meryl went to Stockholm to do her vocal for "The Winner Takes It All." She finished it in one take, and Benny Andersson, former ABBA member, called her a miracle.

The entire cast performed their own singing.

In December 2008, *Mamma Mia* became the highest grossing film of all time in the U.K., passing *Titanic*. *Avatar* has since beaten it.

Mandy Moore, Rachel McAdams, Emmy Rossum, and Amanda Bynes were considered for the part of Sophie. Olivia Newton-John and Michelle Pfeiffer were also reportedly considered for the role of Donna.

Cher was offered the role of Tanya, which would have teamed her with Meryl for the first time since *Silkwood*, but she turned it down. She later said she had to decline the role due to concert tour commitments.

WEEK 43
DOUBT
(2008)

FILM FACTS

DISTRIBUTOR: Miramax
RELEASE DATE: December 12, 2008

DIRECTOR: John Patrick Shanley
WRITER: John Patrick Shanley (based on his play)
PRODUCERS: Mark Roybal, Scott Rudin
ALSO STARRING: Philip Seymour Hoffman, Amy Adams, Viola Davis, Alice Drummond

REVIEW

Has any actor or actress played two lead characters in two major films in the same year as wildly different as Donna in *Mamma Mia* and Sister Aloysius Beauvier in *Doubt*? While Meryl often acts in more than one film in a given year, 2008 has to be considered one of her crowning achievements just in terms of showing her remarkable range. In *Mamma Mia*, she plays a sexy, independent woman dancing through Greece, making out with James Bond, and belting out ABBA songs. In *Doubt*, she plays a stern, demanding nun who hides behind a black veil and manages to scare the children at her Catholic school with merely a glimpse in the hallway. The first character is vibrant and full of life, and the second character is a quiet, internally damaged woman who thinks only the worst of others. These roles couldn't be more different than each other, and yet Meryl commits to them so completely that both characters become fully three-dimensional, totally believable, remarkably played by the same actress. That's the magic of Meryl.

John Patrick Shanley, who won an Oscar for his screenplay for 1987's *Moonstruck*, adapted his Pulitzer-Prize winning play *Doubt* to the screen. Cherry Jones, who played the Sister Aloysius role on stage for more than a year and won the Tony award, might have seemed a likely choice to play the character on film, but Shanley didn't direct the play, and he wanted to make a movie that stood separate from what audience members had already witnessed on the stage. For example, scenes that took place in dark rooms in the theater were shot outside in the movie, with exteriors of 1964 Bronx, New York giving the film a crucial cinematic feel. He uses dutch angles and a subtle music score to infuse in the audience a sense of dread. He also wanted powerhouse A-list actors to give his emotionally resonant story new life, both for those who had already seen the play and for those who were coming to the movie cold. With material this rich, he probably could have convinced any major actor to be in his adaptation, and thankfully, for him and for the viewer, he picked the best four actors he possibly could've.

Philip Seymour Hoffman, in an electric performance, plays Father Flynn, a priest with an actual sense of humor and appreciation for his students who unfortunately never refrains from rubbing the strict Principal, Sister Aloysius Beauvier (Meryl), the wrong way. She's always looking for an excuse to get him to leave, and she finally finds that excuse when Sister James (Amy Adams), an innocent nun without a shade of dishonesty, tells her that she suspects Flynn of spending too much time with Donald, the school's first black student. Without a shred of real proof, Sister Aloysius immediately commits herself to the idea that Father Flynn is up to no good with this boy, and she confronts him about his alleged wrongdoing. When he doesn't give her the answer she wants, she pursues the matter further, potentially ruining the lives of everyone around her.

Easily Meryl's best drama since *The Hours*, *Doubt* is an absorbing film that at one hour and forty minutes doesn't overstay its welcome. Films based on plays can often be stuffy and long-winded, but despite most of the signature scenes running on for big chunks of time, sometimes ten to fifteen minutes a piece, the characters are so well drawn and the dialogue is at such a high level of intelligence that the scenes feel shorter than they actually are. *Doubt* presents the kind of unique story that allows each viewer to bring his or her own beliefs to the movie. There's no handholding here, no easy ending that reveals to the viewer the core mystery at the heart of the film. Is Flynn guilty or not? The viewer is never explicitly told, and it's a smart decision on behalf of Shanley because it provides fodder for debate and interpretation.

This film features one of Meryl's finest performances since *The Bridges of Madison County*, but it is also that rare achievement where every major player is outstanding, always raising his or her game. Each of the four actors with significant roles received Academy Award nominations, with the late Hoffman especially a joy to watch square off against Meryl in two long riveting scenes filled with tension and tears. Hoffman is perfect casting for his character because in a long and varied career he played more than a few disturbed individuals—Allen in *Happiness* and Andy in *Before the Devil Knows You're Dead* come to mind—and his slightly off-kilter quality makes guessing whether he's guilty or innocent all the more difficult. He was one of the best actors of his generation, a true original who always took chances, and watching the two extended scenes when he goes toe-to-toe with Meryl is as mesmerizing as movie scenes get. Adams is also a perfect choice here, genuinely innocent and trusting of those around her, but with an inner sadness when she believes that trust has been broken. And Viola Davis's single, stunning scene, when her character Mrs. Miller begs Sister Aloysius to keep the alleged transgression a secret, stuns and exhilarates. Any actress who's able to upstage Meryl in a scene is worthy of applause, and Davis is spectacular in a single moment that took her career to great heights.

Doubt marked Meryl's first major role in a feature film drama since the aforementioned *The Hours*, and for her performance she received a Screen Actors Guild award and another Academy Award nomination. If Kate Winslet's Oscar nomination in Lead Actress for *The Reader* had been placed in the Supporting Actress category, where it was put at the SAG and Golden Globe Awards, Meryl would have certainly won her third Oscar for her raw, chilling performance in *Doubt*. This is a character we think we know everything about when we're first introduced to her. She's a disciplinarian, the wicked witch of the Catholic school who inflicts fear and pain on her students, especially the unfortunate ones who don't follow the rules. She doesn't take crap from anybody, and she's suspicious of Father Flynn from the start. But as the film continues, the viewer starts to see cracks in her veneer, her lack of ever looking inward to see what's made her so judgmental of others and so bitterly unhappy. When she explodes at Flynn in their second of two major scenes, she seems to be yelling less at him and more at her own frustrations in convincing herself to only see the worst in people.

It is not until the final scene that her character, finally having received her wish for Flynn's removal from the school, allows her intimidating and demanding persona to crumble, when she tells Sister James that she has doubts. Her two lines at the end can be interpreted in more than one way. Does she have doubts that Flynn molested the boy? That she handled the situation correctly? That inherent goodness in humanity is on the way out? Or possibly her own faith in God? Like the core mystery of the movie, her own doubts are left for interpretation, which makes this ending both challenging and effective. It also gives Meryl one of her most memorable movie endings, probably her most emotionally draining since the last scene of *Kramer vs. Kramer*.

Meryl followed up *Doubt* with her endearing portrayal of Julia Child in Nora Ephron's *Julie & Julia*, which also co-starred Adams. Soon after that, she starred in *The Iron Lady*, the film that finally, after nearly thirty years, won her an Academy Award, oddly enough beating out her *Doubt* co-star Viola Davis, who was nominated for *The Help*. Despite approaching sixty at the time of appearing in *Doubt*, an age when most actresses have either ruined their faces with plastic surgery or been relegated to one-dimensional mother roles, Meryl found herself at the most exciting time of her career with one tremendous performance after another that continued to cement her status as our greatest living actress. Who else, after all, could go from a movie like *Mamma Mia* to a movie like *Doubt* and excel at both roles so significantly? Only the best.

AWARDS WATCH

Meryl received her fifteenth Academy Award nomination, for Best Actress. She won the SAG Award for Female Actor in a Leading Role, and received Golden Globe and BAFTA Award nominations for her performance. She tied with Anne Hathaway for Best Actress at the Critics Choice Awards, and she won Best Actress from the Iowa Film Critics, Kansas City Film Critics, North Texas Film Critics, Phoenix Film Critics, and Washington DC Film Critics. She also shared in a Best Ensemble award at the National Board of Review, and earned a Best Actress award from the Online Film & Television Association.

Doubt earned five Academy Award nominations, four for the actors, and one for Shanley's adapted screenplay. It also received five Golden Globe nominations, three BAFTA Award nominations, and five SAG Award nominations. Viola Davis won Best Supporting Actress awards from the Alliance of Women Film Journalists, Black Reel Awards, Dallas-Fort Worth Critics, Houston Film Critics, and St. Louis Film Critics, as well as a Virtuoso Award from the Santa Barbara International Film Festival. Adams won a Spotlight Award from the Palm Springs International Film Festival, and Shanley earned a WGA Award nomination.

FUN FACTS

Meryl hand knitted the shawl she wears in the film.

Hoffman insisted that Adams be a part of the movie and even threatened to leave the project if she wasn't cast.

Only Hoffman was told if his character was guilty or not. None of the other actors knew.

Oprah Winfrey lobbied for the role of Mrs. Miller, but Shanley refused to even let her read.

Davis earned an Oscar nomination for essentially one scene.

Frances McDormand, Sigourney Weaver, Kathy Bates, Annette Bening, and Anjelica Huston were all considered for Meryl's role.

Tom Hanks, David Hyde Pierce, and John Cusack were considered for the part of Father Flynn.

Shanley offered the role of Sister James to Natalie Portman, but she turned it down.

Shanley's first film as director since 1990's *Joe Versus the Volcano*.

WEEK 44
JULIE & JULIA (2009)

FILM FACTS

DISTRIBUTOR: Columbia Pictures
RELEASE DATE: August 7, 2009

DIRECTOR: Nora Ephron
WRITER: Nora Ephron (based on the books by Julie Powell and Julia Child)
PRODUCERS: Nora Ephron, Laurence Mark, Amy Robinson, Eric Steel
ALSO STARRING: Amy Adams, Stanley Tucci, Chris Messina, Jane Lynch, Mary Lynn Rajskub

REVIEW

Julie & Julia is one of Meryl's most enchanting movies ever, a supremely entertaining love letter to Paris, New York, food, and love. The late, great Nora Ephron wrote and directed the film, her last, with wit and affection, and assembled a terrific group of actors who fit their roles perfectly and who infuse the movie with their own unique charms. *Julie & Julia* opened in August 2009, soon after Meryl's smash hit *Mamma Mia* and her multiple-Oscar-nominated *Doubt*, so one could say that she was at the true height of her career, with her masterful performance as Julia Child giving audiences yet another excuse to fall in love with her all over again.

The film is based on two non-fiction books—*My Life in France*, by Julia Child, and *Julie & Julia*, by Julie Powell—and Ephron could have chosen to make either one into its own separate film. In interviews, however, she stated that from the beginning she was only interested in making a movie that blended the Julia Child story in 1949 Paris with the Julie Powell story in 2002 New York, since the parallels between the two were so similar. Both are about women hitting a crossroads in their lives and trying to find something that fills them with joy and purpose. They are also love stories that feature two doting men who truly love their wives and want to see them succeed. It's also, of course, about the love of food!

The first, notably better, story in the movie details a few years of Julia Child's life in Paris, where she moved with her husband Paul (Stanley Tucci) because of his government job. She considers hat-making lessons to give herself something to do with her free time, but she realizes that food is her true passion, and she decides to become a cook. While in the beginning she struggles keeping up with the other more advanced men in her class, Julia quickly becomes adept at cooking, bringing her own flavors and styles to her recipes, and she collaborates with two women to write the ultimate French cookbook for Americans, one that would change her life forever.

The second story concerns a cubicle worker named Julie Powell (Amy Adams) who feels no sense of purpose in her life as she approaches turning thirty, but an idea pops into her head one day that she should try her hand at blogging. Her goal? 365 days. 524 recipes from Julia's famous cookbook, *Mastering the Art of French Cooking*. As the year goes on, her blog explodes, and she and her husband Eric (Chris Messina) see their lives changing for the better, too. Ephron bounces back and forth between the two storylines every five to ten minutes typically, and often finds the right balance between the two.

Ephron had collaborated with Meryl twice before, on the superb *Silkwood* and the disappointing *Heartburn*, but both of those movies she only wrote—Mike Nichols directed them. *Julie & Julia* marked Meryl's only film with Ephron as director, which makes this being her swan song as a filmmaker particularly poignant. It may be silly to suggest that a writer/director's final movie has to be one of his or her better ones, but after the two unfortunate bombs *Lucky Numbers*, with John Travolta, and *Bewitched*, with Nicole Kidman, it's a relief that Ephron's last movie marked a return to form for the artist, who had achieved success with *Sleepless in Seattle* and *You've Got Mail*, and especially her screenplay for *When Harry Met Sally*. *Julie & Julia* shows everything that makes Ephron wonderful—her attention to detail, her infectious sense of humor, her fantastic way with actors, and her obsession with food.

While Meryl is a revelation in *Julie & Julia*, as she tends to be in about every other film, the movie wouldn't have worked if she had been paired with the wrong actor to play her husband, or if lesser actors had been hired to portray Julie Powell and her leading man in the modern day storyline. Thankfully, Ephron chose the very best for all four of the main roles, and even in some of the small supporting ones, too. Tucci enjoyed a terrific chemistry with Meryl in *The Devil Wears Prada*, but actual screen-time with the two of them together was limited in that movie. In *Julie & Julia*, he shares a multitude of charming scenes with her, some with cute banter, some with surprising sexuality, all showing their great love for one another. He's not the most obvious choice for this part, and it was actually Meryl herself who suggested him. It's a masterstroke of casting that brings an extra special element to the movie. Adams, in her second film with Meryl in less than a year, is her typically likable self as the insecure and sometimes narcissistic blogger, and Messina is always a welcome face in any movie he's in. Also, Jane Lynch is a hoot as Julia's sister, and Mary Lynn Rajskub has some funny lines as Julie's friend Sarah.

Meryl received another Academy Award nomination for this film, and if not for Sandra Bullock's beloved performance in *The Blind Side*, she might have taken home her third Oscar. It seemed like every time she was nominated in the 1990s and 2000s, she came close—*really* close—to winning, but one other dynamite figure (Kate Winslet and Bullock particularly) managed to scoop that statue out from under her. She would finally win two years later for *The Iron Lady*, but her performance in *Julie & Julia* is one of her finest and most charming post-*Adaptation*, yet another example of Meryl playing a real-life figure and transforming her performance into something more than just impersonation.

She looks the part in every way, with that curly brown hair and slightly aged look that makes her appear twenty years older than she did in *Mamma Mia*. Child was six-foot-two, so her shoes, as well as some clever camera angles, make the five-foot-six Meryl look much taller. She's got that famously deep, iconic voice that has been parodied for decades, most memorably by Dan Aykroyd on *Saturday Night Live* (a sketch that appears in the movie), but Meryl manages to tread that fine line between goofy and realistic every time she opens her mouth. Everything about her character and performance ring true. The love she feels for her husband, her desire to have a child and her mixed feelings when she learns her sister Dorothy (Lynch) is pregnant, her adoration of cooking and the excitement she feels as she improves in her craft, and finally her desire for her long-in-the-works cookbook to be published. These moments are all fascinating to watch, and Meryl makes the most of each.

Julie & Julia was the perfect movie for me to watch in this, my forty-forth week in My Year With Meryl Streep. It was borderline creepy, in a good way, to be watching a movie about a woman who's anxious to turn thirty, on the eve of my own thirtieth birthday, and to watch a movie about a woman who decides to blog her way through Julia Child's cookbook one recipe at a time for a year, when I was blogging through Meryl's filmography one movie at a time for a year. I enjoyed *Julie & Julia* even more than when I saw it opening weekend back in 2009, partly because I have a deeper appreciation now of Meryl's artistry, but mostly because it spoke to me more at age thirty than it did at age twenty-five. This is a film about following your dreams and finding yourself and falling in love with great food one delicious meal at a time, and it works.

AWARDS WATCH

Meryl received her sixteenth Academy Award nomination, for Best Actress. She won the Golden Globe for Best Actress in a Motion Picture – Comedy or Musical, tied with Sandra Bullock for Best Actress at the Critics Choice Awards, and won Best Actress at the Satellite Awards. She also earned SAG Award and BAFTA Award nominations for her performance. In addition, she won Best Actress from the Awards Circuit Community, Boston Society of Film Critics, Kansas City Film Critics, New York Film Critics, North Texas Film Critics, Oklahoma Film Critics, Phoenix Film Critics, San Francisco Film Critics, Southeastern Film Critics, and Women Film Critics.

Julie & Julia earned a Golden Globe nomination for Best Motion Picture – Musical or Comedy, as well as Satellite Award nominations for Best Motion Picture – Musical or Comedy, and Adapted Screenplay. Francine Maisler won the Artios award for Best Casting in a Feature Film Comedy, and Ephron received a WGA Award nomination. In addition, the film got a Dorian Award nomination for Campy Film of the Year from the Gay and Lesbian Entertainment Critics.

FUN FACTS

Ephron's final film.

To make Meryl appear taller, countertops were lowered, forced perspective camera angles were used, and Meryl wore extra high heels.

The second Meryl film with "Julia" in the title, following her 1977 debut.

In real life, Paul was ten years older than Julia, while Meryl is eleven years older than Tucci.

Meryl gained fifteen pounds for the role.

"Stop by the Train" by Henry Wolfe is included in the soundtrack. Henry is Meryl's son.

Adams' second film in a row with Meryl, following *Doubt*. Unlike their previous collaboration, they share no screen-time in *Julie & Julia*.

WEEK 45
FANTASTIC MR. FOX (2009)

FILM FACTS

DISTRIBUTOR: 20th Century Fox
RELEASE DATE: November 13, 2009

DIRECTOR: Wes Anderson
WRITERS: Wes Anderson, Noah Baumbach
PRODUCERS: Wes Anderson, Allison Abbate, Jeremy Dawson, Scott Rudin
ALSO STARRING: George Clooney, Jason Schwartzman, Bill Murray, Willem Dafoe, Owen Wilson, Michael Gambon

REVIEW

And now for something truly spectacular: Meryl in animated form! Almost every major Hollywood star has voiced a character in an animated film at one point in his or her career—Tom Hanks in *Toy Story*, Cameron Diaz in *Shrek*, Sandra Bullock in *Minions*—and Meryl is no exception. Voicing characters can be challenging, but most actors would say it's a load of fun because it's just you and the microphone, in your PJs, in a studio, with no make-up on, pure imagination at is peak. Woody Allen is famous for voicing his main character in 1998's *Antz* in a mere five days, and Luke Skywalker himself Mark Hamill has made an entire career post-*Star Wars* doing voice work. Meryl is not an actor who necessarily seems an obvious choice to voice an animated character, but she's done it more than you might think.

During the 1980s, when Meryl primarily acted in lead roles in dramatic feature films, she lent her talents to one other arena—animation. She was the narrator—credited simply as Storyteller—for a series of video shorts based on Beatrix Potter's famous children's stories, starting with *Rabbit Ears: The Tale of Peter Rabbit*. In 1994, she lent her voice to *The Simpsons*, playing Bart Simpsons' girlfriend Jessica Lovejoy, in the seventh episode of the sixth season titled "Bart's Girlfriend." In 1999, she played Aunt Esme Dauterive in the sixth episode of *King of the Hill*'s fourth season, "A Beer Can Named Desire." She voiced Blue Mecha in Steven Spielberg's 2001 feature *A.I. Artificial Intelligence*, and even voiced a character in the silliest title on her entire resume—*Higglety Pigglety Pop! Or There Must Be More to Life*, from 2010. Her first animated feature that she lent her voice to was 2006's *The Ant Bully*, a rare bomb in the animated world that cost an estimated fifty million but grossed only twenty-eight million nationwide. She played the role of Queen and teamed with talent like her *Prairie Home Companion* co-star Lily Tomlin, her *Adaptation* co-star Nicolas Cage, and her *August: Osage County* co-star Julia Roberts, but all those big names didn't do much to pull in audiences or bring credence to the voice-work she had been doing since 1987.

All that changed, though, with Wes Anderson's magnificently entertaining 2009 stop-motion animated feature *Fantastic Mr. Fox*, which teamed Meryl with George Clooney, as well as Anderson regulars Jason Schwartzman, Willem Dafoe, Owen Wilson, and Bill Murray. Nominated for the Academy Award for Best Animated Feature, *Fantastic Mr. Fox* is based on Roald Dahl's beloved 1970 children's novel about a fox who every night steals food from three grotesque and mean-spirited farmers: Walter Boggis, Nathaniel Bunce, and Franklin Bean. The men become fed up with Mr. Fox's shenanigans, so they set out to destroy him, with no idea the fight they're about to face. Clooney voices the title character, and Meryl voices his wife Felicity, mother to little Ash and aunt to Kristofferson. She is a stern but loving character who wants only the best for her family, especially when it comes to her husband's questionable safety.

Cate Blanchett was the first choice for Felicity, but she dropped out for undisclosed reasons, and Meryl took over the character. She proved to be an inspired choice. Her calm, breathy voice is perfect for Felicity, who has that desirable mix of truth-telling and sweetness, of no-nonsense and stability. A quick stare from her can put any other creature in its place, and so, while Felicity doesn't get as much screen-time as Mr. Fox, her character leaves an indelible impression on the viewer. It's unclear how many days Meryl worked on this film—with so much time dedicated to her 2008 and 2009 live-action features, it's likely she completed her work on *Fantastic Mr. Fox*, which she reportedly did in Paris, in a week or two at most—but no matter her limited involvement, her casting was a masterstroke to this production, which offers similarly great voice work from Clooney, Murray, and especially Michael Gambon as the appalling Franklin Bean.

Fantastic Mr. Fox marked Anderson's sixth feature as a director, and the umpteenth movie to be made from Dahl's books. While the 1971 *Willy Wonka and the Chocolate Factory* remains the all-time best (with *The Witches* and *Mathilda* close behind), *Fantastic Mr. Fox* is one of the most entertaining and innovative takes on a Dahl story. The writer remains one of the finest children's storytellers who ever lived, and his books live on well after his death, always inspiring new writers and filmmakers alike. Anderson admitted in the behind-the-scenes documentary on the DVD that Dahl is one of his favorites of all time and that it was a dream come true to translate one of his books into a movie. Live action would've been weird for this story, and the stop-motion, versus traditional and computer animation, was ultimately the perfect choice, because it gives a tangible quality to the characters and a bright, cheery setting that can only be achieved in camera. The book itself is short at ninety-six illustrated pages, so Anderson and his co-writer Noah Baumbach had to expand the story, smartly adding a first act and a third act that give more backstory to the central characters.

Even more is given in the film version to the Felicity character, which thankfully allowed Meryl more to do in the storyline. While she has voiced numerous animated characters in multiple projects, *Fantastic Mr. Fox* remains her best work of animation she's been involved in, and likely ever will. While 2008 was a stellar year for Meryl, with a smash musical success and an awards-friendly drama, 2009 marked an even bigger high for her, because not only did her two live-action features net her award nominations and big box office, but she also lent her voice to a wickedly funny and subversive animated film. While it would be a treat for audiences everywhere if Meryl one day appeared in a live-action movie directed by Anderson, handing her talent over to this fantastic piece of animation is easily the next best thing.

AWARDS WATCH

Meryl was nominated for Best Animated Female from the Alliance of Women Film Journalists, and Best Voice-Over Performance from the Online Film & Television Association.

Fantastic Mr. Fox earned numerous awards and nominations, including two Academy Award nominations, for Best Animated Feature and Best Original Score. It was nominated for Best Animated Feature at the Golden Globe Awards, as well as the BAFTA Awards. It won Best Writing in a Feature Production at the Annie Awards, Best Animated Film at the International Cinephile Society Awards, and Best Animated Motion Picture at the Satellite Awards. The Indiana Film Journalists, Las Vegas Film Critics, Los Angeles Film Critics, New York Film Critics, Oklahoma Film Critics, Toronto Film Critics, and Utah Film Critics awarded *Fantastic Mr. Fox* Best Animated

Feature. It also received a Special Achievement Award for Anderson at the National Board of Review.

FUN FACTS

When Meryl was in London filming *Mamma Mia*, she noticed a fox outside her apartment window. She said she and the fox stared at each other, stone still, for twelve minutes. Amazed by the experience, she used it as inspiration for her performance.

Meryl's character name, Felicity, was named after Dahl's widow.

Anderson had the actors record their dialogue outside of a studio and on location, to add to the naturalness.

The color scheme of the movie almost completely excludes green and blue, as Anderson wanted to give the film an autumnal feel.

The first book Anderson ever owned was *Fantastic Mr. Fox*.

WEEK 46
IT'S COMPLICATED (2009)

FILM FACTS

DISTRIBUTOR: Universal Pictures
RELEASE DATE: December 25, 2009

DIRECTOR: Nancy Meyers
WRITER: Nancy Meyers
PRODUCERS: Nancy Meyers, Scott Rudin
ALSO STARRING: Steve Martin, Alec Baldwin, John Krasinski, Lake Bell, Hunter Parrish, Zoe Kazan

REVIEW

As the first decade of the twenty-first century drew to a close, Meryl delivered yet another one of her sensational achievements: her portrayal of Julia Child in Nora Ephron's *Julie & Julia*. For this performance, she went on to win the Golden Globe award and receive her sixteenth Academy Award nomination. But Meryl, a borderline workaholic at this point, had one more film to finish the decade with, one that opened on Christmas Day: *It's Complicated*, which, like *Julie & Julia*, was written and directed by a woman—Nancy Meyers—and featured Meryl in the role of a talented chef.

Unlike *Julie & Julia*, *It's Complicated* has a lazier, sitcom-y feel to it that slows the film down at points and doesn't leave a lot to think about when the end credits start to roll. But like in Meyers' previous fluffy entertainments *Something's Gotta Give* and *The Holiday*, the enormously talented actors involved elevate the material considerably.

Meyers wrote the part of Jane Adler for Meryl specifically and said in the DVD commentary that she pictured Meryl speaking her words all throughout the process of writing the screenplay. Meyers had worked with such Oscar-winning heavyweights as Diane Keaton and Kate Winslet in her previous films, so it must have seemed only natural to pursue the most acclaimed actress of all for her next project. One of the few female writer-directors in Hollywood, Meyers was able to breathe a sigh of relief when Meryl responded to the material immediately and signed on to the project. It doesn't hurt that despite Jane being more like Meryl than most of her other screen creations, it's a juicy role that's featured in almost every scene of the movie and gives her lots to do in both comedy and drama. It also gave her the opportunity to act alongside funny men Alec Baldwin and Steve Martin for the first time.

Jane is a gifted baker and cook who has her own flourishing business in downtown Santa Barbara, but besides her job, not a lot is going well in her life. She is still sad about her divorce from her ex-husband Jake (Baldwin), who left her ten years ago for a much younger woman. Her youngest child has just moved out of her house, leaving her with an empty nest. And when she's in New York for her son's graduation, she gets drunk and has sex with Jake. She tries to put the incident behind her, but Jake keeps coming back for more, and despite her being aware that the affair is a bad idea, she keeps seeing him anyway. In the meantime, someone else pops up in her life: Adam (Martin), her architect who is helping her design a new wing of her home. She doesn't think much of him at first, but when Jake stands her up, she invites Adam to a party, where they both smoke marijuana and have the most fun either has had in ages. Will Jane choose Jake or Adam in the end? And better yet, do we care?

It's Complicated is an entertaining, breezy movie that is nothing special, and certainly not one of the films that will be heavily featured in any Meryl highlights reel. But it goes down easily, like vanilla ice cream, delicious while you're tasting it, not much to think about when it's over. The film is slowly paced, never in a rush, never trying to get to the next big joke. It takes its time and allows for the three central characters to be fleshed out, particularly Jane.

The most joy in watching *It's Complicated* comes from seeing Meryl interact with Baldwin and Martin, two funny actors who are also deft at drama, and who are perfectly matched for her in this film. Baldwin, who hadn't been given a role this good since 2003's *The Cooler*, has a magnetic chemistry with Meryl, especially in their quieter scenes. Martin, who hadn't had a decent movie since 2001's underrated black comedy *Novocaine*, shows a sweetness in the nerdy Adam character that he rarely displays in the movies. Too often relegated to flashy comedic characters in mediocrity like *Cheaper by the Dozen*, Martin has been serious in films like *Shopgirl* and *Grand Canyon*, and to some extent the brilliant *Planes, Trains, and Automobiles*, and his sensitive side thankfully gets played up in *It's Complicated*. His chemistry with Meryl is different than Baldwin's, more sincere and grounded. One of the best scenes in the movie has Meryl and Martin baking a fresh batch of chocolate croissants, and the romance developing between the two feels natural and earned.

The character of Jane is one of Meryl's least challenging roles, which, like Julia in *Defending Your Life*, mostly consists of traits of Meryl herself, as opposed to a creation like Julia Child that had to be molded from the outside in. She gets to show different shades all throughout the movie, the most fun one being a long stretch of time when she's high off marijuana. She's as loose in this sequence as she's ever been in a movie, and the big comedic scenes in *It's Complicated* show that Meryl is always up for something silly. As forced as the situations can sometimes be—the scene involving iChat stretches credibility a bit too far—Meryl sells them the best she can.

She also has solid dramatic moments throughout, like when she gets stood up by her ex-husband and quietly turns out all the lights in her home, and a scene toward the end when a look of unexpected rejection says so much with so little. She makes the viewer sympathize with her, despite the fact that she's cheating with a married man. And she always makes the character grounded in reality, even when she's living in a large dream-like house not even Meryl herself could probably afford, even when she's laughing hysterically as she takes another hit of weed, even when writer-director Meyers is cramming illogical plot developments and the occasional contrived joke down our throats. Even when the movie itself isn't wholly successful, Meryl, unbelievably, makes it work—at least to a certain extent.

Meryl received a Golden Globe nomination for her role in *It's Complicated*, but 2009 was really the year of *Julie & Julia* for her, and by the end of awards season, *It's Complicated* had mostly been forgotten. It was a success at the box office, making 112 million in the United States and over 200 million worldwide, showing that Meryl, sixty years old at the time of the film's release, was a box office draw unlike any actor her age, male or female. She had impressed in movie after movie, but after *It's Complicated*, Meryl was ready to take on a role that would be one of her most daring yet, and certainly her most challenging since any dramatic film she'd made since *The Bridges of Madison County*. Finally, after nearly three decades of superior work with endless nominations and too few wins to show for them, Meryl was about to pick up her third Academy Award.

AWARDS WATCH

Meryl earned a Golden Globe nomination for Best Actress in a Motion Picture – Comedy or Musical. She also won the Audience Award for Best International Actress at the Irish Film and Television Awards, and shared in the Best Ensemble award from the National Board of Review.

It's Complicated received Golden Globe nominations for Best Motion Picture – Musical or Comedy and Best Screenplay. Also, the film earned a Best Motion Picture – Comedy or Musical nomination at the Satellite Awards, and Baldwin got a BAFTA Award nomination for Best Supporting Actor.

FUN FACTS

Meryl asked her alma mater, Vassar College, if they could film the college graduation scene on their campus. They refused, even though Meryl serves on their Board of Trustees and two of her children have attended there.

In the scene where Jane answers a phone call from her daughter Lauren, she is surprised when Jake kisses her, causing her to say, "You're still on the phone" instead of "You're still on the plane." This was a genuine reaction from Meryl, who did not expect Baldwin to kiss her in that moment. Fortunately she kept the scene going, and the mistake was left in the movie.

The film's depiction of recreational marijuana smoking in an innocent manner without consequences is the reason for its R rating.

A body double was used for Baldwin's nude scene.

Martin and Baldwin are to date tied for most times hosting *Saturday Night Live*, with fourteen times each. They also co-hosted the 2010 Academy Awards, where Meryl was nominated for *Julie & Julia*.

All four of Meyers' films made in the 2000s featured actresses in the leading role who had won or would go on to win Best Actress Academy Awards. Helen Hunt, from *What Women Want*, won for *As Good As It Gets*; Diane Keaton, from *Something's Gotta Give*, won for *Annie Hall*; Kate Winslet, from *The Holiday*, won for *The Reader*; and Meryl won for *Sophie's Choice* and *The Iron Lady*.

WEEK 47
THE IRON LADY (2011)

FILM FACTS

DISTRIBUTOR: The Weinstein Company
RELEASE DATE: December 30, 2011

DIRECTOR: Phyllida Lloyd
WRITER: Abi Morgan
PRODUCER: Damian Jones
ALSO STARRING: Jim Broadbent, Olivia Colman, Alexandra Roach, Harry Lloyd, Anthony Head, Iain Glen

REVIEW

We have arrived at one of the more controversial films on Meryl's resume, both in how it depicts the former Prime Minister Margaret Thatcher in her later life and in how Meryl finally won her third Academy Award, beating out the supposed favorite, Viola Davis. *The Iron Lady*, written by Abi Morgan and directed by Phyllida Lloyd, is a strangely unaffecting movie that goes by far too slowly and features a weird hodgepodge of narratives that never mix together well. The greatest disappointment of the movie is that it could have been great, given that Meryl is sensational in it, playing Thatcher as ambitious in her early days, strong and willing to make tough decisions in her Prime Minister days, and losing the light in her later stage of dementia. Everything about Meryl's performance is flawless and screams master class. Therefore, it's a shame that little in the film measures up to her.

The blame has to go to Morgan's screenplay and Lloyd's direction, which never finds a compelling point of view into who Thatcher really was. Abi seemed to think watching scene after scene of the elderly Thatcher getting false glimpses of her husband and marveling at the skyrocketing prices of milk would be fascinating for the viewer, but they're not. If the film had merely begun and ended with the wraparound story of Thatcher as old, there might have been a point to be made about the pursuit of power and its consequences, but the film keeps cutting back to her in this stage, time and time again, to the point where any point that could have been made becomes lost. Lloyd, who previously directed Meryl in the musical extravaganza *Mamma Mia*, a film about as far removed from *The Iron Lady* as you can get, cast the movie well—*Buffy the Vampire Slayer*'s Anthony Head is particularly good as Geoffrey Howe—and she brought a polished look to the proceedings. Clearly, though, she didn't have a handle on the themes of the movie either, because she allowed the odd shifts of narratives to play out the way they do.

The same way that Steven Spielberg's *Lincoln* effectively examines not Abraham Lincoln's entire life, but a small, important nugget of it, *The Iron Lady* could have been a tense, absorbing look into a short period of time in

Thatcher's reign as Prime Minister, maybe focusing on a specific issue she contended with that brought great controversy onto her. Instead, there's too much: we get glimpses of Thatcher as a young woman starting out in her career (Alexander Roach, uncanny as a younger Meryl), and Thatcher as the Prime Minister, and Thatcher as the old lady who's slowly going mad. The film also tries to make us care about the love Thatcher shared with her husband, Denis (an inappropriately wily Jim Broadbent in the older years and a more restrained Harry Lloyd in the younger ones). But since so little of the movie focuses on the older Denis when he's actually alive, the emotional resonance of this relationship gets lost in the process. There's so much going on, with rarely a scene that's allowed to play out long enough to get us invested, that at a certain point it feels like an editor could've taken all of the scenes in the movie, thrown them in a blender, and come out with something that more and less represents the film as it stands now.

All of these story and editing problems fortunately don't weaken Meryl's stellar performance, which represents probably her best dramatic work since *The Bridges of Madison County*. Fairly short at one hour and forty-five minutes—many famous screen biopics like *Gandhi* and *Nixon* have weighed in at over three hours—*The Iron Lady* should have given Meryl a lot more to work with, but she does her best with what's given to her. She is intimidating, clever, and funny in her many scenes as Thatcher in her Prime Minister years, with true-to-life wardrobes, an impeccable accent, and subtle, masterful make-up and hair that won Oscars for Mark Coulier, and J. Roy Helland, the latter figure having worked with Meryl throughout her entire career. Her makeup is even more convincing when she's older, with cleverly hidden prosthetics and Meryl appearing believably like an old woman, and despite these scenes not working as well as they should, Meryl is brilliant at capturing the downfall of this once powerful figure.

Even though just catching a glimpse of Meryl as Thatcher prompted everyone to assume Meryl would be nominated for another Academy Award, her likelihood of actually winning seemed uncertain leading up to the big night in 2012. While she won the Golden Globe, Viola Davis had been picking up steam in recent weeks, winning the important SAG Award for her terrific performance in *The Help*. The only African American actress to have won a leading role Oscar was Halle Berry for *Monster's Ball*, and it seemed possible that Davis would become the second. But in the end, the Academy decided that Meryl's work in *The Iron Lady*, despite the film's shortcomings, was worthy of the big award. It had been twenty-nine years since she'd won her last Oscar for *Sophie's Choice*, after all, and she had lost a whopping twelve times since. She had come close with *Doubt*, and semi-close with *Julie & Julia*. It was time.

The biggest tragedy of her winning is that in the far-off future, people may turn to *The Iron Lady* before they look at much better dramas she appeared in, like *A Cry in the Dark*, *The Bridges of Madison County*, and *Marvin's Room*, the latter of which she wasn't even nominated for. People might think that because Meryl won for this specific performance, it might also be the better movie. While Meryl is amazing in *The Iron Lady*, it's arguably one of her weakest movies, and it's sad, given the great opportunity of having Meryl play the powerful and polarizing figure of Margaret Thatcher, that the filmmakers couldn't have produced a more entertaining and involving film.

AWARDS WATCH

Meryl won her third Academy Award, for Best Actress. She also won the Golden Globe for Best Actress in a Motion Picture – Drama, as well as the BAFTA Award for Best Leading Actress. She was nominated for a SAG Award, Critics Choice Award, and a Satellite Award, and she won Best Actress awards from the Australian Film Institute, Denver Film Critics, Gay and Lesbian Entertainment Critics, London Critics, New York Film Critics, and Southeastern Film Critics. She also won Best Actress at the Rembrandt Awards and the Richard Attenborough Film Awards.

The Iron Lady also won the Academy Award, as well as the BAFTA Award, for Best Achievement in Makeup. The film received BAFTA Award nominations for Best Original Screenplay and Best Supporting Actor, for Broadbent. In addition, Lloyd was nominated for the Audience Award at the European Film Awards, Colman won British Actress of the Year from the London Critics, and Morgan won Best Woman Storyteller from the Women Film Critics.

FUN FACTS

Meryl finally won her first Oscar in nearly thirty years.

Meryl prepared for her role by spending months watching broadcasts of Thatcher, to learn her speech and mannerisms. She also spoke with people who knew her, including former Labour Party leader Neil Kinnock, and sat through a session at the House of Commons in January 2011.

Meryl never met Thatcher in real life, but she did attend one of her lectures in 2001 at Northwestern University.

Meryl donated her salary for the film to the Women's History Museum.

In a rare feat, *The Iron Lady* was nominated for two Oscars, and won both.

WEEK 48
HOPE SPRINGS (2012)

FILM FACTS

DISTRIBUTOR: Columbia Pictures
RELEASE DATE: August 8, 2012

DIRECTOR: David Frankel
WRITER: Vanessa Taylor
PRODUCERS: Todd Black, Guymon Casady
ALSO STARRING: Tommy Lee Jones, Steve Carell, Jean Smart, Elizabeth Shue, Becky Ann Baker, Mimi Rogers

REVIEW

After winning her third Academy Award, Meryl could have taken a much deserved break, but not only did she start shooting *August: Osage County* soon after her big win, she already had another movie due for release later that summer—the David Frankel comedy-drama *Hope Springs*. Unlike *The Iron Lady*, which was the kind of prestige picture made specifically to win awards, *Hope Springs* is a quiet, sometimes funny, often melancholy movie that works more as a rainy day kind of entertainment. Meryl does a fine job, playing a vulnerable, unsatisfied housewife named Kay, but it's actually Tommy Lee Jones, who plays her repressed husband Arnold, who transforms his typical tough guy persona to create an emotionally resonant character.

Vanessa Taylor's screenplay was originally titled *Great Hope Springs* and was for some time on the Black List, the list of most loved unproduced screenplays circulating around Hollywood. It was Meryl's enthusiasm over the project that got it off the ground, and she turned to her *The Devil Wears Prada* helmer Frankel to take the directing reigns. He says in the DVD audio commentary that when Meryl boards a movie—*any* movie—a director essentially has his pick of actors he wants for the other roles. Would Carell have taken the part of the therapist Doctor Feld if not for the opportunity to perform with two acting legends? Probably not. Would Elizabeth Shue, who back in 1996 was nominated for Best Actress at the Oscars alongside Meryl, have taken a brief cameo as a no-name *waitress*? Meryl is so respected that she attracts fantastic actors to her projects, no matter the role's size or stature, and together Frankel and Meryl decided on Jones for the pivotal role of her husband, Arnold.

It's easy to see why Meryl wanted to be in *Hope Springs*. How often do major movies get made, let alone movies released in the summer among superhero blockbusters, that are about two people over age sixty trying to put the spark back into their relationship? Very few, and even fewer that are made with wit and intelligence. The story is simple: Kay (Meryl) has been married to Arnold (Jones) for thirty-one years, but any emotion felt between the two has been lost. They sleep in separate bedrooms, they don't talk about anything, they don't even touch each other anymore. She realizes the marriage is doomed if she doesn't do something to save it, so she drags Arnold to Maine to spend a week in intensive counseling with the renowned Doctor Feld (Carell). By opening up to the therapist and each other, they find what's lacking, and what needs to be fixed, before one of them might decide it's too late.

Hope Springs is not the most visually arresting movie—much of it takes place in one drab room with three people just talking to each other—but the performances are so great and the dialogue is so truthful that even when the movie feels like a series of one-act plays, it works. These scenes crackle with a perfectly timed rhythm that make them pure joy, to the point that some of them seem too short, even at eight to ten minutes. Meryl and Jones have a tremendous chemistry that makes them feel like a real couple, both when they're in a bad place, and when they finally reach a better one.

What works especially well is screenwriter Taylor's insistence that Kay and Arnold not have an easy road toward an authentic reconciliation; until the last few minutes, it's not clear if the two will be able to work through their problems. This element gives the film a welcome level of unpredictability, even though in our hearts we know they'll find love again. While Frankel lays it on too thick at times with some ill-timed songs—Annie Lennox's saccharine "Why" toward the end of the movie is a prime example—and despite the happy ending being a little too abrupt, *Hope Springs* is definitely worthwhile viewing.

The performances are all solid. Carell has the most thankless role as Doctor Feld, simply because he plays a character with no backstory or depth of any kind (although the DVD includes a great deleted scene that shows in explicit detail his marital woes). This is a movie about Kay and Arnold, and to have gone into the history of Feld would have been inappropriate, but Carell is a welcome dramatic presence in a film that plays up his stone-faced strengths.

Jones, the Oscar winner for the smart-talking Samuel in *The Fugitive* and Oscar nominee for the similarly cynical Thaddeus Stevens in *Lincoln*, is wonderfully subdued as Arnold. He's physically perfect casting for this role, a man who's emotionally closed off from his wife and scared to reignite their intimacy, but it's his deeply felt performance that makes this film worth watching. Over the years, Jones has had the tendency to go over-the-top in his movies (think *Natural Born Killers* and *Batman Forever*) and this quieter guy, who resembles more his character from *No Country for Old Men*, is Jones at his best, looking inward and trying his best to come out of his shell. Jones is a pleasure to watch in *Hope Springs*, and his performance should have received more accolades.

Meryl is appropriately dowdy as Kay, with a bland blonde hairdo and thick black glasses that cover most of her face, and unlike many of her previous characters, Kay is someone who doesn't often speak her mind—it takes every ounce of her courage just to ask her husband to come with her to the therapy sessions. Many might think this performance was a step down after her bravura, Oscar-winning work in *The Iron Lady*, but the magic of Meryl is that she refuses to be predictable in her choice of characters and that she's unafraid to take on someone who might not necessarily be the most outspoken. After all, she followed up her frumpy therapist character in *Prime* with her Queen of Evil in *The Devil Wears Prada*; she followed up her dancing and singing in *Mamma Mia* with her quietly damaged nun in *Doubt*.

To look at *The Iron Lady* and *Hope Springs* back to back is to see an actress completely in command of her craft, and not afraid to show her own vanity. She's not expected to look like a bombshell in *Hope Springs*, and her mousy appearance only helps in making Meryl the person disappear into this character that surely millions of women can relate to. So much of her brilliance in this performance comes from moments when she doesn't even open her mouth but instead just sits and thinks. Meryl doesn't have to go big to be great; at this stage in her career, just watching her *be* is more than enough. *Hope Springs* is not a great movie, but it's an endearing one, and it features two of our finest actors in top form.

AWARDS WATCH

Meryl earned a Golden Globe nomination for Best Actress in a Motion Picture – Comedy or Musical. She was also nominated for a Jupiter Award for Best International Actress, as well as a People's Choice Award for Favorite Dramatic Movie Actress. She won the People's Choice Award for Favorite Movie Icon.

Hope Springs also won the BMI Award for Best Film Music, as well as a Jupiter Award for Best International Actor, for Jones.

FUN FACTS

Jeff Bridges turned down Jones' role.

When the project was first announced in 2010, Meryl's longtime collaborator Mike Nichols was attached as director.

The late James Gandolfini was considered for Jones' role, and the late Philip Seymour Hoffman was considered for Carell's role.

Dr. Feld tells Kay a metaphor of fixing a deviated septum. Meryl has a deviated septum in real life.

WEEK 49
AUGUST: OSAGE COUNTY (2013)

FILM FACTS

DISTRIBUTOR: The Weinstein Company
RELEASE DATE: December 27, 2013

DIRECTOR: John Wells
WRITER: Tracy Letts (based on his play)
PRODUCERS: George Clooney, Jean Doumanian, Grant Heslov, Steve Traxler
ALSO STARRING: Julia Roberts, Ewan McGregor, Chris Cooper, Margo Martindale, Julianne Nicholson, Juliette Lewis, Abigail Breslin, Benedict Cumberbatch, Dermot Mulroney, Sam Shepard, Misty Upham

REVIEW

In the first scene of *August: Osage County*, Meryl appears at the bottom of a staircase, confused, pale, her hair stripped down to just a few short strands of gray. She looks as awful in this scene as she ever has on-screen, and immediately, just two minutes in, we know this film is going to feature Meryl in a *very* dramatic performance. If *Death*

Becomes Her features Meryl's most over-the-top performance in a comedy, *August: Osage County* offers probably her most over-the-top turn in a drama. Some of her moments portraying the pill-popping, cancer-riddled, foul-mouthed Violet Weston—the matriarch of a large messed-up family—are mesmerizing, and then there are other moments where she goes arguably too big with her vindictive yelling. She's always entertaining, but there are shades of her trying too hard in *August: Osage County*, a mediocre movie that unfortunately doesn't add up to much.

The film is based on the Tony-award-winning, Pulitzer-Prize-winning play by Tony Letts. After it premiered in Chicago in 2007, the play went on to enjoy a long Broadway run that lasted 648 performances, as well as a run on the London stage. Reviews of the play were mostly enthusiastic, while reviews of the film were much more mixed. Sometimes plays have seamless transitions to the big screen—Mike Nichols' *Who's Afraid of Virginia Woolf*, for example—while others struggle to find the same emotional power on the big screen, like the dull *Plenty*, also starring Meryl. *August: Osage County* ran a whopping three-and-a-half hours on the stage, and by truncating its runtime to barely two hours for the movie, Letts, who also wrote the screenplay, had to lose strong character moments that made the play so engaging for audiences. While a few powerful moments remain in the film, there are so many characters to keep track of and so much angst and extreme hate that never seems truly earned that after awhile, the film feels more contrived than it should. Also, director John Wells, most known as a TV producer, and who had only directed one other movie—2010's *The Company Men*—before this one, doesn't give the film any discernable visual style.

What helps this flawed film the most is the astonishing ensemble cast, one of the most impressive ever assembled for a Meryl movie. Julia Roberts is the other big star in the film, but also on board are Ewan McGregor, Sam Shepard, Dermot Mulroney, Julianne Nicholson, Benedict Cumberbatch, Juliette Lewis, Abigail Breslin, and the late Misty Upham, as well as Meryl's *Adaptation* co-star Chris Cooper and her ...*First Do No Harm* co-star Margo Martindale. Any three of those actors headlining a movie would be something worth seeing, so to have them all in this production makes this mixed bag of a movie worth watching at least once.

Everyone does a fine job, but the three most notable supporting performances from this group come from Nicholson, Cooper, and Roberts. Nicholson gives probably the quietest performance in the movie, and she has a terrific moment at the end when she learns a horrific truth about the man she loves. Cooper has the most honest scene, when after endless hatred has been spewed from one character to another, he confronts his wife (Martindale) and demands that she show more respect to their son (Cumberbatch). For a few years, Roberts had a string of bad performances in flop movies, starting with *Duplicity* and ending with *Mirror Mirror*, and thankfully the role of Barbara gave Roberts her meatiest role since Anna in Mike Nichols' *Closer*. She is in many ways the heart of the film, and she has some nice, authentic moments along the way.

And then there's Meryl, who initially didn't want to play the role of Violet. In interviews she stated that playing this character wasn't exactly something she yearned for, particularly given Violet's non-stop nasty attitude. She was ultimately persuaded, though, and she commits to this character's vitriolic attitude with no restraint whatsoever. While the film is an ensemble piece, Meryl is in lots of the movie, with a moving moment when she gets out of a car and runs through a field, a startling scene outside in the cold where she talks about her late husband, a sad conclusion where she dances to a song and realizes none of her daughters plan to stay, and two memorably whacko dinner table scenes that bring out the craziness in everyone. A moment late in the film is most remembered for the ridiculous line, "Eat the fish, bitch!" that Barbara screams at Violet, but it's also a well-constructed scene of growing suspense through fast-cutting.

The dinner scene with the entire group, though, is the true centerpiece of the narrative. It is here that all the characters come together and share their feelings and pains and morbid thoughts. Violet sits at one end of the table, barking at almost everyone nearby in the rudest ways imaginable: calling one of her daughters ugly, and yelling at her sister's husband, "Blow it out your ass!" As hard as some of what she says here is to take, it's important to remember that the character is in immense physical pain from her cancer and is reeling from the loss of her husband; she's a mean-spirited person to begin with so to add in these two factors bring out the worst in her.

Meryl could have played this scene with a bit more subtlety, though. Sometimes she goes so big it feels like she's projecting on a stage to reach everyone in a large audience. However, her commanding presence among all of these great actors is felt from beginning to end, and she does her best to make some of the more hollow lines of dialogue ring true. There are some inconsistencies to be found in her character's anger—while she calls out her granddaughter (Breslin) for saying something demeaning to her mother, Barbara later screams atrocities at Violet, and yet Violet thinks nothing of it—but overall she is so steeped in madness that eventually anything crazy she does seems warranted. It would be hard for any actress to make a character like this three-dimensional, but Meryl does her best to give Violet sympathetic qualities, and not just turn her into a monstrous matriarchal caricature.

August: Osage County premiered at the Toronto Film Festival, was released in limited release in late December, and then expanded nationwide in early January—obviously this was a movie that the studio heads assumed had Academy Awards written all over it. Unfortunately, the film only received two Oscar nominations: one for Roberts, in Supporting Actress, and one for Meryl, in Lead Actress. While the film didn't please audiences and critics as much as many might have expected, *August: Osage County* offered Meryl yet another fascinating, complex character to play in a performance that is constantly riveting, sometimes flawed, endlessly entertaining, a bit screechy at times, never boring—and always full of surprises.

AWARDS WATCH

Meryl received her eighteenth Academy Award nomination, for Best Actress. She also earned Golden Globe, Critic's Choice, Satellite, and SAG Award nominations for her performance. In addition, she won the Capri Actress Award, and shared in the Outstanding Ensemble nomination at the SAG Awards.

Roberts received Academy Award, Golden Globe, Critic's Choice, Satellite, and BAFTA Award nominations for her performance. She won Supporting Actress of the Year at the Hollywood Film Festival, the Spotlight Award at the Palm Springs International Film Festival, and Best Performance in a Feature Film at the Prism Awards. *August: Osage County* also won the Capri Movie of the Year Award, as well as Not-So-Obviously-Worst-Film from the Oklahoma Film Critics. In addition, Letts got a WGA nomination for his adapted screenplay.

FUN FACTS

Most of the cast members stayed at the same hotel property for the duration of the shoot, which allowed them to rehearse scenes at night before the following day's filming. Only Cumberbatch reportedly stayed someplace else.

Letts wanted the original stage cast to reprise their roles in the film, but none of them did. He also objected to

British actors (McGregor, Cumberbatch) appearing in the movie.

Breslin auditioned for her role with a 103 degree fever.

Chloe Grace Moretz auditioned for Breslin's role.

Jim Carrey was considered for Mulroney's role.

Producer Harvey Weinstein wanted Judi Dench for Violet and Nicole Kidman for Barbara, but Letts voted against the idea.

WEEK 50
THE GIVER (2014)

FILM FACTS

DISTRIBUTOR: The Weinstein Company
RELEASE DATE: August 15, 2014

DIRECTOR: Phillip Noyce
WRITERS: Michael Mitnick, Robert B. Weide (based on the novel by Lois Lowry)
PRODUCERS: Jeff Bridges, Neil Koenigsberg, Nikki Silver
ALSO STARRING: Jeff Bridges, Brenton Thwaites, Odeya Rush, Alexander Skarsgard, Katie Holmes, Cameron Monaghan, Taylor Swift

REVIEW

As Meryl continues to rack up awards and accolades, winning her third Academy Award for *The Iron Lady* and being nominated again for *August: Osage County*, one might assume she would stick to appearing in movies as the lead, and *only* the lead; after all, most people think of Meryl as a leading lady and not a supporting one. Despite winning the Supporting Actress Oscar for *Kramer vs. Kramer* back in 1980, Meryl often plays the main character in her films. Especially after the weirdly anticlimactic year of 2007, which brought audiences three underwhelming dramas with Meryl in lame supporting roles, it seemed likely that she would stick to lead characters. And she did—*Mamma Mia*, *Julie & Julia*, *The Iron Lady*. All successful films, many of them highly acclaimed awards contenders.

And yet, Meryl is anything but predictable, which she proved yet again in 2014, when she gave us supporting turns in not one, not two, but *three* new movies, just like in 2007. She plays a cameo role in Tommy Lee Jones' *The Homesman*, as well as the Witch in Rob Marshall's musical epic *Into the Woods*. First up in the year was this adaptation of Lois Lowry's beloved 1993 novel, which features Jeff Bridges in the title role, cute-as-a-button Brenton Thwaites as the main character Jonas, and Meryl in an icy turn as the Chief Elder, who runs a utopian community that has taken pain and anger away from its inhabitants and in turn ripped everyone of their emotions. At a heavily attended youth ceremony, one eerily similar to the one that opens the similarly themed *Divergent*, Jonas is picked to be the Receiver of Memory, a person who spends time with the Giver to receive past memories. When Jonas learns about what people's lives were like before the society became so bland—and black-and-white—he starts to turn against the system.

Bridges had been trying to make this novel into a movie for twenty years. In 1994 he famously attempted to get a movie made that featured his father Lloyd Bridges in the title role, and despite that failure, his name had been tied to the project ever since. It seemed like it would never get off the ground, but then came the popularity of young adult adaptations—everything from *Twilight* to *The Hunger Games* to the aforementioned *Divergent*. When studio executives finally saw the potential they had with *The Giver*'s story, the project was green-lit, although with some required changes: Jonas's age was bumped up from eleven to sixteen, there would be more action than the book, and the role of Chief Elder would be significantly beefed up for the adaptation (at least the crucial black-and-white element of the novel carried over to the screen). Lowry herself was dumbfounded when Meryl signed on to play a part that had very little time and weight in the book, and only later learned that the role had been expanded for the movie. Good for all involved, given that Meryl's chilling performance is one of the few memorable elements of a mostly dull and uninvolving production.

If Bridges had gotten the chance to direct his adaptation in the '90s, the result probably would have been more pure and faithful to Lowry's book. Unfortunately, the 2014 version was made after the young adult revolution, so too much in it, from the ceremony scene, to the high-tech action, to the unnecessary teen romance, feel familiar and false; it's especially sad given that the book came out more than a decade before any of the others before mentioned. For those who aren't familiar with Lowry's novel, this movie will feel very been-there-done-that, which is a shame. But even if one hadn't seen the other young adult adaptations, this film feels pedestrian all the way through, with a lack of energy throughout, an anticlimactic ending, and two weird casting choices that are distracting. Katie Holmes plays Jonas's mother, who is so much of a stiff, endlessly saying things like "Precision of language," that the role brings her short period of Scientology worship to mind. Also, Taylor Swift pops up for a couple of insignificant scenes that add no emotion or depth to the story, and she looks so unlike herself that it begs the question of why she is even a part of this.

On the positive side, most of the other actors do a fine job, especially Bridges in the title role. It took so long for the movie to be made that he became old enough to take the part he had originally envisioned for his father, and he is quietly riveting as the Giver, with his scarred psyche and husky voice. Thwaites, who broke out in 2014 with roles in *The Signal* and *Maleficent*, is likable as Jonas, with a boyish face that makes the character appear even younger than he is, and Cameron Monaghan, so great on *Shameless*, has a couple of exciting scenes with Thwaites, as the best friend who turns on him.

Meryl does what she can as Chief Elder, starting with giving her long, gray hair that is one of her most unflattering looks in all her decades of moviemaking. However, it must be noted that this is her most insignificant role in a movie since she played Corrine Whitman in 2007's *Rendition*. In at least a third of the movie she appears as a hologram, and in another third she spends her time behind a giant throne, looking down on the others as if she's some kind of God.

When asked in interviews why she agreed to be in the movie, Meryl said she likes to play boss—she is the mother of four kids, after all—and that throughout her entire career she had always wanted to work with Bridges. He had been in talks for the Tommy Lee Jones role in *Hope Springs* a few years back, and so she latched onto the opportunity to work with one of the greats; it's their few select scenes together that give the film the most tension. When she whispers to the Giver about an unfortunate incident that happened to his former Receiver of Memory, there's an immediate sense of history between them, and when she completes a hologram message to him later in the narrative and says, "He's lying," the deception felt in her character cuts deeply.

She has a little bit here and there throughout the rest of the film, but it's her last scene, when she explains to the Giver how important it is not to revert back to the way the world used to be, that is Meryl's best in the film, one that finally shows the character's vulnerability, and her strict desire for no more change. While the film only works halfheartedly, Meryl does what she can with this underutilized villainous role, similar to one the equally brilliant Kate Winslet downsized her talent for in *Divergent*. Thankfully, Meryl would return as another, more complex villain in a much better movie four months following *The Giver*'s release.

AWARDS WATCH

Meryl did not receive any awards or nominations for her performance, but the film won the Truly Moving Picture Award at the Heartland Film Festival and was nominated for Favorite Dramatic Movie at the People's

Choice Awards. In addition, the Denver Film Critics nominated "Ordinary Human" as Best Original Song.

FUN FACTS

Meryl and Bridges' first film together.

Meryl shot some of her scenes in England while she was filming *Into the Woods*.

For many years, Bridges wanted to direct a version of the movie with his father Lloyd playing the Giver. To date, Bridges has never directed a movie.

Holmes played Thwaites' mother, even though she is only ten years his senior.

WEEK 51
THE HOMESMAN (2014)

FILM FACTS

DISTRIBUTOR: Roadside Attractions
RELEASE DATE: November 14, 2014

DIRECTOR: Tommy Lee Jones
WRITERS: Tommy Lee Jones, Kieran Fitzgerald, Wesley A. Oliver
(based on the novel by Glendon Swarthout)
PRODUCERS: Luc Besson, Peter Brant, Brian Kennedy
ALSO STARRING: Tommy Lee Jones, Hilary Swank, Grace Gummer, Sonja Richter, Mirando Otto, William Fichtner, John Lithgow, Tim Blake Nelson, Jesse Plemons, James Spader, Hailee Steinfeld

REVIEW

Throughout her long career, Meryl has bounced around in different genres, starred as the main character in some films and appeared in smaller parts in others, and given audiences something unique and surprising each time out. She has rarely, however, made an appearance in a movie that felt like anything other than a favor to the film's director. There have been films that she appeared in mostly due to the director's persistence—Wes Craven had to write her a heartfelt letter before she changed her mind and signed on to *Music of the Heart*—and there have been films of questionable merit that she has showed up in—the Farrelly Brothers' *Stuck on You* and an awful and stiff 1990 television monstrosity called *The Earth Day Special*, in which she played the character of Concerned Citizen. But not until Tommy Lee Jones' gorgeous looking but dramatically inert 2014 western *The Homesman* has Meryl been given such a tiny, thankless role. Appearing in no more than five minutes at the end of the movie, she does what she can with an underwritten part that gives her almost nothing to do.

When it premiered at the Cannes Film Festival, *The Homesman* looked prime to be a major year-end awards contender. Jones had before directed two television movies and one theatrical feature film—the acclaimed *The Three Burials of Melquiades Estrada*, also a western—and in a career that included terrific performances in films like *Coal Miner's Daughter* and *In the Valley of Elah*, as well as an Oscar-winning turn in *The Fugitive*, Jones looked like he might have finally done what Kevin Costner did with *Dances With Wolves*: excelled as both actor and director in a handsomely made western. The film offers a fantastic leading female role in Mary Bee Cuddy, a part which two-time Oscar winner Hilary Swank plays brilliantly. The supporting cast is filled with impressive names, everyone from John Lithgow to Hailee Steinfeld, from James Spader to Tim Blake Nelson. Even Meryl's daughter Grace Gummer shows up in a major role.

Early reviews were positive, but while the cinematography by Rodrigo Prieto, who shot the similarly stunning *Brokeback Mountain*, is lush and gorgeous (a shot of Jones riding away from a burning building is particularly breathtaking), *The Homesman* is a crushing bore, with little urgency in its sprawling narrative, and with only Swank giving a solid performance, one that unfortunately is tempered with an unexpected (and unnecessary) plot twist. In 1850s Nebraska, Mary (Swank), single and yearning for an adventure, elects to travel across the country to round up three young women who have gone crazy. Toward the beginning of her journey, she encounters an older man George Briggs (Jones) who has been left for dead. Begging to be helped, George convinces Mary to let him join her. The two fight cold winter weather, tired horses, and a scarcity of food, and along the way, Mary starts to wonder if George may be the one who will agree to marry her, since no man ever has.

The Homesman begins strong, when it focuses on Mary's uneventful life at home, but as soon as she sets out on her cross-country trip, the film slows to almost a halt, mainly because George never amounts to a credible or interesting character, and the three crazy women offer little more than occasional screams and tantrums. Despite the wide open terrain featured in many wide establishing shots, so much of *The Homesman* makes the viewer feel claustrophobic, particularly in that middle hour when little conflict is to be had and the quiet quest toward an indiscernible destination becomes the movie's only focus. By the time that destination is reached, little feels learned and accomplished, and the movie's final scene, which features unexpected dancing on a ferry, is weird and unsatisfying.

Jones' *Unforgiven* this is not, but *The Homesman* is not all a missed opportunity. Jones and Swank have a nice chemistry together, and Swank is fantastic in her subtle performance, easily her best since *Million Dollar Baby*. She creates a three dimensional character that the viewer fully understands from her first few scenes on—that is until she makes a decision later in the movie that feels manipulative on the screenplay's part; even if this big twist was featured in Glendon Swarthout's novel, it could have been corrected in the script.

While some of the major actors appearing in small cameos are distracting—Lithgow, for example—Spader is great as a wealthy wiseass named Aloysius Duffy who appears in a brief, enormously tense scene that offers one of the film's few suspenseful moments. Nelson goes a little over-the-top in his cameo, but Steinfeld shares a nice moment with Jones at the end, and Jesse Plemons, from *Friday Night Lights*, is so quietly affecting in his few scenes at the beginning that it's a shame he didn't get more screen-time.

Meryl plays Altha Carter, the woman who the three crazies are ultimately turned over to in the film's conclusion. She appears in three successive scenes that are so short that if someone goes to the bathroom before she appears, he or she might not get back in time before her character disappears. It's nice to see Meryl and Jones together again on-screen so soon after their delightful pairing in the comedy *Hope Springs*, and it's especially unique to see Meryl share a scene with one of her daughters—Gummer, who appeared in *Larry Crowne* and *Frances Ha*.

However, Meryl here is given so little to do and say that almost nothing is discovered about her minor character, who ultimately could have been played by any actress in her fifties or sixties. Altha obviously didn't need to be the focus of the film, but she could have played a bigger role in the narrative in the film's third act, rather than simply saying hello, thanks, and goodbye. *The Homesman* is a mediocre western with little to recommend about it, and anyone going to see it to catch a supporting turn by Meryl will unfortunately be sorely disappointed.

Thankfully, though, after two disappointing roles, Meryl had one more supporting turn to offer in 2014, and this one would not disappoint in any way—yes, Meryl's Oscar-nominated turn as the Witch in Rob Marshall's *Into the Woods* would be the ultimate Christmas present for moviegoers everywhere.

AWARDS WATCH

Meryl received no nominations or awards for her performance, but the film was nominated for the Palme d'Or at the Cannes Film Festival, and Swank earned a Best Actress award from the Boston Society of Film Critics, as well as nominations from the Phoenix Film Critics, San Diego Film Critics, and Women Film Critics.

FUN FACTS

Meryl's third collaboration with Jones following *A Prairie Home Companion* and *Hope Springs*.

Meryl and her daughter Grace share the screen for the first time since *The House of the Spirits*.

In the 1990s, Paul Newman owned the rights to Swarthout's novel, and wanted to direct the film himself.

Jones, Nelson, and Spader were all in Steven Spielberg's *Lincoln*.

Steinfeld's second western following her Oscar-nominated performance in *True Grit*.

WEEK 52
INTO THE WOODS
(2014)

FILM FACTS

DISTRIBUTOR: Walt Disney Pictures
RELEASE DATE: December 25, 2014

DIRECTOR: Rob Marshall
WRITER: James Lapine (based on the musical by James Lapine and Stephen Sondheim)
PRODUCERS: Rob Marshall, John DeLuca, Callum McDougall, Marc Platt
ALSO STARRING: Emily Blunt, James Corden, Anna Kendrick, Chris Pine, Johnny Depp, Christine Baranski, Tracey Ullman

REVIEW

With *Into the Woods*, we come to the end of *My Year With Meryl Streep*, and what a great film to go out on. This funny, fast-paced movie musical that is dark enough for adults to appreciate, while toned down from the stage version enough to appease children, is uneven at times, with a supremely weird third act that throws one surprise after another at the viewer. But the film is an entertaining romp all the way through, with a terrific ensemble cast that features Chris Pine in his most scene-stealing role to date, Emily Blunt in a bravura performance, and Meryl looking like she's having her most fun ever on-screen in her four decades of filmmaking.

Meryl has said in interviews that for decades she had vowed to never play a witch on screen, because as soon as she turned forty, she received offers for three witch parts in one given year (she turned forty in 1989, so the Anjelica Huston role in 1990's *The Witches* seems like it could have been one of them). She didn't like what a witch represented: an older woman, ugly, isolated, with no wants or desires except to bring misery to those around her. Thankfully after nearly twenty-five years she put a hold on that rule just this once to play the Witch in *Into the Woods*, directed by Rob Marshall (*Chicago*), written by James Lapine, and based on the 1987 Broadway musical with music and lyrics by Stephen Sondheim (*Sweeney Todd*). Winning Tonys for Best Score and Best Book, among others, *Into the Woods* ran for 765 performances over nearly two years, and has received national tours, numerous revivals, PBS specials, and reunion concerts. Now the film adaptation has finally arrived, and while it's not perfect, it is one of the better movie musicals of the last ten years, and certainly Marshall's best movie since his Academy-Award-winning debut, *Chicago*.

Fairy tale adaptations are definitely in right now, with *Maleficent* a recent blockbuster. *Into the Woods* is such a welcome delight in that it, like the ABC hit series *Once Upon a Time*, blends numerous fairy tales into one compelling story. The characters of Jack and the Beanstalk, Cinderella,

Little Red Riding Hood, and Rapunzel are all represented here, in an original story about a childless baker (James Corden) and his wife (Blunt) who are unable to start a family of their own, until one day the next-door Witch (Meryl) places a curse on them, forcing them to set out on a quest that could make their desired baby a reality. The duo ends up finding Jack's cow, Rapunzel's hair, Red Riding Hood's cape, and Cinderella's slipper, but will that be enough to appease the Witch? It's not an easy adventure for anyone involved, what with Jack (Daniel Huttlestone) climbing up and down the beanstalk, Rapunzel (Mackenzie Mauzy) being locked away from life and love, Red Riding Hood (Lilla Crawford) trying to evade the hungry Wolf (Johnny Depp), and Cinderella (Kendrick) fleeing from the ball on a nightly basis.

All of these stories and characters being tossed around in a single movie might have been chaotic or confusing in different hands, but Marshall's assured direction and Wyatt Smith's skillful editing keep everything clear from the first scene to the last. The major actors in the film all get at least one stand-out moment (with only Depp being underutilized), and the songs do a terrific job furthering the story and showing the hope and heartache in the characters, rather than ever stopping the movie cold. One element the film handles especially well is understanding that most viewers already know these classic fairy tales through and through and don't need every moment of them visualized on-screen; Marshall, for example, wisely avoids showing Jack up in the Giant's castle or Cinderella dancing with the Prince (Pine) and instead gives us only the essentials that are needed for this particular story. Some have complained that the last forty-five minutes of the movie, which more or less represents the controversial Act II of the stage musical, take the narrative in a misguided direction that feels strained and unnecessary. However, it's in this stretch of the film that the most interesting things actually happen, with the fairy tale endings we know by heart flipped on their heads and often cruelly ripped apart to create a dark, original ending that is in every way unexpected. Not everything in the third act works—it does hit a lull or two—but much of it breaks from the norm, making for a conclusion that feels fresh and exciting.

One of the great joys of *Into the Woods* is seeing talented, likable actors in both big roles and small. Kendrick is one of the highlights of the movie, with her pitch-perfect singing and vulnerable characterization of Cinderella that rings true. Tammy Blanchard and Lucy Punch are appropriately sinister as Cinderella's stepsisters, and Christine Baranski brings a welcome comedic touch to her Stepmother. Huttlestone is a likable find as Jack, and it's always fantastic to see Tracey Ullman, who plays Jack's mother, in a movie. Crawford is a bit shrill, unfortunately, in the role of Red Riding Hood (and Depp gets almost nothing to do), but Mauzy is an effective screen presence as Rapunzel. Billy Magnussen is handsome and debonair as Rapunzel's Prince, but it's Pine as Cinderella's Prince who steals the show; he is hilarious and appropriately charming in the role, and his rendition with Magnussen of "Agony" is one of the film's most memorable sequences. Corden is fine and tender as the Baker, but of these two, Blunt shines, with an emotionally rich, tour-de-force performance that allows her to sing, beautifully, for the first time on film. She's stunning in this.

And then, of course, there's Meryl. *Into the Woods* marks her third and last supporting role in a 2014 film, and after appearing in underwritten parts in *The Giver* and *The Homesman*, Marshall's musical finally gave her a great character in the Witch, who shows depth, power, and fragility in her perfectly placed moments. Like Heath Ledger's the Joker in *The Dark Knight*, the Witch is in *Into the Woods* just the right amount, with Meryl freakishly good in a role that really amounts to two different people. The first is a wounded, bitter, outrageous old witch, with shaggy gray hair, scars and wrinkles on her face, and crusty, yellow fingernails. Meryl has rarely played a character this ugly before, but it's the Witch's love for her daughter Rapunzel that makes her far more than a one-dimensional villain; the Witch slowly becomes someone we're rooting for just as much as the Baker and his wife. The second character is the post-transformation Witch, a stunning beauty with curly blue hair and a regal blue gown that is alternately Meryl's most gorgeous minutes on film. She is a hoot in the third act, with winning moments of both humor and raw emotion.

The number one joy of this movie, though, is getting to hear Meryl sing on-screen once again. She has show-stopping numbers in *Ironweed*, *Postcards from the Edge*, *A Prairie Home Companion*. She danced all around Greece in the musical blockbuster *Mamma Mia*, still to date her most successful movie. And now in *Into the Woods* we get three fleeting but winning Meryl numbers that may mark the best her voice has ever sounded in a movie. Maybe behind all that crazy hair and make-up she felt more free, and maybe the fantastical, theatrical nature of this material convinced her to go bigger, but Meryl is a powerhouse singer *in Into the Woods* like she's never been in a film before. Her "Witch's Lament" is quietly haunting and only sad in that it doesn't go on longer, and her emotionally powerful "Stay With Me" is the clip that runs at awards shows. But it's her final big number—"Last Midnight"—that impresses most of all, with Meryl big and alive like she rarely gets the chance to be on-screen, having what looks to be, after nearly forty years of moviemaking, the ultimate time of her life.

There is a scene toward the end of *Into the Woods* where most of the characters come together to face the angry female giant, and in one single frame Meryl stands with Baranski, her *Mamma Mia* co-star; Blunt, her *The Devil Wears Prada* co-star; and Ullman, her *Plenty* co-star. It's not a majorly significant scene, but it was this moment, when Meryl stands with three previous co-stars, that it hit me: *My Year With Meryl Streep* is finally over. What a joy it has been for the last fifty-two weeks to watch this actress evolve, surprise, affect, and entertain. She is the best we have, the most awarded and nominated actress in film history, the most incredibly talented movie star in the world, and in *Into the Woods*, she gives us yet another of her astonishing performances.

AWARDS WATCH

Meryl received her nineteenth Academy Award nomination, her first in the Supporting Actress category since *Adaptation*. She was also nominated for a Golden Globe, Critic's Choice Award, and SAG Award for her performance.

Into the Woods was nominated for two more Academy Awards, for Production Design and Costume Design. The film also received Golden Globe nominations for Best Motion Picture – Comedy or Musical, and Actress in a Comedy or Musical, for Blunt, and it received two BAFTA Award nominations, for Best Make Up/Hair and Costume Design. In addition, *Into the Woods* won Movie of the Year at the AFI Awards, Best Live Action Family Film from the Phoenix Film Critics, Best Ensemble in a Motion Picture at the Satellite Awards, and the Creative Impact in Directing Award at the Palm Springs International Film Festival.

FUN FACTS

Meryl's nineteenth Oscar nomination for *Into the Woods* makes her far and away the most nominated actor of all time. Way behind her are Jack Nicholson and Katharine Hepburn, who each had thirteen nominations.

This film marks the first time an actor has been nominated for an Academy Award for playing a witch.

Meryl's first Disney movie.

While filming a scene, Meryl's foot reportedly got caught in her costume as she jumped on a table, causing her to fall backward, head first, toward the concrete floor. Everyone froze in fear thinking Meryl would be seriously injured or worse, but Blunt stepped in and caught Meryl before she hit the floor.

Most of Meryl's songs in the film were sung live, even though she had pre-recorded them.

Catherine Zeta-Jones, Michelle Pfeiffer, Kate Winslet, Nicole Kidman, and Idina Menzel were all considered for the Witch.

Meryl was the first person to be cast in the movie.

At 125 million and counting, *Into the Woods* is one of Meryl's most successful films to date.

CONCLUSION

Meryl Streep is a worldwide treasure. For nearly four decades, she has impressed audiences in a variety of entertaining films—and there's currently no stopping her. Scheduled for release in 2015 are *Suffragette*, about foot soldiers who took part in the early feminist movement, in which she has a supporting role; *Ricki and the Flash*, written by Diablo Cody, in which she plays an aging rock star trying to connect with her estranged kids; and *Florence Foster Jenkins*, from director Stephen Frears, that features her as a New York heiress who dreams of becoming an Opera singer. Will any of these performances net Meryl her twentieth Academy Award nomination? Whether they do or don't, you know she will deliver her best each time out, just like she's been doing since 1977. It was my privilege to spend a year of my life watching her films, and I look forward to both revisiting her classics and catching up on her newest gems in the many years to come.

ABOUT THE AUTHOR

Brian Rowe graduated from Loyola Marymount University, where he studied English & Film. He has written twelve novels and dozens of short stories. He is currently pursuing his MA in English-Writing at the University of Nevada, Reno, and is hard at work on his next novel.

My Year With Meryl Streep is Brian's second work of film criticism, following *The Sandra Bullock Files*.

ALSO BY BRIAN ROWE

Happy Birthday to Me
Happy Birthday to Me Again
Happy Birthday to You
The Vampire Underground
The Zombie Playground
The Monster Apocalypse
Over the Rainbow
Magic Hour
The Sandra Bullock Files: From Speed to Gravity

CONNECT WITH BRIAN ONLINE

Brian's Web Site
http://brianrowebooks.com

Made in the USA
San Bernardino, CA
20 August 2015